Adam Khoo has soul force. In less than three decades on this planet, across several lifetimes of failure, then emerged with stunning brilliance to claim success as his birthright! His story resonates within these pages. With eloquent courage, immeasurable compassion and intrepid determination, Adam offers inspiration to legions of students imprisoned in dystopian dungeons with beliefs about their mediocrity their only evidence of reality. Genius is exposed by opportunity, and never imposed by authority. Adam's gift is an opportunity to bring forth light from obscurity. May this book illuminate the manifold pathways of excellence.
— **DILIP MUKERJEA**, Best-selling Author of *Superbrain*, *Brainfinity*, *Braindancing* and *Surfing the Intellect* (collectively known as The Brain Quartet)

The book takes the reader on an exhilarating journey of self-discovery. It is not just about learning, but stretching and realising one's potential. It packs in enough tips and strategies to help the reader cope and succeed in myriad situations.
— **CHIA MIA CHIANG**, Former Principal, Ngee Ann Polytechnic (2000–2014), President, Nanyang Academy of Fine Arts

Adam Khoo typifies the graduate NUS aims to produce — goal-directed, creative and enterprising. In this readable and helpful manual, Adam shares the practical strategies and techniques that have contributed to his success.
— **PROF SHIH CHOON FONG**, Former President & Vice-Chancellor (2000–2008) National University of Singapore

This second edition of Adam's masterpiece I Am Gifted, So Are You! emphasises the point that the genius in each person can be unleashed with proper guidance and motivation. Timetested super learning strategies have been skillfully integrated in the enlarged scope and content of this volume to ensure success of individuals. This is a book that would cater to all who believe that the driving force lies within themselves and are prepared to dream dreams and dare to reach for the highest in life.
— **DR ONG TECK CHIN**, Former Principal, Anglo-Chinese School Independent (1994–2010)

Adam has certainly blazed the trail for academically slow learners, late developers and low achievers. More importantly, he has also given hope to many neighbourhood schools and their teachers to hold on to the belief that their pupils can achieve and excel if only we give them the opportunities to bloom.
— **NG GEK TIANG**, Former Principal, Ping Yi Secondary School (1984–1989) Senior Inspector of Schools, Ministry of Education (1989–1991) Former Principal, Crescent Girls' School (1991–1996) Assistant Director, Pastoral Care and Career Guidance, MOE (1997–1998)

This book will empower you to gain control of your thinking and, in so doing, will allow you to unleash the full potential of your mind. Compulsory reading for all students and educationalists.
— **DR KENNETH LYEN**, Consultant pediatrician and bestselling author of over 11 books on child development, creativity and education.

I am GIFTED, so are YOU!

Adam Khoo

With Foreword by Tony Buzan

Latest *Power-Packed* Edition

mc Marshall Cavendish Editions

© 2002 Times Editions Private Limited
© 2006 Marshall Cavendish International (Asia) Private Limited

This updated edition is published in 2014
First published in 1998
Reprinted 1998, 1999 (twice), 2000, 2001, 2002
Revised 2002
Reprinted 2002, 2003 (twice), 2004 (twice), 2005, 2006, 2007, 2008, 2009, 2010, 2013

Published by Marshall Cavendish Editions
An imprint of Marshall Cavendish International
1 New Industrial Road, Singapore 536196

All rights reserved

No part of this publication may be reproduced, stored in a retrieval system or transmitted, in any form or by any means, electronic, mechanical, photocopying, recording or otherwise, without the prior permission of the copyright owner. Request for permission should be addressed to the Publisher, Marshall Cavendish International (Asia) Private Limited, 1 New Industrial Road, Singapore 536196. Tel: (65) 6213 9300, Fax: (65) 6285 4871. E-mail: genref@sg.marshallcavendish.com

The publisher makes no representation or warranties with respect to the contents of this book, and specifically disclaims any implied warranties or merchantability or fitness for any particular purpose, and shall in no events be liable for any loss of profit or any other commercial damage, including but not limited to special, incidental, consequential, or other damages.

Other Marshall Cavendish Offices:
Marshall Cavendish Corporation. 99 White Plains Road, Tarrytown NY 10591-9001, USA • Marshall Cavendish International (Thailand) Co Ltd. 253 Asoke, 12th Flr, Sukhumvit 21 Road, Klongtoey Nua, Wattana, Bangkok 10110, Thailand • Marshall Cavendish (Malaysia) Sdn Bhd, Times Subang, Lot 46, Subang Hi-Tech Industrial Park, Batu Tiga, 40000 Shah Alam, Selangor Darul Ehsan, Malaysia

Marshall Cavendish is a trademark of Times Publishing Limited

National Library Board Singapore Cataloguing in Publication Data

Khoo, Adam, 1974-, author.
I am gifted, so are you! / Adam Khoo. – Second edition. – Singapore : Marshall Cavendish Editions, 2014
pages cm

ISBN : 978-981-4561-48-8 (paperback)

1. Learning, Psychology of. 2. Study skills. I. Title.

BF318
153.15 -- dc23   OCN880860152

Printed in Singapore by NPE Print Communications Pte Ltd

DEDICATION

Dedicated to the genius within you.

Most of all, from me to my parents, Vince, Betty and Joanne, my grandparents, my sister Vanessa and my wife Sally.

ACKNOWLEDGEMENTS

No worthwhile project can ever come into being without the combined effort of a team of rather talented individuals. Therefore, I need to thank many wonderful people for their invaluable contributions and for making this book a reality.

My parents for their years of support and editorial help on the first drafts of the original manuscript, my wife who played a big part in helping me with this second edition and Kenneth Wong for his beautiful illustrations.

Heartfelt thanks also go out to Tony Buzan, Dilip Mukerjea and Vanda North for their faith and support. Also to Asha Kumaran and the team at the former Oxford University Press. Without your faith and vision, this book would never have seen the light of day.

This book is also, in no small part, due to some very inspiring educators whose personalities, talents and friendship have influenced me profoundly on my journey. Thanks to my partner and mentor Ernest Wong for being the first to tell me that I am gifted; Dr Tad James and all the good people at Advanced Neuro Dynamics who introduced me to the world of NLP; then to some of the giants of personal development, Dr Richard Bandler, John Lavalle, Robert Dilts, Anthony Robbins and Eric Jensen.

I would also like to thank all the academics who have helped shaped my beliefs and attitudes: Prof Wee Chow Hou, Dr Kulwant Singh and Dr May Lwin for their support and interest in my work; also the other dynamic lecturers at NUS. Going back further, I must thank the dedicated teachers and Principals of Ping Yi Secondary School (1987-90) who did not give up on me: Mrs Ng Gek Tiang, Mrs Pearl Goh, Mr Heng, Miss Grace Lee and Mdm Markati Yusoff. Other people I must thank are Mrs Lee Phui Mun (Principal, Victoria Junior College), Ms Phua Puay Shan and teachers at Victoria Junior College (1991–1992).

My gratitude also goes out to my ex-colleagues for powerful and memorable times at our camps; in particular, thanks to Ms Theresa Wong, Lee Say Keng, best friend Jo Pang, Gary Tan, Tan Minyi, Zachary Low, Kenneth Wong,

Audrey Ng, Audrey Tan, Eunice Lee and Mark Tan. A special thank you to all those who have supported me like Gary Lee, Petrina, Shannaz, Vincent, Michelle, Jie Yao and Maximillian Tung.

More special thank yous, this round to Dr. Tony Tan & Mrs. Mary Tan and to Andrew Tan for giving me my first break into corporate training. Others who believe in me and whom I must thank are Jeffrey Chin and the ninth and tenth Management Committee (Faculty of Business Administration, NUS) for giving me the opportunity to conduct my courses there.

A special thank you to Patrick Cheo, Eric Ng, Benny Lee and Koh See Kwang for their dedication in helping me build up Creatsoul Entertainment and with whom I have had a lot of fun working. Also, thanks go out to Jack Tan and staff of Razes Entertainment for supporting us all the way! Not forgetting the management and staff of Adcom (S) Pte Ltd, Event Gurus Pte Ltd and Adam Khoo Learning Technologies Group Pte Ltd.

This book is also dedicated to my friends Dr Dennis Wee, Dave Rogers, Dr Kenneth Lyen, Gay Chee Cheong, Tommie Goh, Zeng Guangwei, Ng Soo Ann, Ng Soo Gin, Ng Soo Ming, Kimmie Leong, Andrew and Evonne Wee, Shirley Chew, Tan Lye Poh, Alvin Woon, Melvyn Koh, Melvyn Lu and David Ong who introduced me to the Young Entrepreneurs' Organization.

Also to LC Seah, Samuel Chia, Jeffery Goh, Parvindar Singh, Ong Tze Boon, Bernard Goh, Genevieve Theseiria, Mike Moey, Roger Khoo and all the members of the YEO.

And finally, to Marshall Cavendish for making this edition a reality.

ABOUT THE AUTHOR

At the time when this book was first published in 1998, Adam Khoo was an undergraduate in the National University of Singapore (NUS) Business School. He ranked among the top 1% of students in NUS, earning himself a place in the prestigious Talent Development Programme (TDP), an extension of the Gifted programme. He was also placed on the Dean's List every consecutive year for his outstanding academic achievements.

Today, Adam Khoo is an entrepreneur, best-selling author, peak performance trainer and professional stocks & FX trader. He holds an honours degree in Business Administration and was awarded the NUS Business School Eminent Business Alumni Award in 2008 and the NUS Outstanding Young Alumni Award in 2011. He is also a Licensed Master Practitioner and Trainer in Neuro-Linguistic Programming™ (NLP™) by the Society of NLP, USA.

A self-made millionaire at the age of 26, Adam owns and manages multiple businesses with a combined annual turnover of $30m. His business interests include pre-school education, learning centres, conference management, corporate training and advertising. He is the Executive Chairman of Adam Khoo Learning Technologies Group Pte Ltd, one of Asia's largest training & education companies.

Adam is known as one of the most dynamic and powerful speakers in Asia. Over the past two decades, he has trained over 500,000 students, teachers, professionals, investors and business owners to achieve excellence in their various fields of endeavour. He does this by imparting them his highly actionable success strategies in accelerated learning, peak performance, wealth creation and entrepreneurship. He has worked with hundreds of schools, multi-national corporations and non-profit organisations in Singapore and around the region.

His success and achievements have been featured in *The Straits Times, The Sunday Times, The Business Times, The New Paper, Lianhe Zaobao, Berita Harian*, Channel News Asia (CNA), MediaCorp Channel 8 Money News, MediaCorp

News Radio 93.8, *The Hindu, Malaysia Sun, The Star* and even on Brazilian national TV. In 2007, Adam was ranked among the 25 richest Singaporeans under the age of 40 by The Executive magazine.

A life enthusiast with an unceasing passion for helping others, he believes every person deserves to succeed in life. He continues to inspire thousands of people around the world by sharing his success strategies and life insights on his personal website. You too can connect with him on www.adam-khoo.com and www.facebook.com/adamkhoosuccess.

ABOUT TONY BUZAN

Tony Buzan, holder of the world's highest 'Creativity IQ', is the originator of Mind Mapping®, Founder of The Brain Trust, Chairman of the Brain Foundation and developer of the concept of Mental Literacy.

He is one of the world's most consistent, best selling authors, having written and published, more than 80 books on the brain, creativity, and learning. To date, Mr Buzan's books have been translated into 30 languages and achieved sucess in more than 100 countries. His classic bestseller, Use Your Head, has sold more than one million copies worldwide.

Tony Buzan is also a much sought-after speaker, having been rated by Forbes (USA) as one of the top lecturers in the world, along with such personalities as Margaret Thatcher and Henry Kissinger.

He is also a Fellow of the Institute of Training and Development and an elected member of the International Council of Psychologists. In addition, he is also an advisor to International Olympic coaches and athletes and to the British Olympic Chess Squad.

Tony Buzan, along with Raymond Keene, organised the first ever Mind Sports Olympiad at the Royal Festival Hall, London in August 1997. Such activities are all part of Tony Buzan's dedication to helping people unleash more of their brain power. He has unquestionably influenced millions of people all over the world in the way they approach thinking and intelligence.

FOREWORD BY TONY BUZAN

It is a particular pleasure for me to write the Foreword to Adam Khoo's *I Am Gifted, So Are You!*

His title is correct. He is gifted! This does not need to be proven in any other way for you than by reading this book which you now hold in your hands. Every page glistens with intelligence, wit, humour and creativity. What is particularly interesting about Adam's personal case is that for many years of his life, 'gifted' was not a term that was regularly applied to him, thus my even greater pleasure in recommending this book to you. On my lecture tours around the world focusing on the development of human intelligence and the creation of thinking and learning organizations, one of the first things I talk about are the stories of those who were 'delinquent', 'poor students', 'slow', 'backward', 'naughty', 'wicked', 'bad', 'educationally subnormal', 'disruptive', 'suffering from Attention Deficit Disorder Syndrome', 'not destined for university', 'failures', 'dunces', etc.

My case has always been that the inherent intellectual capacity and basic creative brilliance of all human beings is far greater than we have ever thought and have regularly been told about.

It is wonderful, therefore, when an individual who is deeply seconded in the 'non gifted' camp for some extraordinary reason, finds his or her way to the 'gifted camp'.

The way in which this gigantic and apparently impossible leap is made is virtually always through self-realization. Self-realization is also always nearly based on learning how the brain and body work individually and in concert. This includes, almost obviously, learning about the fundamental nature of memory, thinking, reading and learning, while finding out about the fundamental, physiological and biological operations of the brain and the body.

Enter Adam!

From being a 12-year-old 'non gifted', Adam, by learning about himself and especially learning how to learn, within a very short period of time, as you will find out when you read his personal story in Chapter 1, graduated from being near the bottom of a class of students who were at the bottom of all the other classes, to being in the top 10%, then in the top 5%, next in the top 1%. He did this not only on a short-term basis, but year after year after year.

CONTENTS

Foreword by Tony Buzan   xi

SECTION I: I AM GIFTED, SO ARE YOU!

CHAPTER 1	How a Dumb Kid Can be Gifted	1
CHAPTER 2	The Process of Successful Learning	7
CHAPTER 3	Are You Ready to Succeed?	16
CHAPTER 4	I Believe I Can Fly…So I Can	21

SECTION II: SUPER LEARNING STRATEGIES

CHAPTER 5	You Have the Brain of a Genius	36
CHAPTER 6	Power Reading for Information	50
CHAPTER 7	Mind Mapping®: The Ultimate Note-Making Tool	67
CHAPTER 8	Super Memory for Words	106
CHAPTER 9	Super Memory for Numbers	132
CHAPTER 10	The Pattern of Memory	150
CHAPTER 11	Mastering The Art of Application	158

SECTION III: YOUR PERSONAL DRIVING FORCE

CHAPTER 12	Dare to Dream: The Power of Goals	171
CHAPTER 13	Motivation — Moving Beyond Procrastination	194
CHAPTER 14	Formulas for Scoring 'A's	203
CHAPTER 15	The Time of Your Life	215
CHAPTER 16	Getting Empowered… In an Instant	229

SECTION IV: EXAMINATION STRATEGIES

| CHAPTER 17 | The Final Countdown | 247 |
| CHAPTER 18 | The Final Battle | 256 |

Chapter 1

How A Dumb Kid Can Be Gifted

CAN A DUMB KID BECOME GIFTED?

First I would like to congratulate you on picking up this book. The fact that you are now investing your time and effort in reading it clearly shows that deep inside you know instinctively that you are capable of a lot more than what you are achieving now. Whether you are already a good student, an average one or an underachiever, you have the potential to produce fantastic results. You know and believe that you have within you, a gifted person waiting to be unleashed!

Almost every day, I go around giving seminars and training thousands of students and teachers on how to unleash their learning genius and produce straight A results. Newspapers and TV programmes have referred to me as a master of learning and a genius. They talk about how I have helped many students, even the most 'hopeless ones', turn around to be scholars who succeed in all other aspects of their life as well.

I can tell you that the person who is most shocked by all this is…myself. After all, not too long ago, everybody referred to me as a lazy, indifferent and stupid kid who will never amount to anything. How could someone who was once called 'dumb' now be called 'gifted'? People who meet me now cannot believe that I was once a below average student who kept failing exams and who was almost doomed to have no future. Well, the strange thing is that it is absolutely true. I do not care how many times people may have given up on you or told you that you were dumb, hopeless, good for nothing and slow. You, like me, have the power to turn everything around in a short period of time and become gifted!

In this book, I want to share with you exactly how you can achieve this. And remember, I am not teaching you how to succeed from the perspective of someone who was born smart and who has succeeded all his life. I am teaching you from the perspective of someone who was once labelled an underachiever and a below average student. So if you are not doing too well in school right now, I know exactly how you feel. I was there before, at the bottom.

JUST ANOTHER UNDERACHIEVER

For me, my failure as a student began right from day one when I entered primary school. As a young kid, I hated reading. All I wanted to do was to play computer games and watch TV. As a result, I didn't pay much attention in class and the 'F's started showing up in my report cards. That made me hate teachers, studying and school even more! Well, things got worse and worse. By Primary Three, I was expelled from St Stevens Primary School for misbehaviour and relocated to Ngee Ann Primary School. There, I still continued to play and ignored my studies totally. As a result, when the Primary School Leaving Examination (PSLE) results were announced, I did so badly that I was rejected by all the six secondary schools that my parents listed as their choices. Instead, I was dispatched to Ping Yi Secondary School, a relatively new public school that no one we knew had heard of.

While I was not expected to suddenly shine at this new school, no one expected that I would backslide so far that my exasperated Secondary One mathematics teacher would call up my mother to ask why I could not even do a Primary Four mathematics problem. At that time, passing a subject was the greatest achievement of my life. As a result, my results always hovered between 40% and 55%. In my entire cohort of over 160 students, I was among the bottom ten.

My parents panicked and sent me for lots of private tuition. But that didn't help at all. It came to a point when they thought that the only solution would be to send me for an overseas education. They thought if I stayed on in Singapore, where the education system was so competitive, I would never qualify to get into any tertiary institution.

FOR THINGS TO CHANGE, I MUST CHANGE FIRST

It was at the lowest ebb of my school career that my father learned of a motivational programme for teenagers designed to teach them how to study and take charge of their lives. Deciding that they had nothing to lose except their money, my parents enrolled me in the five-day camp.

So, on a Sunday morning in 1987, I was dropped off at a local hotel and put under the charge of the Master Trainer, Mr. Ernest Wong. I was a mere 13-year-old among other students aged between 12 and 20. On that day, I was far from thrilled at having my precious school holidays burnt. But at the end of the five days, I was a completely changed teenager. What I learnt and experienced had transformed my whole attitude and outlook of my studies and my life.

During the programme, I was exposed to a powerful personal transformation technique known as Neuro-Linguistic Programming™ (NLP™), that taught me how to take charge of my mental state and eliminate my limiting habits and beliefs. I was also astounded by the power of accelerated learning strategies and how I could use it to literally increase my brain-power for memory, reading and concentration.

I learnt that everyone, even the most mediocre students among us, had the potential to become geniuses and leaders. The only things holding us back were our disempowering beliefs and negative attitudes.

This one idea had a tremendous impact on me. I used to believe that I was just not as smart as those kids in the top schools and in the gifted programmes. That no matter how hard I studied, I would never be as good as they are. So why even try?

But now, I believed that it was possible to accomplish anything I set my mind on. That if someone could score straight 'A's, so could I. If someone could get into the gifted programme, so could I! One of the reasons why this technology had such a great impact on me was because I was young and naïve and did not have any negative pre-conceived beliefs. I wholeheartedly accepted what I was told.

Intrigued and challenged, I left the camp with newly acquired super learning skills, ready to claim my birthright of success, For the first time in my life, I set my sights on getting straight 'A's.

GETTING INTO ACTION...WITH 'A' GOALS AHEAD!

Once I left the camp, I was extremely charged up and excited about the future ahead. I felt like I could do anything. So the first thing I did was to set three really big goals. My first goal was to top my school in one year. My second goal was to do well enough to get a place in Victoria Junior College (the top junior college in Singapore). My final goal was to get into the National University of Singapore and become one of the top students there. Impossible dreams? That's what everyone thought.

I Am Gifted, So Are You!

Back home and in school, I swung into action. Up went the self-drawn motivational posters on my walls. I started using all the learning strategies I had learned in the camp. I started taking whole-brained notes in class and started speed-reading in front of my friends. When asked a question by the teacher, I was able to rattle of all the points in perfect order, thanks to the super memory techniques I had learnt.

Naturally, everyone became curious. My teachers asked me what had gotten into me. I responded by telling them that I was going to top the school. They looked at me as if I was crazy. My friends asked me where I was planning to go after I had finished secondary school. I replied that I was going to Victoria Junior College and then to the National University. They all burst out laughing. 'That's crazy! None of us will ever make it there! Only students from top schools can make it there, not us!' Instead of discouraging me, their comments inspired me even more! I was out to prove a point and to change history. That a lousy student from a non 'elite' school could indeed achieve all that!

GETTING RESULTS

Within three months, I had pulled my grades up from an average of 52% to 70%. This enabled me to rise from the bottom of the school to rank among the top 18, all in one memorable year, 1987.

From there I went on to top my school (in terms of Aggregate points, best of six subjects) in the GCE 'O' level examinations with six 'A's and eight points, and was admitted into Victoria Junior College, the college of my choice. I scored straight 'A's for my best three subjects and got a place in the National University of Singapore (NUS) to study Business Administration.

Starting from the first year of university, my grades earned me a place on the Dean's list (honour roll) every consecutive year. I was also admitted into the

NUS Talent Development Programme (TDP). The latter is an extension of the 'gifted programme' offered to the top 1% of students at the university.

I achieved this not as a 'mugger', but as a student who still found time to start his first business in event management at the age of 15 with a couple of friends. The company, Event Gurus Pte Ltd, exists to this day and is extremely successful. I also spent much of my time as an Executive Trainer at the Super-Teen™ programme, helping thousands more students to unleash their true genius.

IF I CAN, THEN SO CAN YOU!

I begin this book with my life experience not to impress you, but to impress upon you the fact that if someone like me who was at the bottom and who was labelled as a lousy student could end up topping a national university and being in a gifted programme, then I believe anyone can!

You just need to create the desire within you to aim for what you want, believe in yourself and learn the strategies to achieve success. This is what this book is all about. I want to share with you all I have learned because the journey to self-discovery is the most exciting one anyone can embark on. Are you ready to create an extraordinary new life for yourself? Then turn the page and read on!

Chapter 2

The Process of Successful Learning

SUPER STUDENTS AND SLOW STUDENTS — SAME BRAIN, DIFFERENT STRATEGIES

After hearing about my success story, many students respond by saying that they could never achieve all that because they are just not smart or talented enough. First, understand that it is not your inherent lack of ability that sets you apart from the 'superstar' students. Rather, it is the learning strategies used by these students that get them excellent results.

You and almost every student on the planet have basically the same brain and nervous system. (We will learn more about this in Chapter 5: You Have the Brain of a Genius). Why then can some students learn easily and tackle

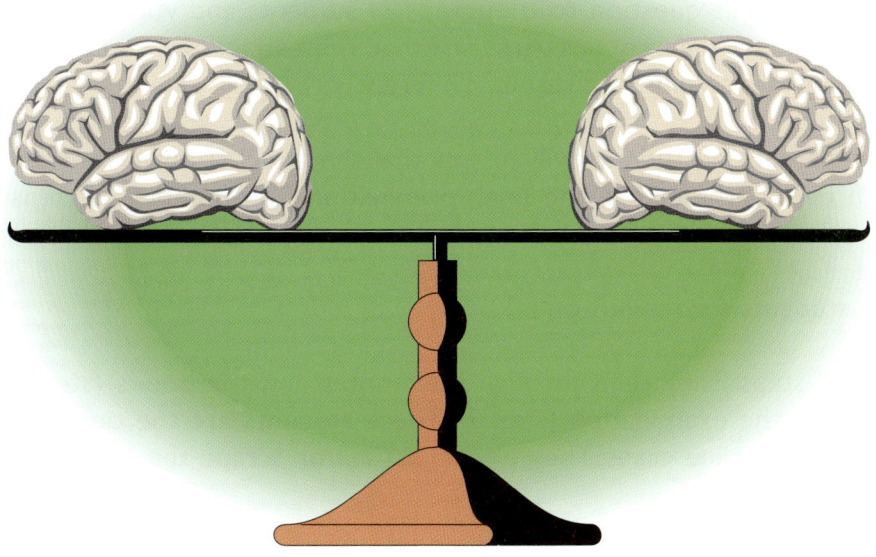

difficult questions effortlessly while other students may read a page four times and still not understand or remember what they just read? The reason is that the former have somehow learnt or instinctively used the right strategies to access a greater portion of their brain power whereas the others have not. They have learnt the secret of 'learning how to learn'.

I believe that success leaves behind clues. If you can learn and duplicate the learning strategies of super students, you will be able to produce the same results! You too will be able to memorise easily and apply what you know to difficult problem questions that are set.

> **IF IT IS POSSIBLE FOR OTHERS, IT'S POSSIBLE FOR ME. IT IS ONLY A QUESTION OF STRATEGIES!**

DIFFERENT STUDENTS, DIFFERENT STRATEGIES, DIFFERENT RESULTS

Let me ask you a question. When do you start studying for your end of the year examination? Here's another question. How do you study for it? How many steps do you go through?

I have posed this question to thousands of students and you know what? I get thousands of different answers! Isn't that interesting? No wonder different students produce different results. Different strategies, different results!

Ninety percent of students will answer that they start studying between one and three months before the final examination. The number of steps they take varies between one and five! Here's what I have found out!

Some students study with only …

a. Two steps. They read through their notes and textbooks (step 1) and go for the examination (step 2). These students are the ones who are the borderline cases. They either just fail or scrape through.

b. Three steps. They read their notes and textbooks, commit them to memory and go for the examination. These students are the 'C' and 'D' students.

c. Four steps. They read their notes and textbooks, commit them to memory, practise answering various questions and go for the examination. These are the 'B' students who will occasionally get an 'A'.

What I discovered about many super students was that successful learning and guaranteeing that 'A' required a total of nine steps. And studying began not from one to three months before the examination, but on the first day of school! That's right. Learning begins on day one.

> **SUCCESSFUL STUDYING IS A NINE-STEP PROCESS THAT BEGINS ON DAY ONE!**

THE NINE-STEP PROCESS OF SUCCESSFUL STUDYING

Yes! Believe it or not, studying begins on the first day of the course you are taking and there are altogether nine steps you must master! Each of these nine steps is covered in-depth throughout this book.

Step 1: Set Very Clear Goals

Many students think that the first step to studying should be to read their notes or their textbooks. I believe that before you do that, the first thing you must do is to set very clear goals on the results you want to get for the subjects you are studying. How many 'A's are you going for?

This is very important because the goals you set will determine how you study and therefore your results! If you set a goal to score 100% in

mathematics, will you study very differently as compared to setting a goal to score 60% instead? Of course! When you are going for 100%, your brain knows that it cannot afford to make a single mistake. Chances are, this will cause you to study every relevant point in the syllabus! As a result, you may score that 100% and if not, you will get 90% or more!

However, if you set a goal to score 60% instead, then your brain will know that it can afford to lose 40% of the marks. Chances are, you won't bother studying everything, skipping chapters that you do not understand or do not like! After all, you can afford to not know 40% of the information. The result will be either scoring that 60%, barely scraping through at 50% or even failing!

What's even worse is that when you do not set a goal, your brain will automatically lock on to the lousiest score it can get away with (i.e. 50%). That's suicidal!

You will learn more about this in Chapter 12: Dare to Dream.

Step 2: Planning & Scheduling

You can set all the fantastic goals you want. But you won't achieve them unless you come up with a plan and schedule your time so that you will know when to do what.

In Chapter 15: The Time of Your Life, you will learn how to create a master plan to reach your goals and how to master your time through scheduling.

I Am Gifted, So Are You!

Step 3: Taking Consistent Action

Everybody can set goals and develop great plans and schedules. However, it is the students who are able to get themselves to take consistent action every day who produce great results. It is the ability to constantly follow through every day to read their textbooks, make their notes and revise that makes the difference.

Unfortunately, if you are like most students, you fall into the trap of being lazy and procrastinating all the time. Sometimes, you just do not feel like studying, especially after you feel lousy about something. By the time you actually sit down and get some work done, the exams have arrived!

I will share with you how to get yourself to take consistent action in Chapter 13: Motivation — Moving Beyond Procrastination, Chapter 14: Formulas for Scoring 'A's and Chapter 16: Getting Empowered…In An Instant

The Next Four Steps Are on Applying the Super Learning Strategies You Will Learn in Section II.

Step 4: Power-Reading for Information

This is the first of the super learning strategies. You must begin by power reading textbooks and relevant reading materials for important information. Remember that not all the words in a textbook are important. You need to extract only the words (known as Keywords) that give you the information. You will learn this in Chapter 6: Power Reading for Information.

Step 5: Mind Mapping®

After gathering all the information-rich keywords, you must then make Whole-brain notes called Mind Maps® that help you re-organise the information in a way that saves you time and activates your brain power. This will be covered in Chapter 7: Mind Mapping®: The Ultimate Note-Making Tool.

Step 6: Super Memory

The next step is to use Super Memory techniques to easily and effortlessly absorb all the important information. Many educational systems are moving towards higher order thinking and away from pure memory based questions. However, remember that unless you can absorb and retain information, you will not be able to use it in higher level critical thinking! Before you can achieve level two, you must always master level one first. You will learn all this in Chapters 8, 9 and 10.

Step 7: Magic of Application

You can memorise all the facts and figures perfectly, but unless you can apply your knowledge to the many different types of questions that are set in the examination, you will not score an 'A'. In Chapter 11, we will explore strategies on how to apply what you have learnt and activate your thinking skills.

Step 8: Exam Preparation

The last super learning strategy is knowing how to prepare for the examination. This starts two months before the examination and is covered in Chapter 17: The Final Countdown.

Step 9: Taking the Exam

The last yet most important step in the Successful Learning Process is taking the examination. Remember, examinations are a game. In Chapter 18: The Final Battle, you will learn the secrets of how to master this game.

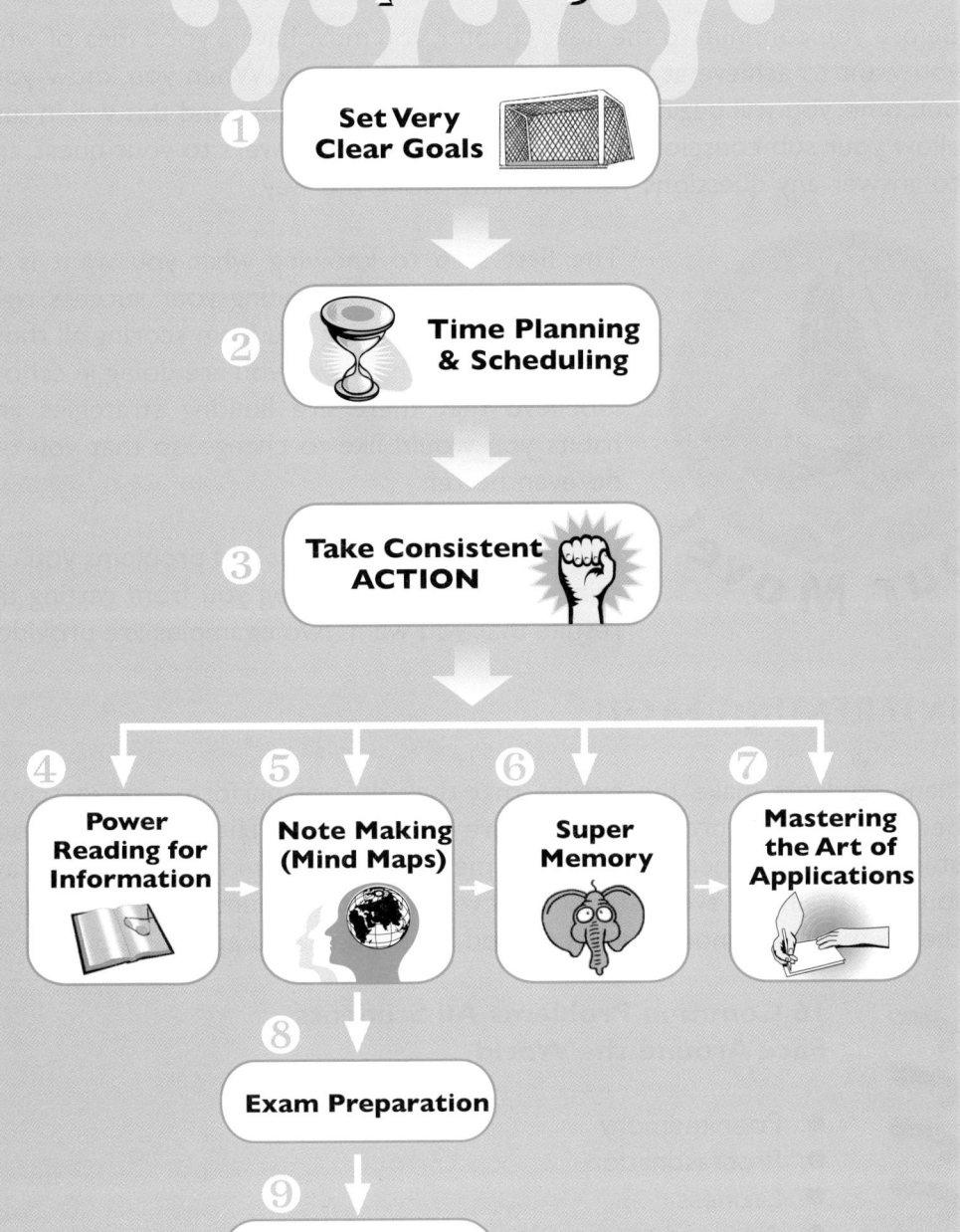

WHAT IS LIMITING YOU NOW AND WHAT DO YOU WANT INSTEAD?

Before you continue to the next chapter, you must have a good idea of what you want to achieve at the end of reading this book. When you know your outcome, you will begin to read with a sense of purpose and this will in turn allow your sub-conscious mind to search for the answers to your quest, and to answer any questions you may have along the way.

The first step to knowing what you want is to take stock of what is limiting your success right now. What's preventing you from scoring all those 'A's? No matter how well you are doing in school, I believe that there are limiting strategies and habits you would like to change, so that you can do even better.

Write down all the reasons and problems you can think of that are preventing you from getting the results that you want. Two examples are provided.

INTERESTING FACT!

Many students make the excuse that they do not perform well in school because of many problems they have with learning. They think that good students do not encounter these same problems. From my research, I have found that almost every student in every country around the world shares the 16 most common problems listed below. So…you are not alone!

16 Common Problems All Students Face Around the World

- Poor memory
- Procrastination
- Laziness
- Addicted to computer games, TV and the Internet
- Difficulty in understanding what is taught
- Easily distracted

- Short attention span
- Day-dreaming in class
- Examination anxiety
- Making careless mistakes
- Pressure and stress from parents
- Too much to study and not enough time
- Lack of motivation
- Giving up easily
- Boring teachers
- No interest in what I am learning

Now that you are aware of what your problems are, I want you to list all the skills and abilities you will need in order to score the results that you truly desire. Two examples are provided.

As you read this book, and learn the tools that I share with you, I want you to:

 **CROSS OUT EACH OF YOUR LIMITATIONS** as you become free of them.

And

 **TICK EACH SKILL AND ABILITY NECESSARY FOR SUCCESS** as you begin to acquire them.

By the time you get to the last chapter, you will have acquired all the skills and abilities needed for success and be free of your limitations, forever! But before we start on the journey of learning, you must first ask yourself…

Chapter 3

Are You Ready to Succeed?

WINNER'S & LOSER'S FRAME OF MIND

Before you go on and learn all the strategies of 'A' students, you must first ask yourself whether you are ready to succeed. 'Of course I am ready to succeed', you may say. 'Everybody wants to succeed!'

Unfortunately (or fortunately), this is not true. Although thousands of students have read this book and have gone through my training programmes, not all of them change and start succeeding in what they do!

5%   **Winner's Frame of Mind**
I WANT to Succeed

95%   **Loser's Frame of Mind**
I WOULD LIKE/WISH to Succeed

The reason is that they start off with the wrong Frame of Mind. If you have the wrong Frame of Mind, you will never succeed no matter what secret techniques I share with you. Before going further, you must understand and get into the right Frame of Mind. This way, you will benefit immensely from this book.

I have discovered that there are two distinct Frames of Mind. You can have that of a Winner or that of a Loser. Unfortunately, only 5% of students have the Winner's Frame of Mind. The 95% majority have the Loser's Frame of Mind. What's the difference? And how can you get into the mindset of the Winner?

DO YOU REALLY WANT TO SUCCEED?

Winners operate from the frame of mind that they WANT to succeed in what they do! They WANT to score 'A's and they WANT to produce great results! Conversely, losers operate from the frame of mind that they WOULD LIKE to succeed or they WISH to succeed. There is a big difference!

When you WANT to succeed, it means that it is a must for you! You will not accept anything less. If you do get anything less, you will do whatever it takes to get what you want (provided it is ethical). What does this mean? It means that if you have to study ten hours a day, you will study ten hours a day. If it means that you have to totally change the way you study, you will do it! If it means that you have to sacrifice your favourite computer games, you will do it. You will do whatever it takes to get those 'A's. In my experience, if you are that committed to achieve something, you will definitely achieve it! Often, students ask me if I think they can score straight 'A's. My answer is, 'It's not whether you can score straight 'A's. The question is whether you are willing to do whatever it takes!' Students who operate from this frame of mind are the ones who will benefit from this book and achieve what they want.

Unfortunately, many students do not WANT to succeed. They simply WOULD LIKE to succeed or think they SHOULD succeed. To these students, scoring 'A's and getting into top universities will be great! But it is not a MUST for them. In other words, they do not mind living without it. There is hardly any commitment and power behind their desire. As a result, they are not willing to do whatever it takes. They are only willing to try things as long as it is not too difficult, too much work or outside of their comfort zone. They are not willing to spend their weekends studying or to change the methods which they use to study. They are not willing to follow everything I teach in this book. To them, it may be too much trouble. This is the kind of students who will go through this book and wind up having the same results as before.

As a friend and a mentor, I urge you to read this book from the Frame of Mind of a Winner! I believe you can achieve great things but you must make it a MUST for yourself! You must be willing to do whatever it takes, no matter how uncomfortable or tough it may be!

Winner's Frame of Mind
They are the 5% who WANT to succeed
It is a MUST to Succeed
They are Willing to Do Whatever it Takes

Loser's Frame of Mind
They are the 95% who WOULD LIKE to succeed
It is okay even if they do not succeed
They are only willing to do what they feel like doing

WINNERS ARE IN CONTROL, LOSERS ARE NOT!

The other characteristic of Winners is that they are in control of their lives, whereas Losers are not!

Winners always take responsibility for whatever happens in their lives! They believe that whatever happens, they caused it somehow. For example, if they failed an exam, it is because they caused it. If their parents do not trust them, it is because they caused it. If they are in the worst class, it is because they caused it. If they are top students, it is also because they caused it. It is extremely powerful to put the responsibility on yourself. Why? Because if you believe that you are the cause of everything, then you have the power to change and improve your life! You are in control. To benefit from this book, you must believe like a winner that you are in control. That if you change what you do and apply all the strategies you learn, you will experience all the success!

Again, those students who will not benefit from this book are the ones who operate from the Loser's frame of mind. They never take responsibility for what happens in their lives. Instead, they always make EXCUSES, BLAME EVERYONE ELSE or DECEIVE THEMSELVES. If they fail badly in school, they make excuses such as, 'I am in a lousy class', 'I have got no time', 'I was born lazy', 'I was born with a bad memory', 'The subject is not interesting', 'My parents are not well educated too'.

They also tend to blame everyone except themselves. They blame their teachers for being boring, they blame the exam for being too difficult, they blame their friends for being distracting or they blame their parents for nagging too much. Worst of all, some students deceive themselves that things are really not that bad. Their mathematics is not as bad as it looks. They are in fact working hard when deep inside they know that they are not.

If you make excuses, blame everyone else or deceive yourself, then this book is not going to work for you too! Why? Because by doing so, it means that you are not in control of your life. Other people and other things are causing you to fail! It is not your fault. This makes you a victim, powerless to change your life at all. 'Life is cruel and unfair' is a common phrase used by these people. So all the strategies and techniques in this book are not going to help at all!

Winner's Frame of Mind
They are the 5% who WANT to succeed
It is a MUST to Succeed
They are Willing to Do Whatever it Takes
They take responsibility for what happens

Loser's Frame of Mind
They are the 95% who WOULD LIKE to succeed
It is okay even if they do not succeed
They are only willing to do what they feel like doing
They make excuses for themselves, blame other people and deceive themselves

GET IN CONTROL AND DO WHATEVER IT TAKES

To sum up this short chapter, you must have the frame of mind of a winner if you are going to get the most out of this book. You must WANT to succeed in learning. You must do whatever it takes. With this level of commitment, you will achieve all the 'A's. Next, you must first take full responsibility for all the good and bad results you are experiencing in your life right now. From now on, do not make excuses for yourself and do not blame other people.

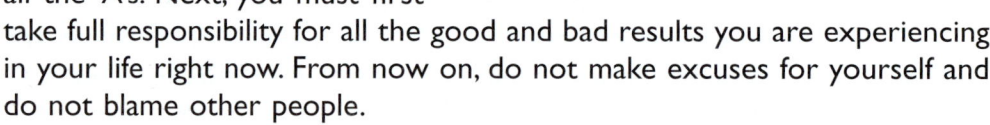

Understand that you are in control! By changing your strategies and your actions, you will change your life! Get ready to begin the journey by learning one of the most powerful ingredients of success…your beliefs!

Chapter 4

I Believe I Can Fly… So I Can!

LUKE SKYWALKER: 'I DON'T BELIEVE IT!'
YODA: 'THAT IS WHY YOU FAILED!'
(FROM THE MOVIE 'STAR WARS: THE EMPIRE STRIKES BACK')

'A' STUDENTS CAN BECAUSE THEY BELIEVE THEY CAN

Many people ask me what was it I had learnt that dramatically changed my results and my life. While many strategies and new skills I learnt allowed me to produce straight 'A's, what made the greatest impact was the change in my beliefs. In the past, I used to believe that I was a lousy student. I used to believe that learning was boring and difficult. That no matter how hard I studied,

I believed that I would never be an 'A' student. Once I had new beliefs like 'I am a genius' and 'Learning is fun and easy', my whole life changed! The same thing goes for you! Before you can achieve 'A's, you must believe you can and that it is fun and easy! It all starts with your beliefs.

I know this may seem very simplistic to you, but it is not! Your beliefs are extremely powerful because they are like the operating system in your brain. They determine the kind of goals you set. They determine the kind of actions you take. They determine whether you will try something or not. They determine whether you give up easily after a setback or you will persevere.

I am not suggesting that merely by believing something you can definitely make it real. No way! Turning beliefs into reality takes the necessary skills and actions to back it up. The point is that when you believe something, your brain is commanded to find a way to make it happen. It will tap all your potential and open up the possibility of producing those results! But once you do not believe that you can do something, your brain gives a command to shut down all your resources to make it happen. It cuts off all possibilities. You will not even have given yourself the option of aspiring for 'A's.

THE CYCLE OF SUCCESS & FAILURE

In general, the beliefs you have will determine the kind of actions you take. The kind of actions you take will determine how much of your potential you will tap. In turn, this will determine the results you get. Finally, the results you get will reinforce the belief you started with.

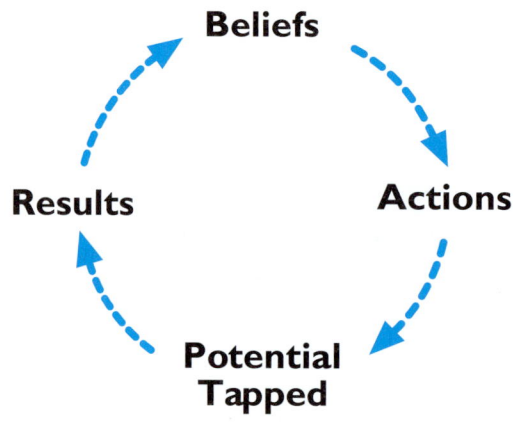

Let's say you have a set of empowering beliefs like 'I am intelligent', 'I can score straight 'A's' and 'Learning is fun and easy'. Now, with these positive beliefs, what kind of actions will you take? Obviously, you will set high goals of achieving straight 'A's. You will put in a lot of effort into your studies as you find it fun. You will study with passion, utilising your time efficiently and putting in more hours than all your friends. Now, by taking all this action, you are going to tap a lot (maybe 90%) of your potential! As a result, you will get great results. Even if you do not get exactly what you want, you will still perform better than a lot of other people. In turn, the 'A's you get will reinforce your belief that 'Studying is easy', 'I am intelligent' and 'I can score 'A's'. Whatever you believe, you will create! It is a self-fulfilling prophecy. This is what I call the cycle of success. So top achievers begin being top achievers by first believing in themselves!

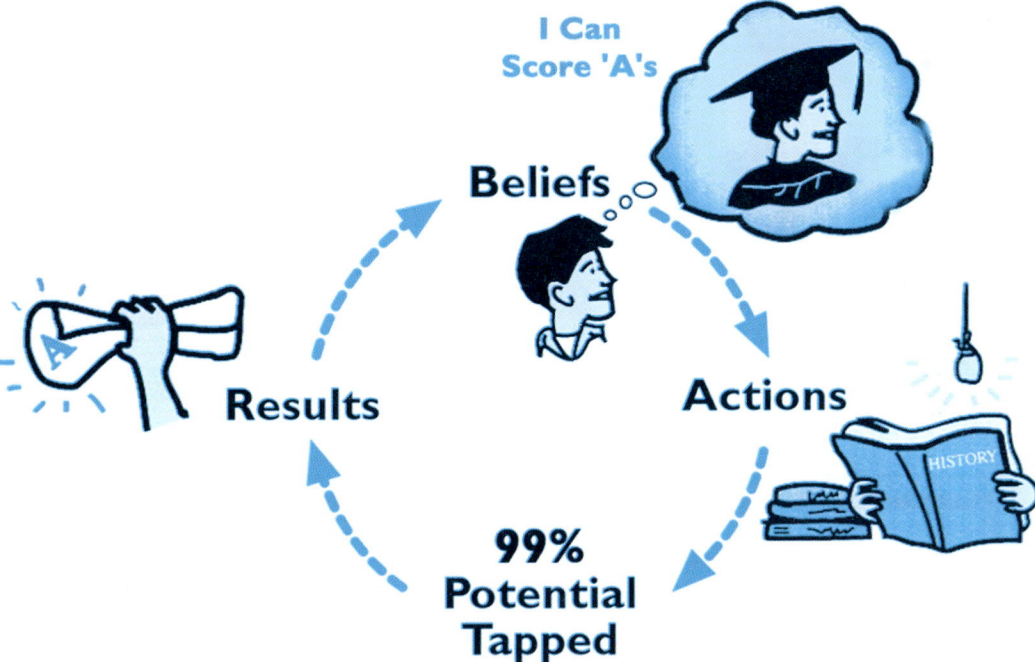

What would happen if you had a set of negative beliefs like 'I am a lousy student', 'No matter how hard I study, I will still screw up', 'There is no way I can score 'A's', 'Studying is boring', 'It's all too difficult'. Do you think you will take action and study hard? No way! You will probably avoid studying and end up doing anything else like surfing the Internet and playing computer games. You will put in a lot less effort as you wouldn't enjoy doing something that's boring and something that you are not good at. With such weak action, you will not tap much of your potential (maybe only 20%) and you will get lousy results. Again, the lousy results will just reinforce all your lousy beliefs.

Many students I know are caught in this trap called the cycle of failure. They keep failing because they think they will fail. And the more they fail, the more they think they will continue to fail.

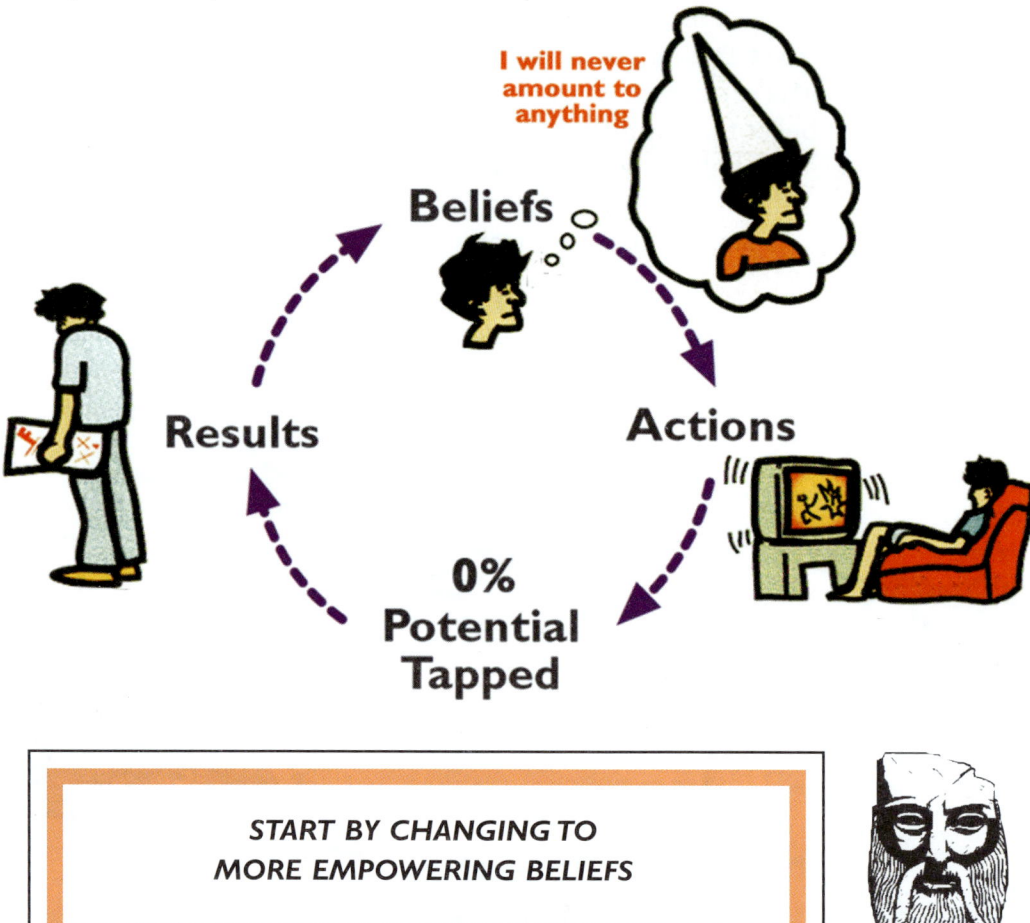

**START BY CHANGING TO
MORE EMPOWERING BELIEFS**

If you happen to be in the Cycle of Failure, you must break the pattern! To do this, you must change your beliefs first (I will share this with you in an upcoming section). Changing your beliefs will cause everything else to change! So, begin to believe that you are an 'A' student, believe that learning is easy and can be fun, believe that you can score 'A's easily. Once you do this, you will automatically take different sets of actions. You will do what 'A' students do. If you are not sure how, then pick a role model (a friend who is scoring excellent results) and model his or her everyday behaviours and strategies in learning. Remember, if you can duplicate these strategies, you can duplicate the results.

> **What Would You Do, If You Were An 'A' Student?**

YOUR BELIEFS ARE TRUE...ONLY TO YOU!

When I tell some people to change their beliefs, they often say, 'Are you crazy? What do you mean change my beliefs? How can I change my beliefs? My beliefs are true! What if I really am lousy and forgetful? What if learning really is boring? I cannot change that!'

What you must remember is that beliefs are never real! They are only true to the person who believes them. If a belief is really true, it would be a fact! Instead, beliefs are nothing but opinions. And no matter what belief you have, there is always someone else that believes something opposite. For every person that believes that mathematics is boring, there is someone else who believes it is fun.

The difference between successful students and lousy students lies in their different beliefs. So, instead of asking if a belief is really true (it is only true if you believe it), you must ask if the beliefs will empower you to succeed. If they empower you, then you must adopt the belief. If it limits you, then you have to abandon the belief.

WHERE DID MY BELIEFS COME FROM?

The whole trouble is that you did not consciously decide to pick your beliefs. If you did, then you would have picked only positive ones. Instead, we wind up with all sorts of beliefs (many of which are lousy) from our parents, our friends, our teachers and our past experiences.

Without meaning to do so, sometimes the people who love us may unknowingly give us beliefs that destroy our lives. Dr Georgi Lozanov, the founder of accelerated learning said that we were all born geniuses, but in the process of growing up, we have been de-geniused by negative suggestions from people. Like our parents, friends or teachers telling us that we are 'lazy', 'good for nothing', 'stupid', 'bad in maths', etc… After we hear it for a while, we slowly begin to believe it, and we live our lives according to these damaging beliefs, thinking they are real and never questioning them again.

HAS THIS HAPPENED TO YOU?

Another way our beliefs are formed is by making inaccurate generalisations of our past experiences. Perhaps when you took your very first mathematics test, you failed badly. Chances are if it happened just one more time, you would have begun to form a belief that 'you are not good in maths'. This is a generalisation you make of a past experience and if you hold on to this belief about yourself, you will fail again, thereby reinforcing it over and over again until it becomes true.

The point is that you may not be bad at maths at all! Perhaps the relevant concepts were not explained properly to you or perhaps you used the wrong techniques or misread the question. We all make mistakes now and again. But using the wrong techniques and believing that you are inherently bad in mathematics are two very different things.

When you tell yourself that you used the wrong methods, it does not make you feel hopeless and lousy. It means that if you learn the concepts and techniques properly, you can score that 'A'. However, if you start saying that 'I failed because I am just bad at maths', then it means you can never be good no matter what you do.

YOU ARE MORE THAN JUST A LABEL

Throughout our lives, we constantly make generalisations about all sorts of things, based on our past experiences. We especially make these generalisations about ourselves and they end up becoming beliefs we have about ourselves.

As a result, we collect a whole lot of labels which we then stick onto ourselves. Some of these labels are 'I'm a lazy person', 'I'm irresponsible,' 'I'm forgetful' or 'I'm lousy at drawing'.

Then, besides the labels we put on ourselves, there are those that others such as our parents, teachers and friends give us. Over time, we forget that these labels are just generalisations and inaccurate beliefs. We are so used to them that we treat them as realities that we live by. The quality of life you are living right now is a direct result of the labels you have collected and pasted on yourself.

LESSONS FROM LIFE

My 'bad at maths' label

In Singapore, many parents drill their children on the multiplication tables (up to multiples of 12) before they enter primary school. In this way, they will have a head start over the rest. However, it has become such a norm that many teachers expect most kids nowadays to have a good understanding of multiplication.

Similarly, my parents tried to teach me and get me to memorise my multiplication tables when I was six years old. For some reason, I just could not understand the meaning of 'multiply'. I understood addition was putting things together and subtracting was taking something away, but I just could not understand what multiplying meant. As a result, I could not do it. My parents were extremely frustrated and thought that I was just dumb. 'Why can't you remember like your cousins?' they would ask. My mum did not help my beliefs by saying that I inherited her 'bad maths' gene. (She failed maths in school too.) Soon, I began to really believe I could not do maths and began associating maths with frustration and failure. Hating maths, I would day-dream in class and not even attempt to do my homework. Needless to say, I failed maths repeatedly. Yes, I had been given a 'bad at maths' label that I carried all the way to Secondary One. I did eventually learn what multiply meant in primary school. A teacher used an example of 3 x 2 as having two boxes of three flowers each. Unfortunately, at that time, the damage had been done to my confidence and beliefs.

Then something happened that changed my beliefs and my life forever. It was the beginning of a new class called Additional Maths. It was a course that everyone said was very tough, much tougher than elementary maths. It so happened that before the first lesson on 'mathematical functions', I spent the night before reading up the chapter in the textbook I had just bought. None of my friends in class bothered to do the same.

The next day, when the maths teacher gave the class lesson on this new topic, everyone was confused. It so happened that because I had read through the chapter, it made some sense to me although I did not understand everything fully. When the teacher asked for a problem to be solved, no one could do it. I was the only one who could give a correct answer and a clear explanation. Everyone looked at me in shock and a few comments filled the air, 'This guy's really smart', 'He's a natural at additional maths', 'He's a maths genius'. The reason for my sudden spark of genius was simply because I had bothered to read ahead.

The feeling was so good, that it motivated me to keep ahead of the teacher so I would go in as a 'genius'. My friends began asking me for help with their homework and I kept receiving praise from the teacher. People began giving me a new label as 'a maths genius' and gradually I began to expect that of myself. My entire beliefs had changed. I began to work hard to maintain my new image and started scoring 'A's consistently. Maths suddenly became fun. Eventually, I scored 'A1's for both additional and elementary maths for the Ordinary Level exams and went on to major in maths in junior college where I scored 'A's for both Further Maths and College Maths.

> **WHY WAIT UNTIL SOMEONE GIVES YOU A 'GIFTED' LABEL? YOU CAN GIVE IT TO YOURSELF NOW!**

BELIEFS...THEY ARE REALLY POWERFUL

You have just learnt that the beliefs you have about who you are and what you are capable of can make an incredible difference in how you will live your life.

If you believe that school is boring, then you will find it boring and get average results. If you believe that learning is fun, you will find it fun and will probably get better grades. If you believe that Chinese is the most difficult language in the world to learn, then you will probably never master it.

Remember that our beliefs are never absolutely true. They are merely opinions and generalisations. But if we believe in them, they will indeed become true. In fact, beliefs are so powerful that they can literally affect you physically and alter your body's biochemistry.

Since the 1940s, doctors have discovered that when you take a medicine and it cures you, it is not so much the ingredients that cure you. What really cures you is your own belief that you will get cured. This is called the placebo effect. In an experiment where they gave cancer patients sugar water and told them that it was a new powerful drug that would melt their tumours, the tumours literally disappeared and the patients got cured. What cured them was a change in their beliefs! Here's another amazing story about beliefs that many of us are familiar with.

LESSONS FROM LIFE

The four-minute mile.

For thousands of years, people believed that it was impossible for a man to run a mile in less than four minutes. Many made this generalisation and formed this belief because anybody who attempted had failed.

Doctors reinforced this belief by showing evidence from their study of the human body that it was physically impossible to achieve this feat. Then in 1954, a man called Roger Bannister refused to believe this. He formed a new belief that it was possible.

After lots of training mentally and physically, he accomplished this supposedly impossible feat. That, however, is not the amazing thing.

What's interesting is that until Roger Bannister accomplished this feat, nobody, for thousands of years, could do it. Yet, within one year of Bannister's breaking the record, 37 other runners also did it and in the following year, another 300 did the same.

Why? Because Bannister's achievement had destroyed people's limiting beliefs that it was impossible.

INSTALLING USEFUL BELIEFS

If believing in something can really make it come true, then why do you not throw away all the beliefs that are limiting you in the past and adopt ones that will propel you to greater heights?

Instead of keeping labels others have stuck on you, create your own positive labels. You may want to give yourself a label like 'I am a leader' or 'I am an excellent manager of time'. In the next exercise, we will be doing just this.

STEP 1: Starting right now, write down all your current limiting beliefs. Write down beliefs you have about yourself, beliefs you have about learning, beliefs you have about school, beliefs you have about your teachers and even beliefs you have about life in general. Examples could be 'I am lousy at maths', 'I am lazy', 'School sucks' or 'Learning is difficult'. Fill in the note pad below now.

My Current Limiting Beliefs

1.
2.
3.
4.
5.
6.
7.

I Am Gifted, So Are You!

STEP 2: Now, examine all the negative beliefs you have put down and for each of them, look for all the possible reasons for not believing they are true. If you think hard enough, you can always find an exception to a belief. List down also, how you think that belief was created in the first place. Remember, it was probably a generalisation you made of something you experienced. What could be another reason for it happening? For each of your negative beliefs, fill in the four columns below. The first one is done as an example.

Limiting Beliefts	Why it is not true	It was created because	The real reason is because
1) • I have a bad memory	• I'm able to memorize the lyrics of new songs very easily • I can remember all the names of wrestlers and their achievements	• I cannot recall what I had studied for the exam	• I did not use the correct technique to remember • I did not make the subject matter interesting enough
2)			
3)			

STEP 3: Here, write down what it would cost you if you continued to hold onto these limiting beliefs. Would it mean failing your finals and not making it to university? Would this be a blow to your parents? I want you to feel that it is absolutely necessary for you to rid yourself of these beliefs now.

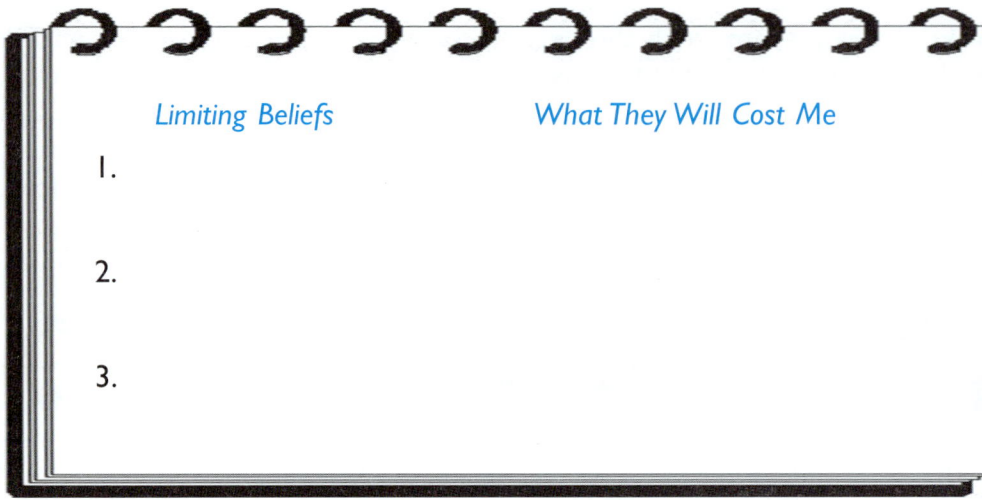

	Limiting Beliefs	What They Will Cost Me
1.		
2.		
3.		

STEP 4: Lastly, write down new empowering beliefs you must have to replace the old limiting ones. What kind of beliefs or labels would you like to have in order to get the results you want? Next, write down reasons and references to back up these new beliefs of yours. Again, if you look hard enough, you will find reasons to back it up.

	New Empowering Beliefs	References
1)	I am a motivated person	When I was preparing for the inter-school basketball game, I practised four hours every day after school, even when I was exhausted.
2)		
3)		
4)		

NO REFERENCES? CREATE THEM!

If you cannot find any references to back up your new beliefs, do what Roger Bannister did. He wanted to believe he could run the mile in less than four minutes but he had no references to back up that belief as he himself never came close to doing it. What's more, no one else in history had done it.

So what Bannister did was that he created references in his mind. He imagined himself accomplishing that feat, over and over again until in his mind, failing was not possible. In the end, he materialised what his mind visualised.

THE 5 BELIEFS OF SUCCESSFUL STUDENTS

Remember that to be a successful student, we must find out what beliefs successful students have. If we can have the same beliefs they have, we will produce the same results in our lives. Below is a summary of five common beliefs that all successful students have.

1. For things to change, I must change first

It is useful to believe that you are responsible for whatever is happening in your life. If you are getting bad grades, if your teacher hates you or your parents treat you like a child, then you must have been responsible for their beliefs either by your actions or by your negative thoughts. By putting the responsibility on yourself, you are putting yourself in charge of your life. Since you created the situations, you can change them.

2. There is no failure, only feedback

Successful students encounter failures too, but if and when they do, they regard failure as 'feedback'. These students treat mistakes or failures as an outcome which they can learn from and constantly change their study techniques or strategies until they succeed. Unlike other students, they do not allow failures to discourage them.

3. If others can, so can I!

Every one of us basically has the same brain capacity or neurological make-up. So why do some of us perform exceptionally well while the rest turn in a mediocre performance? It's because the super performers have learned to access their brain power. This, coupled with their strong powers of concentration, produces the fantastic results you do not even dare fantasise about. But now, with the super learning strategies you are about to learn, you too can tap into your amazing brain and get the same results!

4. Studying is playing.

Absurd notion? Well, think again! Top students enjoy their studies as much as their play. They know that before you can ever be good at anything, you must first love and enjoy it. In this book, you will learn study techniques that will remove the pain from learning and put the joy back into it.

5. Flexibility puts you in control.

> 'YOU MUST UNLEARN WHAT YOU HAVE LEARNED.'
> – YODA TO LUKE SKYWALKER IN 'STAR WARS:
> THE EMPIRE STRIKES BACK'

Successful students know that success depends on flexibility. They are able to change their behaviour and strategies to reach their goals, knowing that those who are inflexible or unadaptable simply get left behind.

As we go on, I will teach you to use your brain in ways that you never have done before. You may even feel uncomfortable at first. This is because society has programmed you to follow certain rules that are not at all useful to learning or behaving. In order to break free from the rut that you are in and scale to greater heights, you must unlearn what you have learnt, and be prepared to learn new things that will transform your life forever.

LESSONS FROM LIFE

Change comes from within

Chris was an angry and frustrated 16-year-old who had a problem communicating with his parents. He felt they did not trust him and the restrictions they imposed on him were ridiculous.

Chris had to be home by 7 pm on weekdays, and on weekends, he was only allowed to stay out until 11.30 pm at night. Most of his friends stayed out way past midnight on weekends, with no questions asked. His entreaties to his father to stop treating him like a child fell on deaf ears. In defiance, Chris would return home past his curfew hour each time, and for this he would be reprimanded by his angry father.

When Chris approached me for advice (after I had directed a few Super-Teen camps, I became an unofficial counsellor to troubled teens), the first thing I told him was that he was responsible for his parents' mistrust of him. Chris was surprised but he listened carefully when I explained that if he wanted things to change, he would have to change his behaviour first. 'How?' he wanted to know and I gave him a few pointers.

So a changed Chris began returning home before his curfew expired. He also began cleaning his own room without been reminded to. His mother was further pleasantly surprised when he began helping out in the kitchen. Then, one night, when he had planned to go out to the cinema, he told his surprised father, 'I think I'll stay at home tonight. I've a class test tomorrow and I do not feel I've prepared enough for it.'

Guess what happened next? Well, his parents began changing the way they regarded him and that changed their behaviour towards him. They began to regard him as a mature and responsible young man and, after a month, gave him more freedom!

Chapter 5

You Have the Brain of a Genius

A LOUSY BRAIN OR AN UNTRAINED ONE?

You often hear people complain that they are not as smart as other people. They say they have a slower brain, a less creative brain or one that just cannot absorb anything. 'If I were smarter, I would do a lot better in school' is one of the most common excuses I hear. Many people ask me if I believe that some students are just more intelligent than others. My answer is always a definite yes. More intelligent students learn faster and produce better results. I always continue by saying that 'your intelligence is your responsibility'. What I mean is that if you are not intelligent, it is your fault. 'But how can I help it if I am not intelligent?' is always the reply.

Well, I believe that a person's intelligence can be trained and anyone can become more intelligent. If you decide today that you want to increase your brain power, your intelligence, your memory and your ability to think, you can! While I acknowledge that there are some people who are born gifted, most gifted people or geniuses were self-trained! I am a good example. I basically trained my brain to be gifted.

HOW EDITH WAS TRAINED TO BE GIFTED

An experiment done by Aaron Stern in 1952 on his daughter Edith proves that intelligence can be trained and that anyone, given the right learning environment and strategies, can be a genius.

What Aaron Stern did was he gave his daughter the most stimulating environment he could think of. From the time she was born, he would play classical music to her, speak to her only in adult language (no baby talk) and teach her lots of new words every day using picture cards. The result of all his effort? At the age of one, Edith could already speak complete sentences. At the age of five, Edith had finished reading the entire volume of *Encyclopaedia Britannica*. At the age of six, she was reading six books a day and the *New York Times*. At the age of 12, she had entered college and at the age of 15, was teaching higher mathematics at the Michigan State University! The good news is you do not have to start at a very young age to train your brain. You can start the training of your brain at any age! But how is it possible to increase your intelligence? To understand the whole process, you have to discover...

THE BRAIN'S INFINITE CAPACITY

To understand how powerful our brain truly is, we need to explore some of the findings researchers have made about the brain over the last 50 years.

Our brain is made up of billions of brain cells called neurones. Although extremely tiny, a single neurone has the processing power that is equivalent to a personal computer. The storage capacity of one neurone is also extremely huge as each cell contains our entire genetic blueprint necessary to recreate another human being just like us! We have on average, 1 million million (1,000,000,000,000) neurones that make up our brain. In comparison, a honeybee that can build and maintain a honeycomb, calculate distances, collect nectar, produce honey, mate, care for its young and communicate to other bees has only 7000 neurones. This indicates that we have tremendous brain power by comparison. In fact, we have so many neurones that even if you have a couple of million less than another person, it wouldn't make a difference at all.

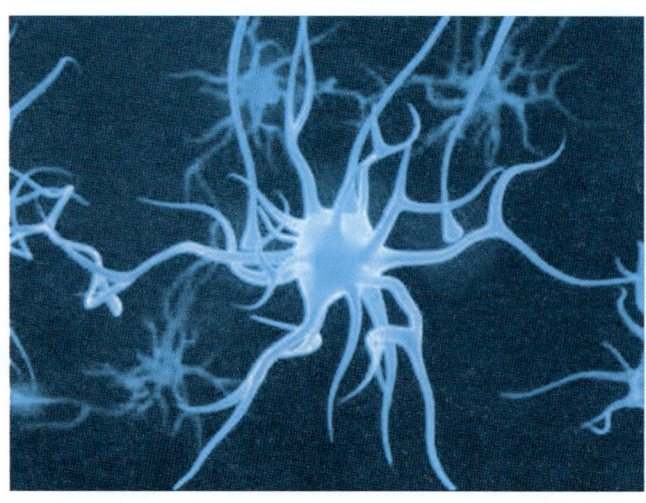

NEURO-CONNECTIONS DETERMINE YOUR INTELLIGENCE

If all of us have basically the same number of neurones, then what really sets students apart in terms of intelligence? What makes one student smarter than another? The answer is the number of connections there are between our neurones. These connections are called neuro-connections.

Twenty weeks after conception, our brain's neurones begin making thousands of connections with one another. These connections determine our range of behaviours and therefore, our intelligence. They are like the 'thought wires' in a robot's brain. If you are really good in solving maths problems, you have probably developed very rich neuro-connections that allow you to analyse, process and solve maths problems. However, with this same set of connections, you may not be able to draw very well. Another student may be brilliant at drawing because he has the necessary thought connections that allow him to conceptualise and render the drawings. The more neuro-connections we have, the more intelligent we are in a particular area.

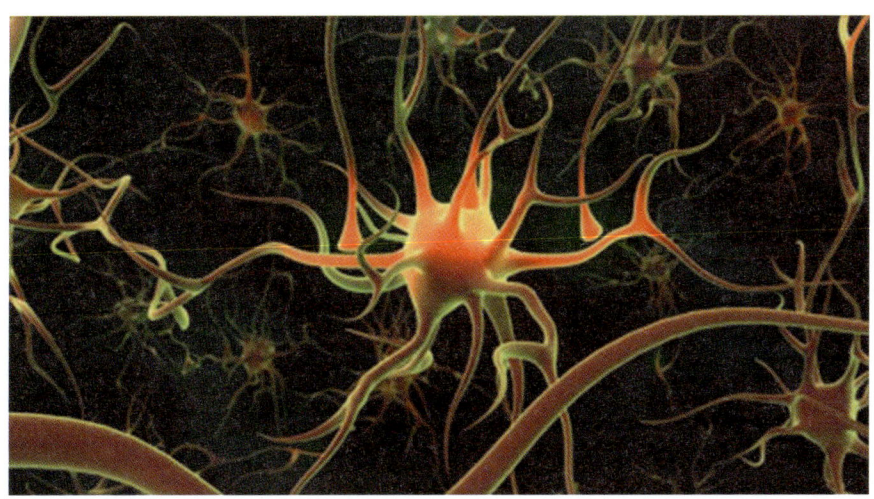

Then, the most important question is what affects the number of neuro-connections we have? This is determined by how much you use your brain. Every time you see, hear or do something new or every time you think, your brain gets stimulated. This is when your brain starts making more connections, making you more and more intelligent.

LET'S FOLD OUR ARMS

Let's do a demonstration to discover the power of neuro-connections. Are you ready to play with me? Remember, the best way to learn is to participate! Great! Now, fold your arms. That wasn't too difficult right? Now, I want you to change direction and fold your arms the opposite way. Go on!

Was that easy? Did you get a bit confused in the beginning? When you eventually did manage to change the direction in which your arms were folded, did you feel comfortable or uncomfortable? If you are like most people you would have been a bit confused at first but after a while, you would eventually figure it out.

Chapter 5 • *You Have the Brain of a Genius*

Now, you may be asking what does this have to do with my brain and with learning? Think about this. How come it was easy for you to fold your arms the first time without thinking about it? Well, you could perform that 'behaviour' because over the years of learning it and doing it again and again, your brain has formed certain thought patterns or neuro-connections to allow you to do that easily. When asked to do something different, something you do not normally do, like folding your arms the opposite way, you fumbled a bit because your brain did not have the necessary connections to perform that new behaviour.

Now, what if you sat in front of a mirror for an hour and practised folding your arms the opposite way? You would definitely be able to fold and change direction easily this time. Why? Because in the process of doing something new over and over, your brain gets stimulated, generating new neuro-connections that allow you to perform that new behaviour rather easily.

IF YOU ARE LOUSY AT SOMETHING... DO MORE OF IT

What is the implication? If you are lousy at maths, what should you do? That's right! You have got to keep doing more and more maths! The reason you are lousy at algebra is because you do not have enough neuro-connections to allow you to understand and apply algebra. By doing more and more algebra, it will become easier and easier! Your brain gets used to it as it creates new connections and thought patterns. The first time you tried ice-skating or roller blading, I bet it seemed really difficult to balance. After a few rounds, it became effortless! Your brain learned to balance.

This sounds really simple. Do more and you get better at something. True. But most students do not follow this basic principle. Ask yourself this: When you are lousy at something like history or maths, do you tend to do a lot more of it or do you do less? I bet the answer will be less. We tend to hate and avoid subjects we are lousy at, giving the excuse that they are boring or that we are just not interested in that subject. At the same time, we tend to do more and more of what we are good at like playing computer games. That's why we get better and better!

The more you use your brain the better it gets. Your brain is just like a muscle. The only way to grow a muscle and get it big and bulging is to stress it, challenge it and carry things that are heavier than what you can normally take. It's the same thing with your brain. The only way to keep getting smarter is to do things which make you think real hard and challenge you! Everyday, find something that you find really difficult to understand or learn and challenge yourself to find out to figure it out. That's the secret to getting smarter.

> **YOUR BRAIN IS LIKE A MUSCLE. USE IT OR LOSE IT.**

DO YOU GET CONFUSED?...GOOD!

Let me ask you a question. Is it good to be confused? Most people think it is bad to be confused or to not understand something. In fact, being confused is the key to getting smarter and better at something. When you are confused about something, it means your brain is facing something beyond its present ability. When this happens, your brain is forced to think and try to figure things out. The process of thinking stimulates your brain, creating more and more neuro-connections and making you smarter. The next time you encounter that same problem, it would seem easier to understand now!

The biggest problem is that most students hate to be confused and they avoid confusing and difficult subjects and chapters. They make the excuse that the subject is not interesting and that the confusing topic will probably not be tested in the exam anyway. As a result, they skip all these difficult chapters and study only those which they easily understand. When questions on these difficult chapters appear in the exam, they will obviously not be able to answer any of them. This typically happens to the 'lousy student'.

'A' STUDENTS GET CONFUSED TOO... THEY JUST RESPOND DIFFERENTLY

How about the 'A' student? Many people have the impression that 'A' students are just smart and that they probably understand things really fast and easily. This is not true at all! There are many chapters and subjects 'A' students find extremely confusing and difficult too. I can testify to this because there were many points that I just found totally confusing even after having read the chapter or even after the teacher had explained it a hundred times in class. The main difference is that when 'A' students are confronted with something difficult and confusing, they do not avoid it or skip it. They look at it as a challenge, something they must solve or figure out. They will spend hours and hours trying to figure out the answer by themselves or by asking friends and teachers. As a result of all this thinking, they stimulate their brain cells to form the connections necessary to slowly understand everything. At the end of the year, they appear to be super smart, being able to answer all those difficult problem sums. This happens not because they were born gifted, but because they have trained their brain to become smarter.

'I DON'T KNOW!' — IT CAN KILL YOUR BRAIN'S GROWTH

Do you know the surest way to stop your neuro-connections from growing? The answer is to say 'I do not know'. And you know what? I know you are guilty of it because I must admit I have done it a few times myself. When you are faced with a question and you answer, 'I do not know!' you are actually telling your brain to stop thinking! This will stop your brain from growing straight away. Instead, you should respond by saying, 'Let me think about it' and start thinking! Giving a bad answer is better than no answer at all because at least it starts the thinking process.

I Am Gifted, So Are You!

6 WAYS TO STIMULATE YOUR BRAIN

1. Listen to Baroque music (a branch of classical music composed in the 1700-1800s).
2. Keep asking and answering lots of questions in the classroom.
3. Challenge yourself by attempting new and more difficult questions and materials every day.
4. Expose your mind to information beyond the textbooks by reading outside the curriculum.
5. Never ever skip difficult topics and chapters, but be excited to figure out the answer!
6. Understand that the only way to get smarter is to make mistakes and get confused first!

6 WAYS TO STOP BRAIN STIMULATION

1. Skipping chapters or information you think are too difficult or confusing.
2. Being afraid of asking questions when you do not know something.
3. Replying 'I do not know!' and not even bothering or thinking about the answer.
4. Only learning things you find easy.
5. Copying answers from friends without finding out how to solve the questions.
6. Being afraid of raising your hand and answering questions in class (it does not matter if you get the questions wrong, as long as you tried to think of the answer).

YOUR INTELLIGENCE IS LIMITLESS

If stimulating your brain increases your intelligence, then is there a limit to how much more intelligent you can become? Well, this depends on how much more neuro-connections your brain can continue to create until it runs out of space! Remember that we have 1,000,000 million neurones and each neurone can make connections with thousands of other neurones.

The total number of possible thought patterns if permutated, would be so large that if we were to write it in normal handwriting, it would be 1 followed by a mind boggling 10.5 million kilometres of zeros. To give you an idea of how big this number really is, let me compare it with something you are familiar with. We all know that the atom is one of the smallest particles in the universe right? Well, do you know how many atoms there are in the universe? It is estimated at only 10 with 100 zeros. (1×10^{100}). Your brain's potential for growth is millions more times bigger than there are atoms in the universe.

10000000000000000000000000
0000000000000000000000000
0000000000000000000000000
0000000000000000000000000
0000000000000000000000000
0000000000000000000000000
0000000000000000000000000
0000000000000000000000000
0000000000000000000000000
0000000000000000000000000
00… 10.5 million kilometres long

YOUR TWO-IN-ONE BRAIN

To learn how to use more of your brain power, you must first understand how it works. The top and central layers of the brain are made up of a left hemisphere and a right hemisphere. Connecting both sides is a mass of fibres known as the corpus collosum. Each half plays a very different role. Our left brain deals with logic, maths, rational thinking, linearity, language, sequence, facts, analysis and so on. Our right brain takes cares of more 'fun' things like rhythm, creativity, lateral thinking, day-dreaming, holism, imagination, colours and feelings.

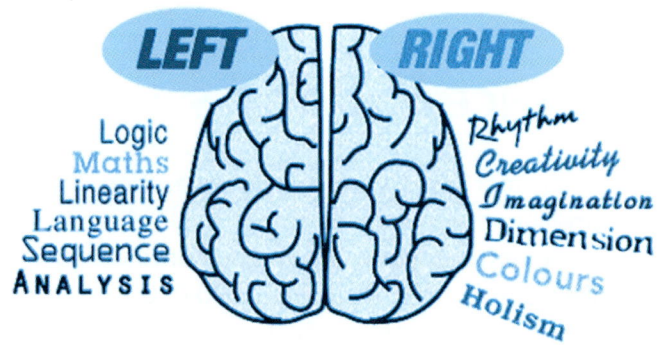

I Am Gifted, So Are You!

LEFT BRAIN GOOD, RIGHT BRAIN BAD?

If you think about it, 90% of the subjects that we are taught in school are left brain based subjects. Core school subjects like geography, history, mathematics, physics, chemistry, biology, English, foreign languages, economics, accounting, law all require left brain functions such as learning facts, analysing information, rational thinking, mathematics and logic.

So if your left brain is constantly being demanded to perform 90% of the time in school, then what about your right brain? It is totally under-utilised. As a result it gets 'really bored' and it ends up distracting you instead!

Do you day-dream a lot in class or end up doodling on your note pad during lectures? Do you know why this happens? It's because most lessons involve your left brain functions and so your right brain has hardly anything to do. So it 'looks for something to do'. Your right brain happily goes off day-dreaming and makes you want to start drawing and doodling on any paper nearby.

Have you also wondered why you always seem to need to turn on the radio or have some music going before you can study? Same reason! It's because your right brain is looking for some attention.

So it seems your right brain is the main cause of your distractions and lack of attention. The answer to solving this problem is to involve both your right and your left brain in the learning process! Not only does it keep your right brain happy and occupied, but this literally doubles your brain power since you now use both sides instead of one!

MOST GENIUSES WERE WHOLE-BRAINERS

In fact, research has shown that the main difference between average people and geniuses is that geniuses have learnt to use both sides of their brain at the same time, no matter what they do. So instead of the average 1%, geniuses are able to tap 4 to 5% of their potential brain power!

Leonardo da Vinci (1452–1519) who is honoured as one of the greatest artists of all time was an accomplished scientist, mathematician and architect as well. Did you know before he painted his masterpieces, he would use mathematic equations to calculate the precise combination of colours to create the desired effect? Yes, his genius came from the fact that he used both sides of his brain simultaneously.

Albert Einstein (1879–1955) used to fail mathematics at school and was considered a slow learner, but his musicality was well developed and he was both a credible violinist and artist. It was only when Einstein learned to use both sides of his brain that he unleashed this genius and formulated the theory of relativity.

He did it by first indulging in a right brain activity, day-dreaming. Einstein loved to day-dream and one day, as he was sitting on a hill day-dreaming as usual, he imagined himself riding on a sunbeam to the far end of the universe, then returning towards the sun.

That day-dream suggested to him that the universe was in fact curved and hence space, time and light had to be as well. This gave birth to the theory of relativity. Other examples of whole-brained geniuses abound, if we look for them.

So, how do we use both sides of our brain to learn simultaneously at the same time? Well, all the super learning strategies in this book are based on this principle of whole-brain learning.

ARE YOU LEFT OR RIGHT BRAIN DOMINANT?

I have noticed that in anywhere around the world, there will always be some students who are more left-brain dominant while others are more right-brain dominant.

Left-brain dominant students usually display the following characteristics. They are normally very neat and organised. They are the ones with neatly combed hair and shirts tucked in their pants. Without fail, their pencil boxes will be well stocked and items neatly arranged. There will always be pens, pencils, a ruler, erasers, etc. Their tables at home are always clean. They will have a place for everything and they will notice and get upset if anyone borrows their things and does not put it back in the right place. These students generally do well in languages, mathematics, crossword puzzles and IQ tests. As a result, they normally excel in school and are the pride of their parents. However, these students tend to be more insensitive and may lack people skills. They are also generally less imaginative, emotional, sociable and creative.

Right-brain dominant students are the complete opposite! Their hair is always in a mess and their shirts un-tucked. They day-dream in class and are usually very talkative and are easily distracted. They are normally very disorganised. Their rooms usually look like pigsties and their study desks are usually buried under books and papers thrown about. Right brain students do not do too well in school as they have short attention spans and find mathematics confusing. However, these students usually excel in sports, arts, music, socialising and creative-based activities. They also get along very well with people and tend to be more in tune with others' feelings.

Which category do you think you most likely fit into? Of course there's also a group of students who are equally strong in both left and right brain functions and would display many of both characteristics!

Which brain dominance is more important? The answer is both! In order to be truly intelligent and succeed in life, functions from both sides of the brain are equally important! In fact, most entrepreneurs and millionaires are more right-brain inclined. This is because it takes imagination, feelings for others and creativity (all right-brain functions) to be an entrepreneur.

TWO BRAINS, ONE SYSTEM

Unfortunately, all students (both left and right brain dominant) are put through the same conveyor belt of the education system where 90% of subjects are taught and tested using left-brain dominant techniques. So what happens? Obviously, right-brain students will be the ones who fail and get kicked into all the lousy classes and schools. How unfair! Pretty soon, right-brain students begin to be labelled as 'slow', 'attention deficit prone', 'stupid' and 'problem students'. And you know what? I was one of them! After a while, these students begin to believe that they are stupid and lousy and that belief seals their fate!

The good news is that if you are a right-brain student, you can begin to learn to use your right-brain functions to learn a left-brain subject! This is exactly what I am going to teach you in this book. Yes! You can use your strong traits like your imagination, music, feelings and artistic ability to learn history, geography, mathematics and even science.

What if you are already a left-brain dominant student and are already doing fairly well in school. Does it mean you do not have to learn these techniques that I am going to share with you? No. If you are already left-brain dominant and doing well, can you imagine what would happen if you learn how to use your right brain that has been under-utilised as well? You will increase your brain power and learning power even more!

LESSONS FROM LIFE, KENNETH'S STORY.

Kenneth Wong (incidentally, he was the illustrator of the previous edition of this book) was a typical right-brain student. He loved to day-dream, draw, and had a short attention span in class. He was extremely creative but had trouble with subjects like mathematics and history. As a result, he was at the bottom of his class at St Joseph's Institution in Singapore. What changed his results was learning super learning strategies like Mind Maps® which allowed him to use his imagination, creative and artistic ability to study left brain subjects like history, science and mathematics. Suddenly, he found learning such subjects fun and easy. In three months, he topped his class and for his 'O' level examinations, scored seven distinctions!

THINK ABOUT IT!

If you are a right-brain dominant student, fear not! You can use a right brain technique to learn left brain subjects in school and excel in them!

By learning how to use both sides of your brain simultaneously to learn, you will more than double your brain power…just like a genius does!

Let's start learning how to learn by doubling our brain power in the next chapter on…

Chapter 6

Power Reading for Information

Now that you have an idea of the power of your brain, let's start on the first of the super learning strategies, Power Reading for Information. Before you can start making notes, memorising or revising, the first step would be to read your textbooks and course materials for the information you need to score that 'A'.

Unfortunately, most students do not read their textbooks or their course materials with the purpose of information gathering. They think reading is for the purpose of just understanding or gaining knowledge. They will then re-read that same material during their revision time in order to try remembering it. If you do this, you will find that when the exam draws near, you will have too much to read, too much to cover and insufficient time to do it.

THE PURPOSE OF POWER READING IS TO GATHER INFORMATION

HOW TO REDUCE YOUR STUDY TIME BY 80% & REMEMBER MORE IN THE PROCESS!

'A' students understand the power of information gathering. They know that it is not the number of words you read that is important, it is the amount of information you get out of it that really matters.

In general, in any textbook, only 20% of the words contain the information you need to fully acquire all the knowledge and to score an 'A'. These words are called the keywords. Keywords include nouns, verbs, adverbs and adjectives. The surprising fact is that the remaining 80% of the words contain no useful information at all. These non keywords are often connecting words like 'is', 'of', 'the', 'has', 'for'. Well, if these words contain no information, what are they doing in the textbook? Their sole purpose is to link the keywords together to form sentences. They are useful in helping you understand what you are reading for the first time, but for the purpose of recalling and revision, they are a waste of time.

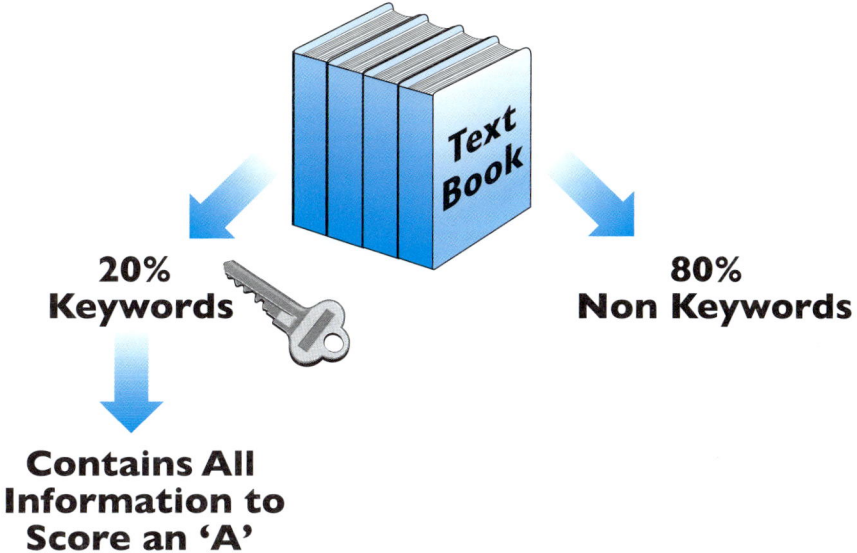

POWER READING IS COLLECTING KEYWORDS

In order to be an effective learner, you must understand that you should only read through your textbooks or course materials just once. As you do, you extract the 'essence' or 'information' in the form of key ideas and keywords.

You then put only these key ideas and keywords into your notes (Mind Maps®), to be ready for revision. You can then ignore and throw away the rest of the 80% of the non keywords forever. So for your upcoming revisions, you just have to go through the 20% of the keywords in your Mind Maps® and get 100% of the information. You will effectively reduce your learning time by 80%!

Gathering keywords from a textbook is like collecting grains of rice from a huge paddy field. It may initially take many hours to go through all the wheat and sift out the edible grains. However, once it is done, we only have to eat the essence of the whole field to get the energy we need.

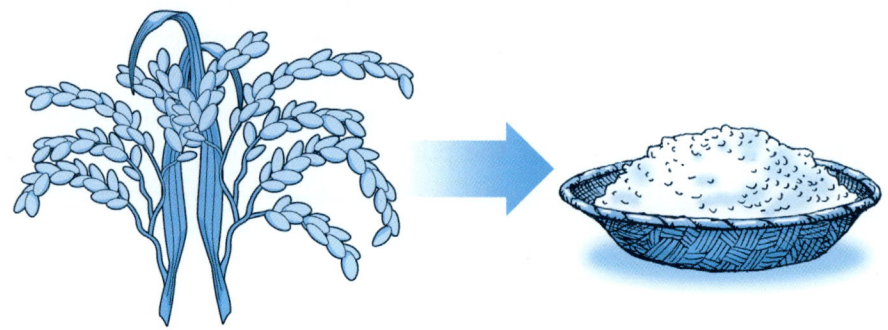

A DEMONSTRATION ON THE POWER OF KEYWORDS

Let me show you the power of keywords. I want you to read the 116-word passage below.

For some time, it has been known that the human brain can be divided into two parts. The left brain and the right brain. It has also been known that the left brain controls the right side of the body and that the right brain controls the left side of the body. It has also been discovered that when the left brain is damaged, it will cause the right side of the body to become paralysed. Similarly, if the right brain is damaged, it will cause the left side of the body to become paralysed. In other words, damage to one side of the brain will cause the corresponding side of the body to become paralysed.

After reading that passage, your brain got a certain amount of information out of it. Again, not all the words contributed to this. The information packed keywords are only the ones in bold.

What would happen if you were to just read the keywords. Would you still get all the information? Read the next passage to find out.

> *human brain divided two parts. left brain right brain.*
> *left brain controls right side body*
> *right brain controls left side body.*
> *left brain damaged, right side body paralysed.*
> *right brain damaged, left side body paralysed.*
> *damage one side brain cause corresponding side body paralysed.*

I am very sure that by just reading the keywords, you would have gotten the same information. None of the information would have been lost. However, read the majority of the non keywords by themselves in the paragraph below.

> *For some time, it has been known that the   can be   into .*
> *The   and the   . It has also been known that the   the*
> *of the   and that the   the   of the   . It has also been*
> *discovered that when the   is   , it will cause the   of the*
> *to become   . Similarly, if the   is   it will cause the   of*
> *the   to become   . In other words,   to   of the   will*
> *the   of the   to become   .*

How much information did you get out of reading all these words? The answer is: nothing. Yet these words form almost 80% of the original passage. This tells you that every time you read your textbooks or course materials, you are actually wasting 80% of your time unnecessarily. In the rest of the chapter, you will learn how to read effectively to gather these keywords to be put into your whole brain notes (Mind Maps®).

Chapter 6 • Power Reading for Information

WHY WE MUST LEARN TO POWER READ

In order to effectively read a textbook and gather information, we must learn how to power read. Power reading is a technique of reading that is designed to increase your reading speed and to increase your concentration and comprehension of reading at the same time.

If you are like most people, you would share the common problem of having poor concentration and poor comprehension while reading. You may also read at a speed which is way below what you are really capable of.

Through power reading, you will be able to read up to three times faster than your current speed. This will give you a big advantage over your friends as you will have a lot more time to relax or move on to note-making and revision.

READING FASTER INCREASES YOUR ABILITY TO CONCENTRATE AND COMPREHEND

Many people avoid reading fast because they think that doing so will reduce their ability to concentrate as well as comprehend what they are reading. In fact, the reason you have poor concentration is because you read too slowly. Remember that lack of concentration is the result of your mind wandering and thinking about other things. The reason it does this (especially the creative right brain) is because it is not fully utilised and it gets bored. Research has shown that our eyes and brain have the ability to absorb over 20,000 words per minute but most people read at the rate of only 200 words per minute, less than 1% of our true potential. If you had a company that employed 100 workers but at any one time, there was only enough work for one of the workers, what would happen? The 99 other workers will get bored and start talking to one another, creating lots of distraction. This is what is happening to your brain when it reads too slowly.

Through many seminars and training programmes, I have proven many times that when I cut down the amount of time I give my students to read a passage, the comprehension level as reflected by tests increases! However, this is provided they use the power reading techniques taught to read effectively.

Let me give you another example using a metaphor. Let's say you were driving down the expressway at 45 kilometres per hour. Would you be concentrating very hard? I doubt it. Your mind will probably be wandering around and be extremely bored. In comparison, what would happen if you were driving at 200 km per hour. I am very sure you would be a lot more alert and your concentration level will be a lot higher! Well, it's the same with reading.

THE EYES HAVE IT

 What determines how fast you read? And how can we increase our speed of reading? The answer lies in the way our eyes move. When asked, many people think that their eyes move smoothly from side to side like a scanner as it reads over a page like what you see below.

What really happens is that our eyes do not move smoothly at all. They move pretty much like a typewriter instead, stopping and moving as we read a page. When we read, our eyes move in a series of pauses like what you see in the following page.

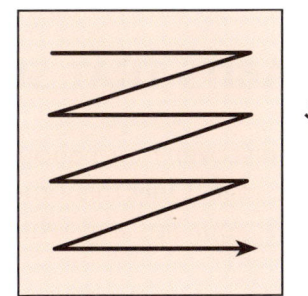

Chapter 6 • Power Reading for Information

Our eyes must pause to pick up information. Every time our eyes pause, we require more time, between ¼ of a second to one second, to read. The more pauses there are, the longer it takes to read and the slower our reading. speed. The key to power reading is to reduce the number of pauses our eyes make as they read.

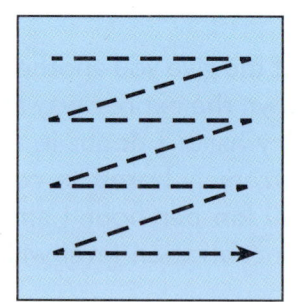

For people who read one word at a time, their eyes will pause at every single word. Assuming that each eye pause takes ½ a second, it will mean that in one minute, they will only be able to read up to 120 words. This reading speed of 120 words per minute (wpm) is considered below average.

In order to read faster, you must not read one word at a time. You must read chunks of words at each eye pause. If you can read two or three words at a time, your reading speed would be 240–360 words per minute. This is the speed of an average reader.

With a bit of training, you should easily be able to read chunks of five to seven words at a time, giving you a power reading speed of between 600–840 words per minute. This is what students who attend the five-day Super-Teen™ training are able to do after a few exercises.

DO A QUICK CHECK ON YOUR READING SPEED
To get a quick gauge of your current reading ability, set a stopwatch to one minute and see how many words you can read at that time.

If reading at 600–850 wpm seems so simple and if all it takes is for us to read chunks of words, why do so many people have problems with reading? Why do so many people read slowly? The reason is because of …

HABITS THAT SLOW DOWN YOUR READING

To discover more about your own reading habits, I want you to re-read the last page. Only this time, be consciously aware of what is happening to your eyes, your lips and what is going on inside your mind.

Now, counter-check to see if you are guilty of any of the slow reading habits listed below.

1. Mouthing Words

As you read, do you notice that your lips move? If they do, then you have the habit of silently mouthing words, a habit that you picked up from primary or grammar school when you first started learning to read by reading aloud in class. Mouthing words slows down your speed as you are limited by how fast your lips can move! By consciously stopping this, you can slowly remove this habit.

2. Subvocalisation

Some people do not move their lips as they read, but instead, they have a voice inside their head reading out the words to them. This is called subvocalisation. This is almost just as bad as your speed is limited to how fast that voice in your head can talk. Because it is such a common habit ingrained in many of us, it is almost impossible to remove that inner voice. Instead, you must begin to practise subvocalising on only the keywords and not every single word. The other way is to drown that voice out and slowly remove that habit by playing very fast beat music (without lyrics) as you read.

3. Regression

Another common problem of readers is having the tendency to keep skipping back and reading over the same words. This habit wastes a lot of time and normally causes the reader to read at less than 100 wpm. Over 90% of regression is caused by apprehension, fear of missing out and lack of confidence in reading. This can be reduced dramatically through getting into the habit of reading fast and trusting your own ability. The other reason could be due to the reader's poor vocabulary or poor command of the language. This issue must be addressed separately.

4. Reading word for word

As mentioned, reading word for word will only allow you to read at 120 wpm. Many people think that this is the correct way of reading as we all first started learning to read by reading aloud, one word at a time.

In power reading, your task is not to read words, but to read for information. It is perfectly alright to read groups of words at one time, focusing only on the keywords.

5. Short eye span

Your eye span is the number of words your eyes can pick up at a glance or at every pause. Most people without much training will have an eye span of about three or four words. If you are a frequent reader, you should have an eye span of about six or seven words. The greater your eye span, the more number of words you will be able to pick up at each eye pause. In order to reach 600–850 wpm, you must train your eye span to reach six or seven words. We will talk about how to accomplish this in the next section.

You can check your current eye span by covering a sentence with a piece of paper. Focus your eyes on the sentence that is being covered. Then, move the paper away for a split second and cover the sentence again. How many words were you able to pick up from that sentence? The number is your rough eye span.

POWER READING TECHNIQUES TO INCREASE YOUR SPEED AND COMPREHENSION

Now that you understand what determines your reading speed, concentration and the bad habits of poor readers, here are a few powerful techniques you can use right now to power read.

1. Use a Pencil as a Pacer

When your eyes have nothing to guide it as it reads, it will tend to dance all over the page, slowing down your reading. Whenever you read, use a pencil to guide your eyes over each sentence. It will increase your focus and concentration. The other reason for using a pencil is to pace your eyes. Just as you need someone to pace your speed as you run a marathon, you should use the pencil to pace your speed of reading. Move your pencil slightly faster than your normal reading speed, it will train your eyes to catch up and get into the habit of moving faster.

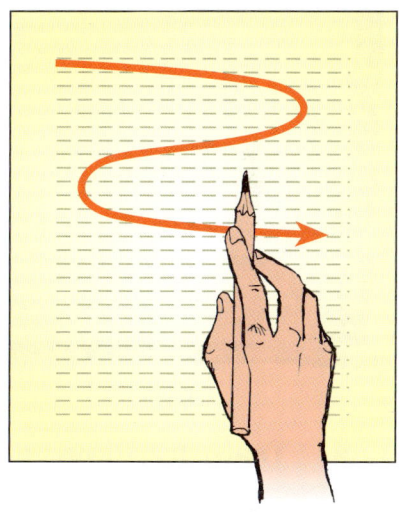

2. Look Out for Key Ideas and Circle Keywords

As you read the text, scan through the non keywords and circle the keywords only. At the same time, look out for the key ideas in each paragraph. It is common that each paragraph will contain a single key idea with supporting points. Knowing this will improve your information gathering process.

3. Increase Your Eye Span to Read Groups of Five to Seven Words at a Time

Go through the exercises A to D on pages 62–66 to gradually increase your eye span. At the same time, consciously read groups of five to seven words at a time as you go through the text.

1 When	2 You	3 Read	4 Word	5 for	6 Word
7 it	8 really	9 slows	10 down	11 your	12 reading

1 When you read word for word	2 it really slows down your reading

4. Train by Playing High Tempo Music as You Read

When you read at home, you can play high tempo music (without lyrics) to train your brain and eyes to read faster. We tend to read at a speed that matches the speed of music we listen to. You will find that when you read without the music, you will be tuned to a higher speed.

The myth that reading in silence improves concentration is not true. In fact, reading in total silence makes your mind wander. The other reason for reading with loud and fast music is so that it will drown your inner voice that slows you down and cuts out potentially distracting background sounds.

5. Read the Chapter from Back to Front

Another technique that most students do not realise is that you should always read the back of a chapter before proceeding to read the front. Why? Because the back of every chapter normally contains a summary of that chapter as well as questions that test you on that chapter. When you read the summary and the questions, your mind will have an idea of what the chapter is all about. Also, your mind will also know what to look out for. It will then be able to read the text with a purpose. You will become a reader actively looking out for information.

In addition, you should always scan through the headings and subheadings of a chapter before you begin reading the words in detail. Previewing the chapter will prepare your mind and make reading more effective.

6. Keep Pushing and Stretching Yourself

Have you ever seen how runners train? They are known to tie weights to their feet as they run in training. This feels extremely uncomfortable, but it trains the muscles to become stronger. When they take off the weights, they will feel very light in comparison and will be able to run very fast.

You can use this same technique in power reading. As you train yourself in power reading, use your pencil to push yourself at a speed beyond what you are comfortable with. For example, if you currently read at only 100 wpm, keep forcing yourself to go at 300–400 wpm. It does not matter if you feel totally confused and uncomfortable. The purpose of this is to stretch and overload your system. After lots of drills and practice, your brain's potential will get used to it. Remember, this must be done with lots of practice for it to be effective.

Now that you have learnt how to Power Read for information, the next step in the super learning strategies is to master creating whole-brain notes called Mind Maps® using the key ideas and keywords you have picked up from the text.

EXERCISE A1

A	B	C
N	D	F
K	V	L
S	Q	I
W	M	P
X	U	G
O	Y	R
V	Z	J
E	T	N
B	L	A
P	N	H
V	W	F
C	X	Z
R	O	A
D	J	Z
G	P	K
Z	F	T
Q	R	U
E	C	S
Y	H	X
F	A	N
U	I	P
H	S	W
L	G	D
M	H	V
J	Z	Q
T	K	O
I	X	Y
K	E	E

EXERCISE A2

Now that you have an idea of the power of your brain, let's start on the first of the super learning strategies, Power Reading for Information. Before you can start making notes, memorising or revising, the first step would be to read your textbooks and course materials for the information you need to score that 'A'. Unfortunately, most students do not read their textbooks or their course materials with the purpose of information gathering. They think reading is for the purpose of just understanding or gaining knowledge. They will then re-read that same material during their revision time in order to try remembering it. If you do this, you will find that

Instructions to exercise A_1–E_1: Focus your eyes on the centre letter and without moving your eyes, read the centre letter and the letter on the left and then on the right, e.g. 'B, A, C', 'D, N, F' move your eyes down and read the entire list of alphabet letters in this order! Centre, Left and Right.

Instructions to exercise A_2–E_2: Focus your eyes on the centre line and use your peripheral vision to read the passage as you move your eyes down. Remember, do not move your eyes from the centre line!

I Am Gifted, So Are You!

EXERCISE B1

A	B	C
N	D	F
K	V	L
S	Q	I
W	M	P
X	U	G
O	Y	R
V	Z	J
E	T	N
B	L	A
P	N	H
V	W	F
C	X	Z
R	O	A
D	J	Z
G	P	K
Z	F	T
Q	R	U
E	C	S
Y	H	X
F	A	N
U	I	P
H	S	W
L	G	D
M	H	V
J	Z	Q
T	K	O
I	X	Y
K	E	E

EXERCISE B2

Now that you have an idea of the power of your brain, let's start on the first of the super learning strategies, Power Reading for Information. Before you can start making notes, memorising or revising, the first step would be to read your textbooks and course materials for the information you need to score that 'A'.

Unfortunately, most students do not read their textbooks or their course materials with the purpose of information gathering. They think reading is for the purpose of just understanding or gaining knowledge. They will then re-read that same material during their revision time in order to try remembering it. If you do this, you will find that when the exam draws near, you will have too much to read, too much to cover and insufficient time to do it.

Have you ever seen how runners train? They are known

EXERCISE C1

A	B	C
N	D	F
K	V	L
S	Q	I
W	M	P
X	U	G
O	Y	R
V	Z	J
E	T	N
B	L	A
P	N	H
V	W	F
C	X	Z
R	O	A
D	J	Z
G	P	K
Z	F	T
Q	R	U
E	C	S
Y	H	X
F	A	N
U	I	P
H	S	W
L	G	D
M	H	V
J	Z	Q
T	K	O
I	X	Y
K	E	E

EXERCISE C2

Now that you have an idea of the power of your brain, let's start on the first of the super learning strategies, Power Reading for Information. Before you can start making notes, memorising or revising, the first step would be to read your textbooks and course materials for the information you need to score that 'A'.

Unfortunately, most students do not read their textbooks or their course materials with the purpose of information gathering. They think reading is for the purpose of just understanding or gaining knowledge. They will then re-read that same material during their revision time in order to try remembering it. If you do this, you will find that when the exam draws near, you will have too much to read, too much to cover and insufficient time to do it.

Have you ever seen how runners train? They are known to tie weights to their feet as they run in training. This feels extremely uncomfortable, but it trains the muscles to become stronger. When they take off the

EXERCISE D1

A	B	C
N	D	F
K	V	L
S	Q	I
W	M	P
X	U	G
O	Y	R
V	Z	J
E	T	N
B	L	A
P	N	H
V	W	F
C	X	Z
R	O	A
D	J	Z
G	P	K
Z	F	T
Q	R	U
E	C	S
Y	H	X
F	A	N
U	I	P
H	S	W
L	G	D
M	H	V
J	Z	Q
T	K	O
I	X	Y
K	E	E

EXERCISE D2

Now that you have an idea of the power of your brain, let's start on the first of the super learning strategies, Power Reading for Information. Before you can start making notes, memorising or revising, the first step would be to read your textbooks and course materials for the information you need to score that 'A'.

Unfortunately, most students do not read their textbooks or their course materials with the purpose of information gathering. They think reading is for the purpose of just understanding or gaining knowledge. They will then re-read that same material during their revision time in order to try remembering it. If you do this, you will find that when the exam draws near, you will have too much to read, too much to cover and insufficient time to do it.

Have you ever seen how runners train? They are known to tie weights to their feet as they run in training. This feels extremely uncomfortable, but it trains the muscles to become stronger. When they take off the weights, they will feel very light in comparison and will be able to run very fast. You can use this same technique in power reading. As you train yourself in power

EXERCISE E1

A	B	C
N	D	F
K	V	L
S	Q	I
W	M	P
X	U	G
O	Y	R
V	Z	J
E	T	N
B	L	A
P	N	H
V	W	F
C	X	Z
R	O	A
D	J	Z
G	P	K
Z	F	T
Q	R	U
E	C	S
Y	H	X
F	A	N
U	I	P
H	S	W
L	G	D
M	H	V
J	Z	Q
T	K	O
I	X	Y
K	E	E

EXERCISE E2

Now that you have an idea of the power of your brain, let's start on the first of the super learning strategies, Power Reading for Information. Before you can start making notes, memorising or revising, the first step would be to read your textbooks and course materials for the information you need to score that 'A'.

Unfortunately, most students do not read their textbooks or their course materials with the purpose of information gathering. They think reading is for the purpose of just understanding or gaining knowledge. They will then re-read that same material during their revision time in order to try remembering it. If you do this, you will find that when the exam draws near, you will have too much to read, too much to cover and insufficient time to do it.

Have you ever seen how runners train? They are known to tie weights to their feet as they run in training. This feels extremely uncomfortable, but it trains the muscles to become stronger. When they take off the weights, they will feel very light in comparison and will be able to run very fast.

You can use this same technique in power reading. As you train yourself in power reading, use your pencil to push yourself at a speed beyond what you are comfortable with. For example, if you currently read at only 100 wpm, keep forcing yourself to go at 300–400 wpm. It does not matter

Chapter 7

Mind Mapping®: The Ultimate Note-Making Tool

Welcome to Chapter 7. I must congratulate you for making it this far. I think the fact that you have committed yourself to reading the last six chapters signifies that you are really serious in producing successful results in your life. I want you to know that research has shown that 80% of people who buy a book never read past the first chapter. What a terrible waste. Again, these are the people who 'would like' to succeed but are not willing to do whatever it takes. So, give yourself a pat on the back and let's begin.

Now that you have learnt to Power Read and pick up the key ideas and keywords from your textbooks or course materials, you need to use them to make your own personalized notes!

MAKING NOTES: THE KEY TO SCORING 'A'S

After modeling thousands of 'A' students, I have discovered that one common strategy they use is that they all make their own personalized notes. Many of them tell me that their notes hold the secret of their success. When I ask them why, they tell me that their notes help them to organize the information in a way that helps them to understand and remember. Their notes also cut down their revision time as it contains only important and relevant points that they need to know.

In other words, there are three main reasons why you must make notes. Making your own notes helps you to:

1. Save time
2. Increase your ability to remember
3. Understand better

CONVENTIONAL LINEAR NOTES: ARE THEY BEST?

Whenever I ask students to show me their notes, I would discover that 95% of them would make notes in the conventional linear style. Linear notes are notes that are written in sentences, usually from left to right. There are two basic forms of linear notes.

Form 1

The first form of linear notes is made up of chunks taken up from the text. It is essentially identical to the original text except that only the more important concepts are included.

The Three States Of Matter

Matter has three states. They are solid, liquid and gas.

In solids, molecules are arranged closely, forming a regular pattern. Forces between them hold them in fixed positions. Because of the strong forces, individual molecules can only vibrate about their fixed positions.

In liquids, molecules are further apart and do not form any regular pattern. Forces between them are weaker and hence, the molecules are not fixed in positions. They can move among one another.

In gases, molecules are much further apart. They move at very high speeds and collide into one another.

Form 2

The second method is normally referred to as writing in point form. Here, short sentences or phrases are ordered and numbered, with each sentence containing a relevant main point that needs to be learnt.

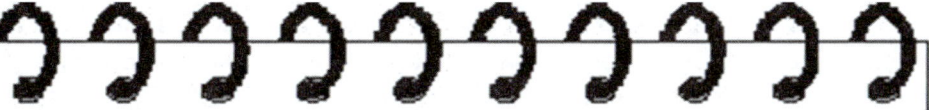

The Three States Of Matter

I. Solids
1. Molecules are arranged closely, forming a regular pattern.
2. Forces between the molecules hold them in position.
3. Molecules vibrate about their position.

II. Liquids
1. Molecules are not arranged in a regular pattern and are farther apart.
2. Molecules are not held in fixed positions.
3. Molecules can move among one another. Hence liquids can flow.

III. Gas
1. Molecules are very far apart.
2. Molecules move at high speeds, colliding into one another.

Although the linear style is the method used by the majority of students (95%) and it is the style many of us have been taught to use, we must ask ourselves if this form of note taking is really the most effective method. Just because everyone does something does not mean that it is the best method.

THE DISADVANTAGE OF LINEAR NOTES

Let me ask you this. Is it 5% of students who score all the 'A's or is it the 95%? The answer is the 5%, the minority! Is it 5% of the students who find learning difficult or is it the 95%? The answer is the 95%, the majority who find learning difficult and boring. So obviously, what the majority is doing does not seem to be working! To get outstanding results, we must do things the majority does not do! We said that 'A' students make notes for three reasons. They are to save time, to help them remember and to help them to understand better. Let's investigate if linear notes help accomplish all this.

Do Linear Notes Result in Saving Time? No!

Do linear notes really help you to cut down unnecessary information and help you to save the most amount of time? The answer is no! Although linear notes extract the main points from the textbook, they still contain the non keywords (that make up 80% of the words), which are unnecessary for learning. So 80% of your time is still wasted unnecessarily when you use linear notes.

Do Linear Notes Help You to Remember Best? No!

The next important question is: Do linear notes help you in remembering? Well, if they did, then all students will have no problems remembering and we know this is not true. In Chapter 8 on Super Memory for Words, I outline the seven principles of super memory. In other words, anyone can have a super memory provided they use these seven principles that trigger our brain's memory power: association, visualization, making something outstanding, colours, holism, rhythm and imagination. Do linear notes use all these super memory principles? Not even one principle is used.

I Am Gifted, So Are You!

Linear notes have no pictures for you to visualize.

Linear notes do not show how the different ideas or points are associated together. Instead, all the ideas and points are just listed out.

Linear notes do not make information outstanding at all. In fact, they make information boring and monotonous.

Linear notes make use of very little colours. Most of them are done in black or blue ink.

Linear notes are not holistic. At one glance, you cannot see the 'big picture'.

Linear notes make no use of your imagination at all!

It is no wonder why most students complain of a very bad memory, because the notes they use do not tap their powers of super memory.

Do Linear Notes Help You to Maximize Your Brain Power? No!

In the chapter on your brain, we said that geniuses are able to produce outstanding results because they are able to use both sides of their brain simultaneously. Unfortunately, linear notes are a left-brain method of learning. It does not utilize any of the right-brain functions, and so it does not maximize your brain power.

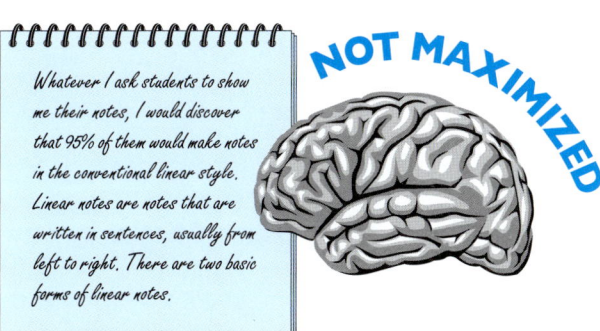

Whatever I ask students to show me their notes, I would discover that 95% of them would make notes in the conventional linear style. Linear notes are notes that are written in sentences, usually from left to right. There are two basic forms of linear notes.

MIND MAPPING®: THE ULTIMATE NOTE-MAKING TOOL

So, if linear notes are so ineffective, then what makes an effective note-making tool? In general, the note-making technique we use should utilize only keywords, incorporate all the seven principles of super memory and it should incorporate the use of both sides of the brain.

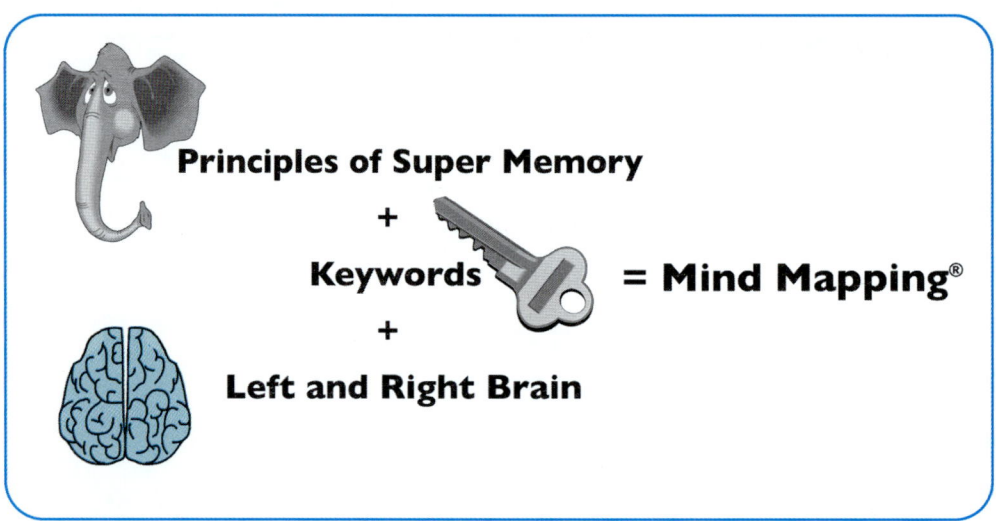

The one note-making tool that achieves all this is the Mind Map® developed by Tony Buzan. That is why I call the Mind Map® the ultimate note-making tool.

THE ADVANTAGES OF MIND MAPPING®

Shown below is an example of a Mind Map® on Weathering, a chapter in geography. Let's make a comparison and see what are the advantages of making our notes in this way.

1. It Saves You Loads of Time as it Uses Only Keywords

If you look at the Mind Map® on Weathering, it would be interesting to note that it contains ten pages of information from the textbook. I was able to condense ten pages into a single page because I only used keywords and images. This is achieved without leaving out any important information. All the information required to score an 'A' is still intact, even the minor details!

For example, looking at the Mind Map®, you can see that the definition of mechanical weathering is the breaking down of rocks into smaller rocks by a physical force. These 15 words are reduced to just five words in the Mind Map®.

Can you imagine the advantage you will have over your friends? When you are revising your materials just before the exam, you will be able to cover an entire chapter of 20 pages in just two or three sheets of Mind Maps®! Your friend may find that he has to take an hour revising a chapter while you can finish it in 20 minutes!

2. It Utilizes all the Seven Principles of Super Memory

You will also notice that the Mind Map® makes use of all the seven principles of super memory that will trigger your ability to absorb quickly and recall fast.

a. Visualization
The Mind Map® has lots of pictures for you to visualize, one of the most important principles of memory. In fact, the entire Mind Map® is like one big picture.

b. Association
The Mind Map® shows very clearly how the points are all associated and linked together. For example, you can see immediately that there are four points associated with 'Weathering'. They are 'Denudation', 'Mechanical Weathering', 'Chemical Weathering' and 'Rate of Weathering'.

I Am Gifted, So Are You!

You can also see right away that there are two points linked to Mechanical Weathering. They are the 'Definition of Weathering' and the 'Types of Weathering'.

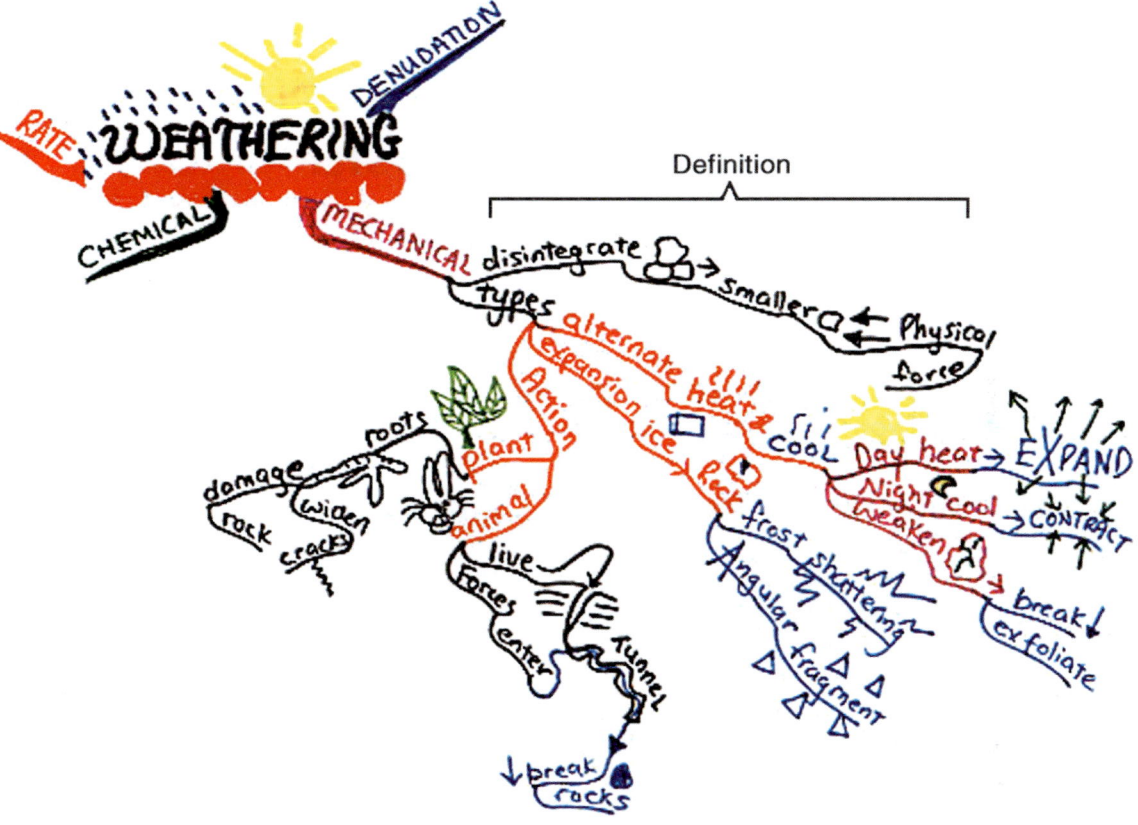

c. Make Things Outstanding

Instead of boring and monotonous words, the Mind Map® allows you to make points and ideas STAND OUT by using different colours, sizes and pictures. This will make the ideas stick to your mind.

$$S\,{\scriptsize I}\,Z\,{\small E} \qquad COLOURS$$

In addition, you can clearly see that Mind Maps® use lots of colours and force you to activate your creative imagination. Finally, Mind Maps® give you a holistic picture of what you are learning.

3. It Uses Both Sides of Your Brain Simultaneously.

Finally, it can be seen clearly that Mind Maps® utilize both the right-brain and the left-brain functions. It is a whole brain learning device that boosts your brain power to the level of a genius.

DRAWING A MIND MAP®: STEP-BY-STEP

Now that you understand the power of Mind Mapping®, the question would be: How do I start drawing one? In this section, I will outline for you the steps on how to build a Mind Map® and the Mind Mapping® laws to follow.

For illustration purposes, let's say you wanted to draw a Mind Map® on yourself. So if your name is John, the title of your Mind Map® would be 'John'.

STEP 1: Draw the Topic at the Centre

The first step in building a Mind Map® would be to draw the topic of the Mind Map® at the centre on a piece of paper (placed horizontally).

Laws to Follow:

1. The topic at the centre can be drawn with as many colours as you wish.

2. It should not be enclosed within a border or a box. The idea is to make the topic outstanding and memorable.

3. You may wish to supplement the image with words, if the topic is an abstract one.

4. The rule of thumb is to keep it the size of two 50-cent coins.

In this case, the topic is 'John', so you can draw an image that represents 'John'

 **STEP 2: Add the Sub-Headings**

The next step would be to add the sub-headings to the topic at the centre.

> Laws to Follow:
> 1. The sub-headings should be in CAPITAL LETTERS resting on a thick branch. This is to make it more outstanding
> 2. They should all be attached to the centre.
> 3. They should be joined at angles (not horizontal), to allow further branches to radiate more easily.

In this case, we can add four sub-headings such as 'Character', 'Family', 'School' and 'Goals' for example.

 **STEP 3: For Each Sub-Heading, Add the Main Points and the Supporting Details.**

Laws to Follow:

1. Only Keywords and Images should be used.

2. Whenever possible, you can use symbols and abbreviations to help you save space and time.

Everyone has their own ways to abbreviate common words. Go ahead and develop more creative abbreviations for yourself. Here are some I use regularly

Not available	~~Available~~
Without	w/o
Because	∴
For	4
Causes	⇒
Increases / decreases	↑/↓
Greater than / less than	>/<
Change	△

3. Each Keyword/image should rest on a line

I Am Gifted, So Are You!

4. There should be a maximum of one word on one line. This is so that even more keywords and ideas can be connected to any existing keyword.

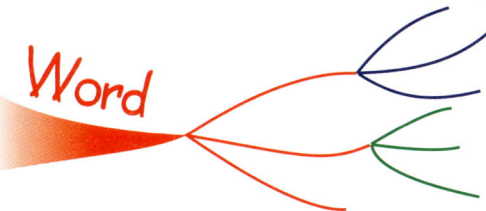

5. All branches should radiate from a single point.

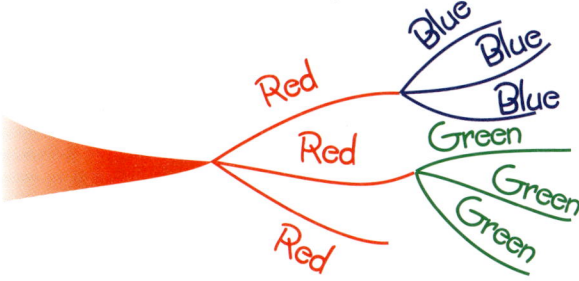

6. All the branches that branch out from the same point should be in the same family colour.

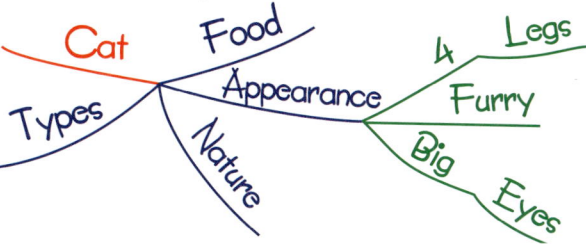

7. We change colours when we go from one level of ideas to a more specific level.

In this case, we add the main points to the various sub-headings as follows:

For example, in the sub-heading 'character', the four main points added are 'generous', 'humorous', 'stubborn', 'determined'.

It is important to note that a Mind Map® is NOT a summary of a chapter in a textbook. It should not just contain main points, leaving the important supporting details out. It should have all relevant supporting details and sub-points. Adding the supporting details and sub-points, you will see the following:

For example, under the main point 'generous', many supporting details such as 'donates money to charities and good causes' and 'volunteers at the hospital and the old folks home' are added.

Note: You will notice that the Mind Map® is developed and read from inside to outside. In other words, the ideas radiate out from the centre. As such, notice that ideas and keywords on the left-side of a Mind Map® is written and read from right to left.

STEP 4: In this last step, let your imagination go wild and add even more pictures and images that will make the ideas more outstanding and stick into your mind.

THE STRUCTURE OF A MIND MAP®

Typically, the Mind Map® is structured in the following way.

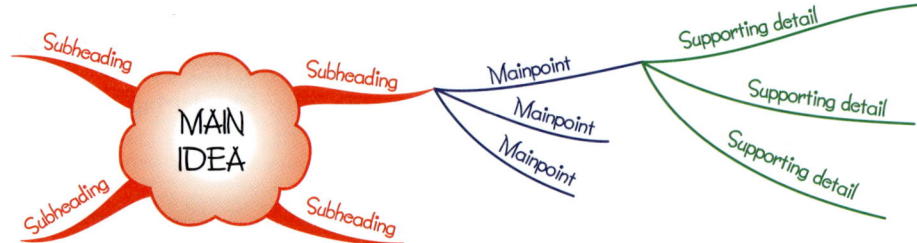

THE FLOW OF INFORMATION

Note that unlike all other forms of written communication, Mind Mapping® does not flow in a linear fashion from left to right and downwards.

Instead, Mind Map®s are drawn, written and read starting from the centre and moving outwards and then in a clockwise direction. Therefore, you will see that in the left-hand section of the Mind Map®, words are read from right to left (starting from the inside and moving outwards). The arrows positioned around the Mind Map® show the way the information should be read. The sequence of the numbers is another guide to the flow.

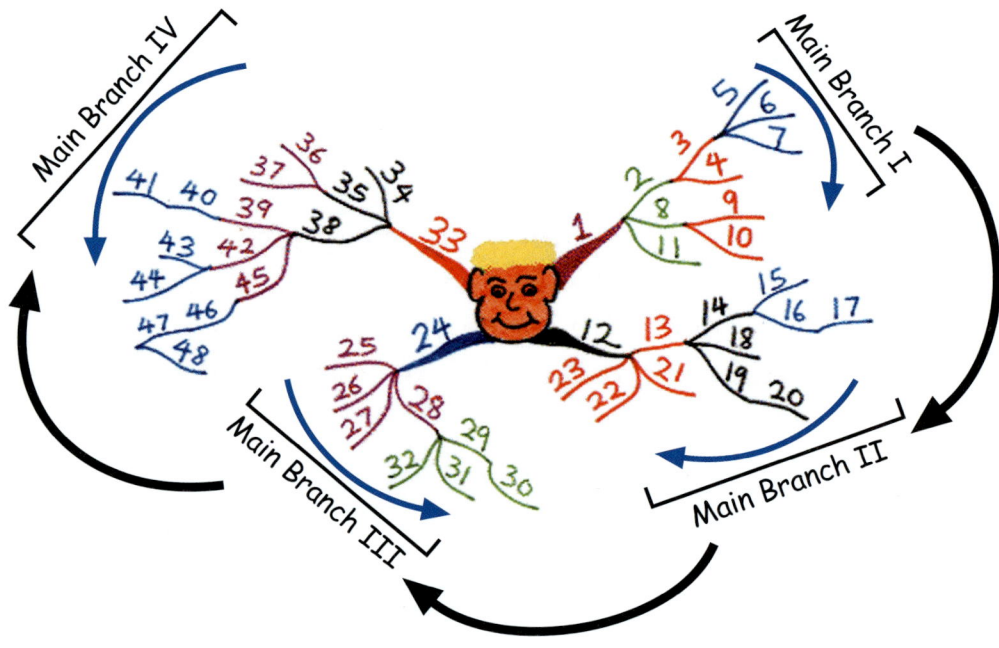

I Am Gifted, So Are You!

The four main structures labeled I, II, III, IV in the Mind Map® on page 82 are called main branches. The Mind Map® has four Main Branches, because it has four sub-headings. The number of sub-headings always equals the number of main branches. Also, note that the main branches of the Mind Map® are read clockwise, starting from main branch I to main branch II and finally to main branch IV. See the black arrows in the diagram.

However, keywords are written and read from top down within each main branch. See the blue arrows in the diagram.

THE POWER OF MIND MAPPING®: A CASE STUDY

Now that you understand the basic steps and laws on how to develop a Mind Map®, let me guide you through the process of converting a typical page of text into a Mind Map®. We will use the topic of 'The Three States of Matter', from a physics curriculum. In doing so, I want to show you how powerful a Mind Map® can be in helping you save time, remember and understand more effectively.

Before we begin the process of Mind Mapping®, I want you to experience the difference between learning from a Mind Map® as compared to learning from conventional linear notes. So, I want you to read the text below on the 'Three States of Matter' like you normally would. Please do this now.

The Three States of Matter

Solids
The molecules in a solid are arranged in a regular pattern and are packed close together. There is little space between them so solids cannot be compressed. They are held in fixed positions by strong inter-molecular forces. As a result, they can only vibrate about these fixed positions.

The inter-molecular forces consist of attractive forces and repulsive forces. The attractive forces prevent the molecules from breaking free and leaving their fixed positions. The repulsive forces prevent the molecules from collapsing. As a result, solids have a fixed shape and a fixed volume.

When heat is applied to a solid, the molecules' energy increases, causing it to vibrate more. As a result, the space between the molecules increases, causing the solid to expand.

Liquid
Molecules in a liquid are slightly further part than in a solid. However, they are still close enough such that a liquid cannot be compressed either. The forces between the molecules are not as strong as those in a solid. As a result, the molecules can move amongst one another throughout the liquid. This is why liquids have no definite shape and take the shape of the container. However, liquids have a definite volume because the attractive forces between the molecules prevent them from breaking away and leaving the liquid.

When heat is applied to a liquid, the molecules vibrate and move with more energy. This caused the molecules to move slightly further apart and the liquid to expand.

Gases
The molecules in a gas are much further apart. As a result, there is a lot of space between them and the gas can be compressed.

The molecules move randomly at high speed, colliding with one another and the walls of the container. The inter-molecular forces are present only at the point of collision. Most of the time, the inter-molecular forces are negligible and so the gas has no definite shape and volume.

Have you finished reading the text? Good. Now, I want you to turn the page and answer the following questions. You are not allowed to turn back to the text for reference.

A TEST ON HOW MUCH YOU REMEMBER

> Please write down your answers to the following in the space below.
>
> 1. Write down all the points you remember on the section on 'solids'
>
> 2. How many things do you need to know about solids? How many main ideas are there?

Please finish writing down your answers before you proceed further! Now, I want you to check your answers with the text. Did you manage to list down all the points? Did you manage to write down how many main ideas there are? I bet the answer is no.

Whenever I ask this question in all my seminars, I notice that most of the time students will not be able to list down all the points about 'solids'. They will definitely miss out a few points. In addition, the points they list are never organized in the right order. The reason is because linear notes are very bad devices for remembering as they do not allow you to remember points in a systematic order. Yet we know that in order to get full marks for a question in the exam, we need to produce all the relevant points!

DRAWING A MIND MAP® ON 'THE THREE STATES OF MATTER'

Now it's time to convert 'The Three States of Matter' into a Mind Map®. Let's begin.

 **STEP 1: Power Read for Keywords**

The first step is to begin by reading the text again, only this time, use what you learnt in 'Power reading' and gather the important information by circling the keywords. An example is given below.

The Three States of Matter

Solids

The molecules in a solid are arranged in a regular pattern and are packed close together. There is little space between them so solids cannot be compressed. They are held in fixed positions by strong inter-molecular forces. As a result, they can only vibrate about these fixed positions.

The inter-molecular forces consist of attractive forces and repulsive forces. The attractive forces prevent the molecules from breaking free and leaving their fixed positions. The repulsive forces prevent the molecules from collapsing. As a result, solids have a fixed shape and a fixed volume.

When heat is applied to a solid, the molecules' energy increases, causing it to vibrate more. As a result, the space between the molecules increases, causing the solid to expand.

▶▶ 86 *I Am Gifted, So Are You!*

 ## STEP 2: Draw the Topic at the Centre

As you learnt earlier, the first thing to do would be to draw the topic at the centre of your paper (placed horizontally).

 ## STEP 3: Add the Sub-headings

Next, attach the first sub-heading to the centre. In this case, we attach 'SOLIDS' to the centre. It is best to fully develop this entire sub-heading before drawing the next two, i.e. 'LIQUIDS' and 'GAS'. This is to enable better spacing and avoid branches getting 'cramped up'.

 ## STEP 4: Add the Main Points and the Supporting Details.

As you read through the keywords you have circled in the text, begin by adding the main points and the supporting details to the first sub-heading on 'SOLIDS'. Again, fully develop 'SOLIDS' before adding points and details to 'LIQUIDS' and 'GASES'.

The first paragraph shows

'The molecules in a solid are arranged in a regular pattern and are packed close together. There is little space between them so solids cannot be compressed. They are held in fixed positions by strong inter-molecular forces. As a result, they can only vibrate about these fixed positions.'

This can be converted into the Mind Map® as follows:

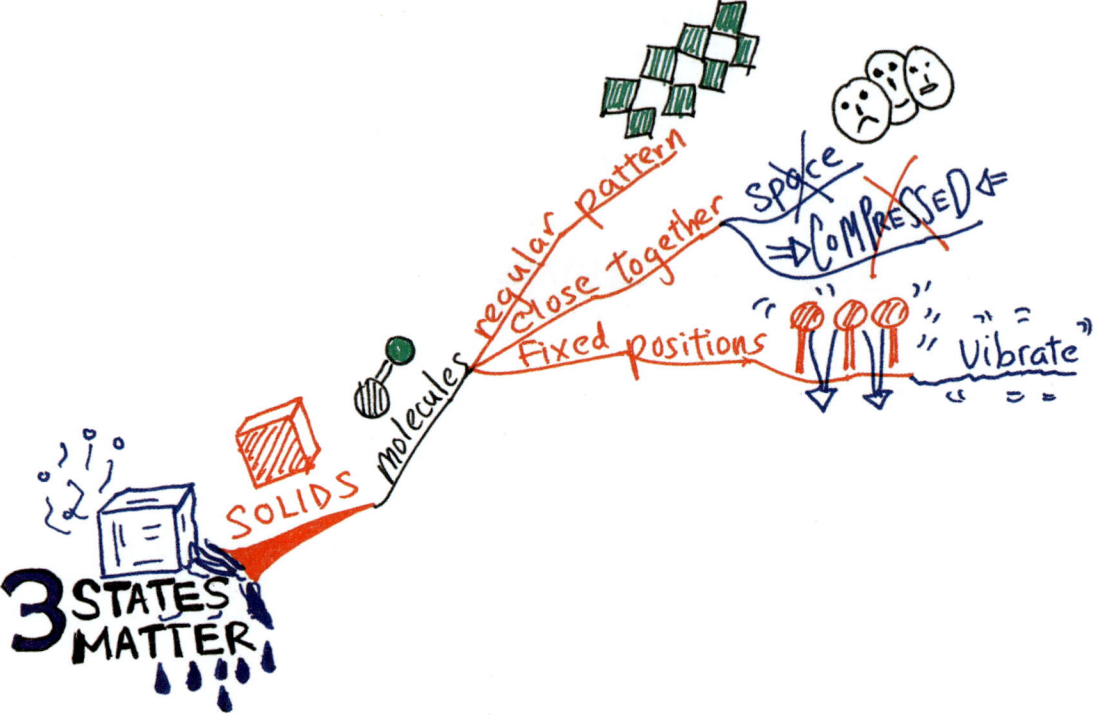

You can see that this entire paragraph is based on 'molecules' which has 3 sub-points. Also, notice the use of lots of pictures to aid recall.

The second paragraph shows

'The inter-molecular forces consist of attractive forces and repulsive forces. The attractive forces prevent the molecules from breaking free and leaving their fixed positions. The repulsive forces prevent the molecules from collapsing. As a result, solids have a fixed shape and a fixed volume.'

This second paragraph is based on a new main point 'forces'. So we can create a brand new branch for this as follows. Again 'forces' has two sub-points. This can be added to the Mind Map® as follows:

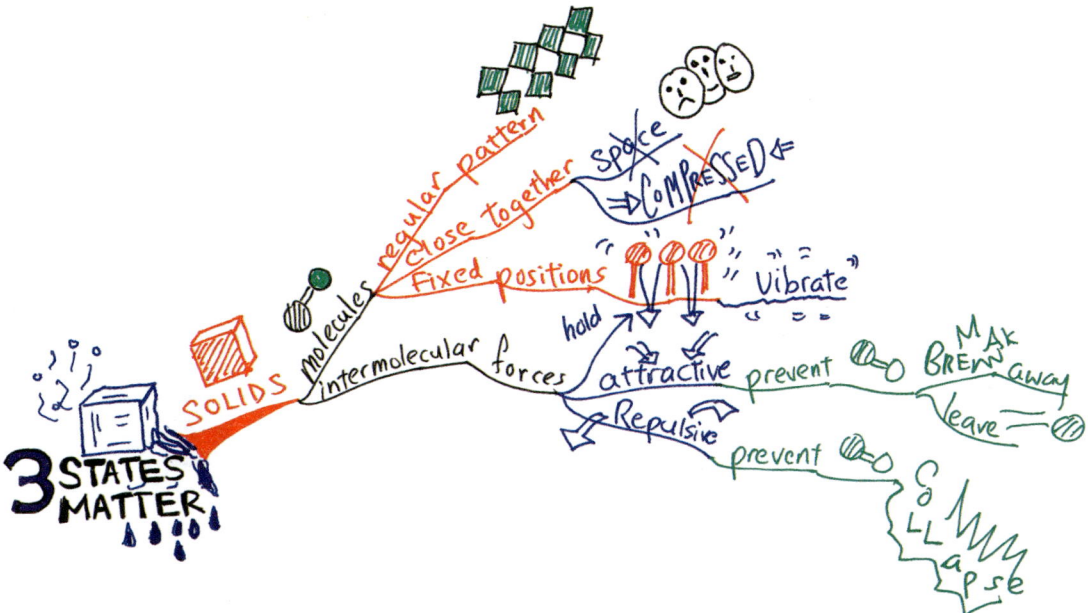

Adding all the main points, sub-points and supporting details from the section on 'solids' into the Mind Map®, we will have the following:

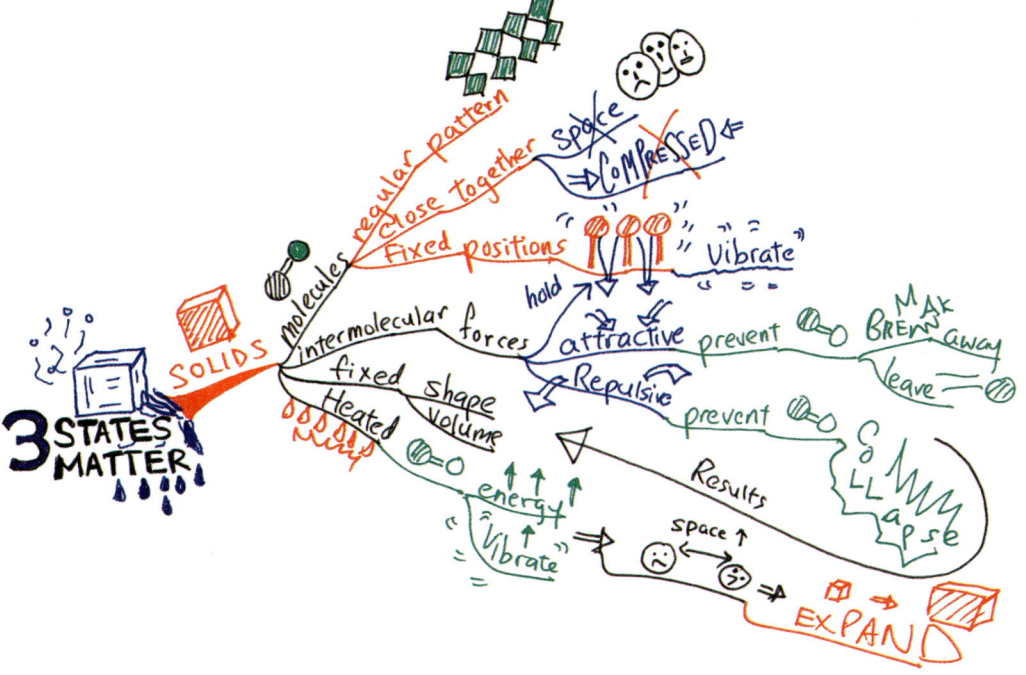

MIND MAPS® VERSUS LINEAR NOTES: THE DIFFERENCE

Before moving on to complete the other two sub-headings on 'LIQUIDS' and 'GASES' and the entire Mind Map®, let's see how the Mind Map® has helped us so far. Let's make a comparison between the linear notes and the Mind Map® on the first section on 'Solids'.

1. Yes! The Mind Map® Saves You Time

Solids Linear Note-Taking Method

The Three States of Matter

Solids
The molecules in a solid are arranged in a regular pattern and are packed close together. There is little space between them so solids cannot be compressed. They are held in fixed positions by strong inter-molecular forces. As a result, they can only vibrate about these fixed positions.

The inter-molecular forces consist of attractive forces and repulsive forces. The attractive forces prevent the molecules from breaking free and leaving their fixed positions. The repulsive forces prevent the molecules from collapsing. As a result, solids have a fixed shape and a fixed volume.

When heat is applied to a solid, the molecules' energy increases, causing it to vibrate more. As a result, the space between the molecules increases, causing the solid to expand.

Solids Mind Map® Method

If you count the number of words under the section on 'Solids', there are 123 words you would have to read under the linear notes. However, we have reduced this to only 28 words in the Mind Map®. And the best thing is, we have captured all the important information! You have effectively reduced your learning time by 80%!

2. Yes! The Mind Map® Helps You Remember

Now, let's see if the Mind Map® does a better job in helping you recall all the facts. I want you to study the Mind Map® above closely. From the Mind Map®, you can see that under 'solids', there are four main points you need to remember: 'molecules, 'forces', 'fixed shape and volume' and 'heated'.

Under molecules, there are three sub-points and their supporting details: 'regular pattern', 'close together' and 'fixed position'.

Under 'intermolecular forces', there are two sub-points and their supporting details. They are 'attractive' and 'repulsive'. And so on and so forth.

By going through the Mind Map® in this way, you can see that all the information is organized into systematic groups! Together with the outstanding pictures and the other principles of super memory, this will help you remember all the points! Go through the Mind Map® thoroughly in this way before you read the next section. Do it now!

Next, without referring back to the text on 'The Three States of Matter', answer the same questions about solids.

SECOND TEST ON HOW MUCH YOU REMEMBER

> Please write down your answers to the following in the space below.
>
> 1. Write down all the points you remember on the section on 'solids'
>
> 2. How many things do you need to know about solids? How many main ideas are there?

If you had gone through the process of drawing and reading the Mind Map®, you would be able to effortlessly write down all the main points, sub-points and supporting details. You would also be able to tell immediately that there are four main ideas that you need to know for 'solids'. They are 'molecules', 'forces', 'fixed shape and volume' and what happens when the solid is 'heated'.

I Am Gifted, So Are You!

COMPLETE THE MIND MAP®

Alright, get your coloured markers ready! It is time for you to start Mind Mapping®. On the blank page labeled 'Your Mind Map®', draw and complete the Mind Map® on 'The Three States of Matter'. It is important for you to know that there is no one correct way of organizing information in a Mind Map®.

As along as you organize the information in a logical and systematic way, it is perfectly acceptable. For the sub-heading on 'solids', you can choose to follow my version or you can re-create your own. Have fun!

A sample Mind Map® is provided on the next page for your reference!

YOUR MIND MAP®

MIND MAP® ON THE 3 STATES OF MATTER

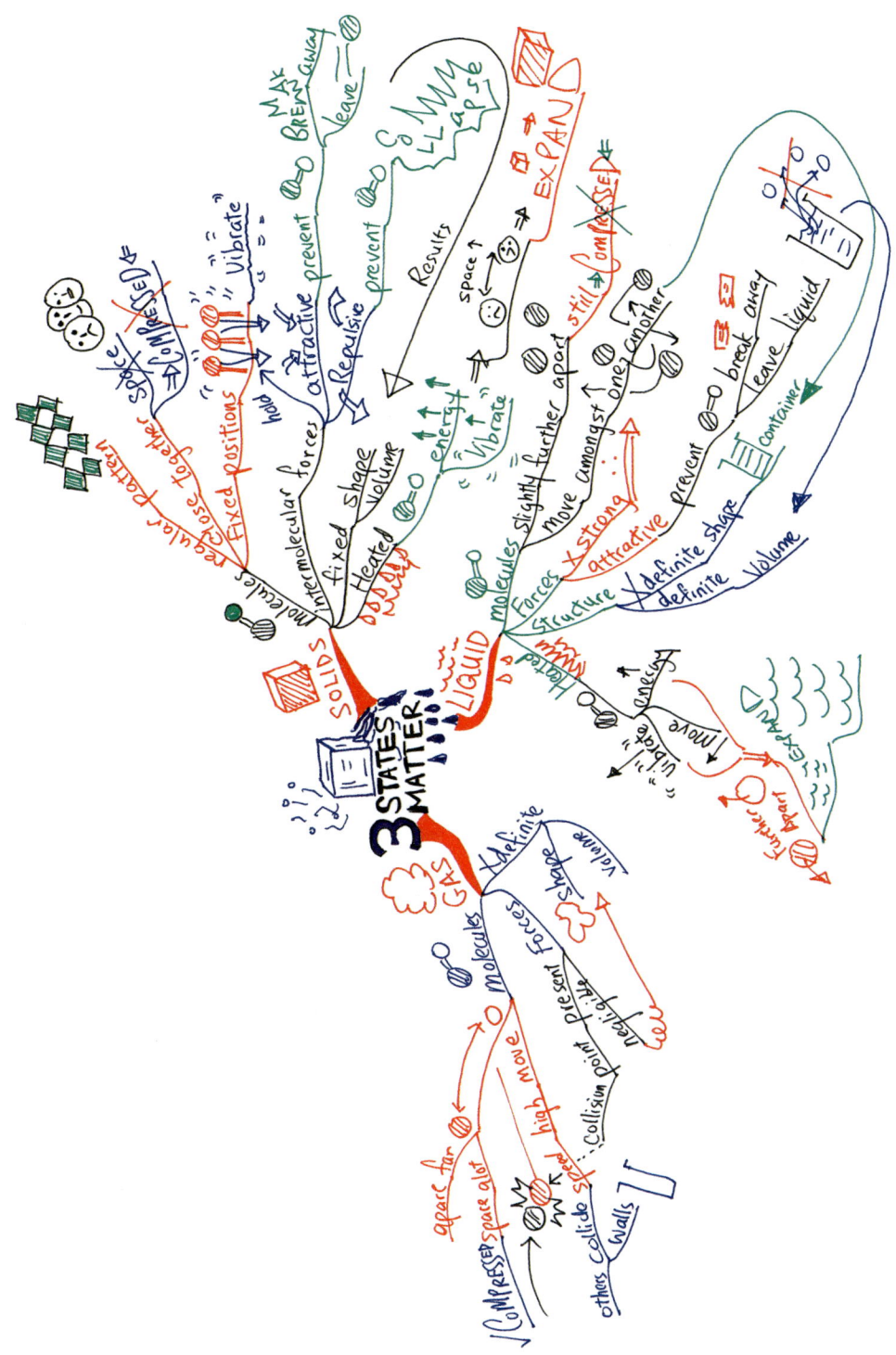

Chapter 7 • Mind Mapping®: The Ultimate Note-Making Tool

ARE YOU READY TO DRAW YOUR FIRST COMPLETE MIND MAP®?

At this stage, you should be well versed on how to create a Mind Map®. However, I believe that practice makes perfect and I want to make sure that by the time you finish this chapter, you are going to be a master at Mind Mapping®. So here is another example for you to practise.

First, Power Read the extract from a geography book on the following page and pick out the keywords. Next, prepare the following materials you will need for your Mind Map®.

1. One or two pages of blank paper of at least A4 size. Art paper is excellent for drawing Mind Maps®.

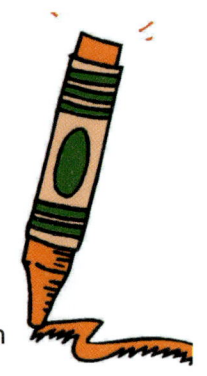

2. A set of colour pens or markers. Be sure to get those with very fine tips.

Great! You are now ready to begin drawing your Mind Map®. When you have finished, check out a sample version on page 101.

ROCKS AND LANDFORMS

Rock Types

There are numerous types of rocks that differ in their colour, appearance, texture, structure, hardness, composition, permeability, degree of resistance to denudation, and other physical and chemical characteristics. The three main types of rocks are igneous rocks, sedimentary rocks and metamorphic rocks.

Igneous Rocks

1. Igneous rocks are formed by the cooling and solidification of molten rocks such as magna and lava within the earth's crust or when they reach the surface.

2. There are two main types of igneous rocks:

    a. plutonic or intrusive rocks which have cooled slowly at great depths of the earth's crust. Granite is the most common of the plutonic rocks.

    b. volcanic or extrusive rocks which are formed by the cooling and solidification of lava after a volcanic eruption. The best known volcanic rocks are baketchup.

Sedimentary Rocks

1. Sedimentary rocks are derived or secondary rocks formed from the deposition and accumulation of materials on land surface or underwater(in lakes, seas and oceans) after million of years.

EXTRACT

2. The sediment and rock fragments that eventually form sedimentary rocks are brought down by various agents of denudation and deposition. They are washed off by rain, rivers or waves, caused to slide down mountains slopes by frost and snow, dragged away by glacier or blown into the air by winds and storms.

3. Thick layers of sediment become deeply buried, compacted or cemented into layers of rock strata, undergoing gradual and physical and chemical changes. Sedimentary rocks are thus also known as stratified rocks. Subsequently earth movement such as folding and faulting may lift these sedimentary layers to greater heights. The sedimentary rocks found up the Himalayan Ranges are believed to be from the seas and Indian Ocean and lifted during the Alpine earth movement some 35 million years ago.

4. Sedimentary rocks are thus looser and less consolidated then igneous rocks or metamorphic rocks. Due to their nature of formation in areas with many living creations, they often contain fossils.

5. Successive deposits of various sediment in land and on sea eventually form various forms of sedimentary rocks, e.g. gravel becomes conglomerate, sand forms sandstone, clay is compacted into shale and lime emerges as limestone.

Metamorphic Rocks

1. No one has actually seen the process of the formation of metamorphic rocks, as this occurs deep within the earth's crust, mostly in a semi-molten state and under superheated conditions. All metamorphic rocks

EXTRACT

EXTRACT

were originally igneous or sedimentary rocks and have become changed in both their appearance and character. They exist in a large number of varieties and are often of much greater value then their original rock type.

2. The metamorphosis (i.e. the process of change) of these rocks may have resulted from the following :

   a. heat, which causes the mineral constituents to re-crystalise,

      e.g. at more than 2000°C

   b. stress, which brings about the alteration in the rock structure, e.g. during folding and faulting

   c. pressure: at depths of 50 kilometres below the surface of the earth so that unstable minerals in rocks undergo chemical adjustment to form new rocks.

   d. water, which dissolves some rocks and deposits other minerals

3. Metamorphic rocks are changed rocks with new chemical and physical Properties, quite different from their original rock type. Many have banded structure, with wavy bands. They can be fine or coarse-grained.

4. Metamorphic rocks, having undergone metamorphism or change, become more valuable. For example, shale is changed to slate and schist, sandstone into quartzite and limestone into marble.

EXTRACT

DRAW YOUR MIND MAP® HERE

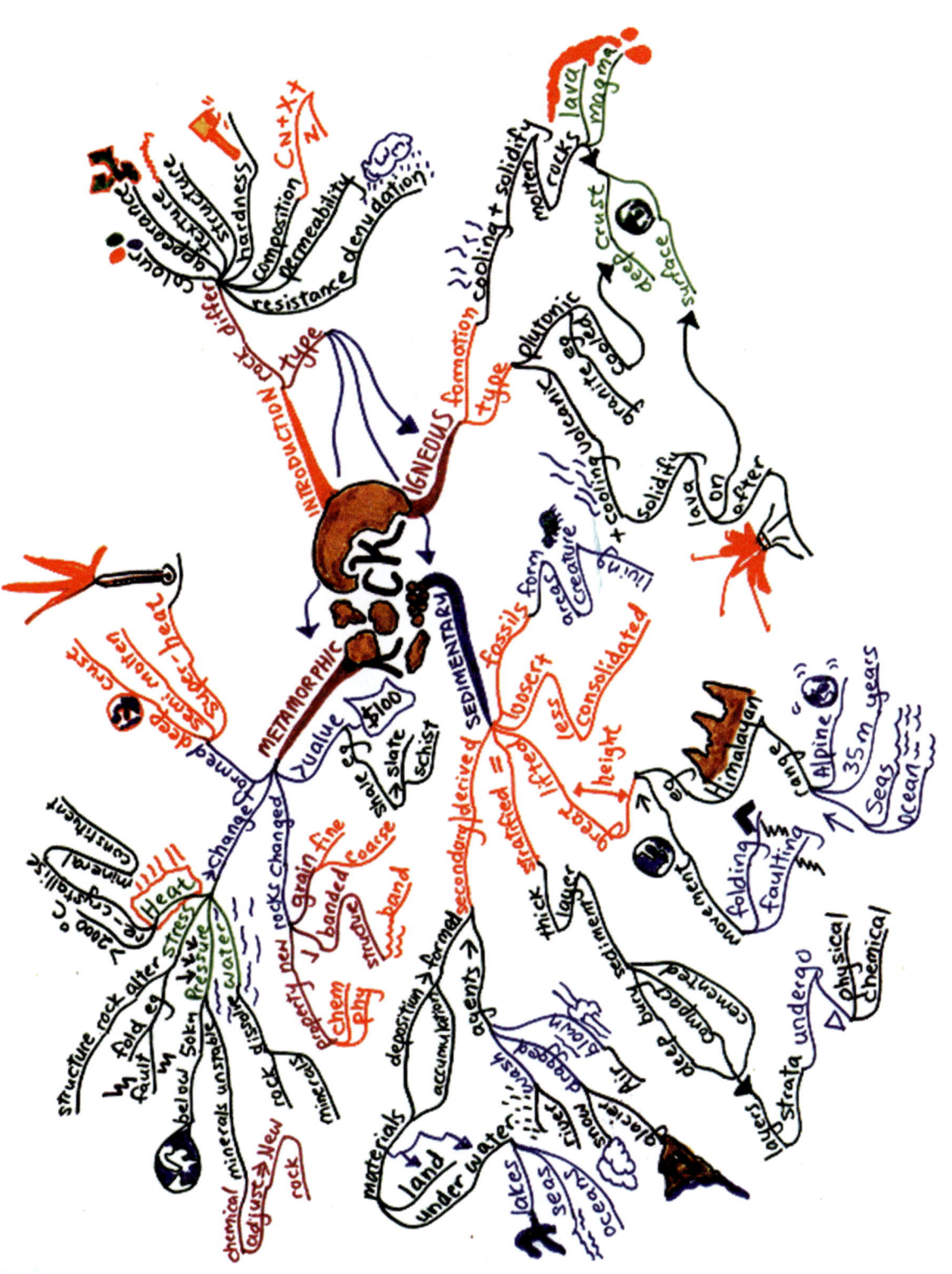

Chapter 7 • Mind Mapping®: The Ultimate Note-Making Tool

TYPES OF MIND MAPS® TO MASTER

There are basically three types of Mind Maps that you can use to help you organize and learn your study materials effectively.

1. Syllabus Mind Map®

The first type of Mind Map® is the Syllabus Mind Map® (also called the Macro Mind Map®). The Mind Map® is done on the table of contents of the subject textbook that you are studying.

This Mind Map® gives you an overview of the entire subject. It is useful to create giant Syllabus Mind Maps® and paste them on your wall. They give you an idea of how much material you have to cover in preparing for the examinations. You should create one Syllabus Mind Map® for each subject you study. Below is a Syllabus Mind Map® for 'O' level physics.

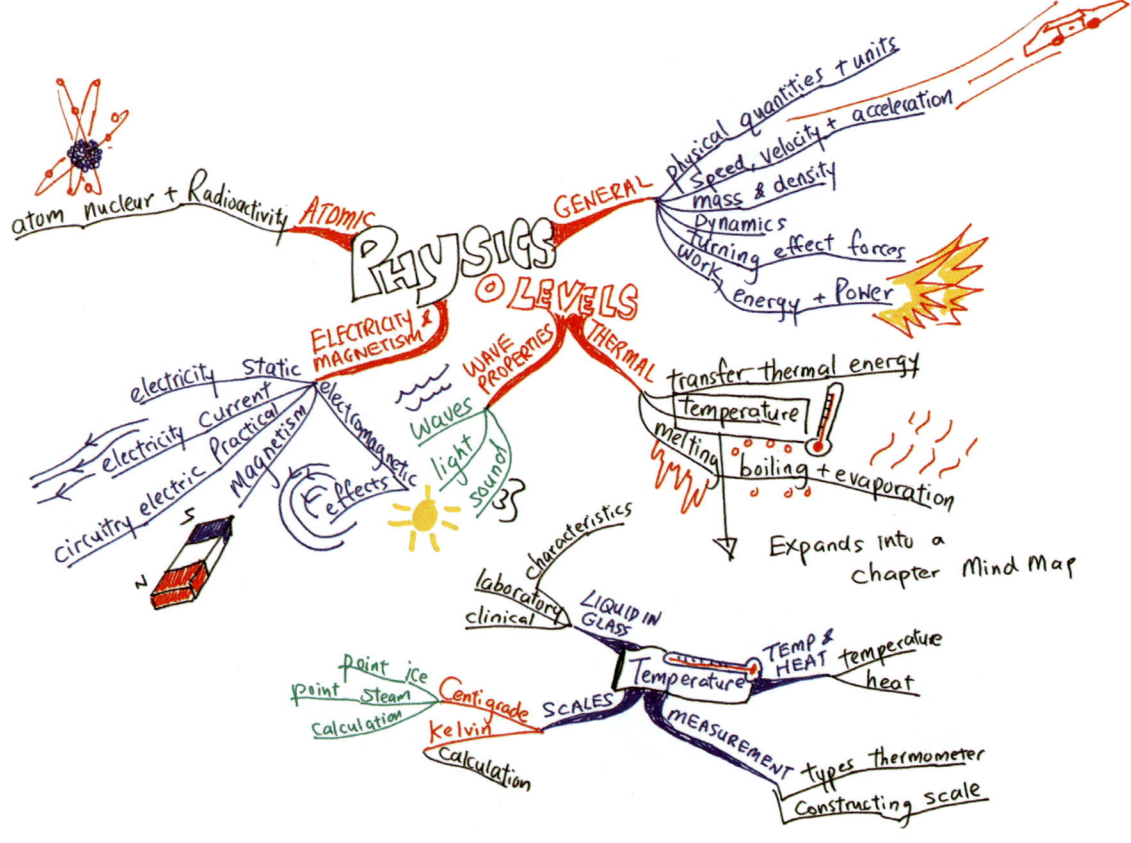

2. Chapter Mind Maps®

Next, you have to do Mind Maps® for each of the individual chapters in the textbook. For short chapters of between 10 and 12 pages, you should be able to condense all the information into one page of Mind Map®.

As for chapters of 20 pages or more, you may require 2 or 3 pages of Mind Maps®. So if for example, you are doing a Mind Map® on the chapter 'Matter', then you can title your Mind Maps® 'Matter 1', 'Matter 2' and so forth.

Another thing to remember is that ideally, a Mind Map® should not be just a summary of all the main points in the chapter. It should contain all the important information down to the last detail.

Feel free to incorporate tables, graphs, flowcharts and other diagrams within your Mind Map® if necessary. Below is an example on a chapter Mind Map® on 'Speed, Velocity & Acceleration in Physics'.

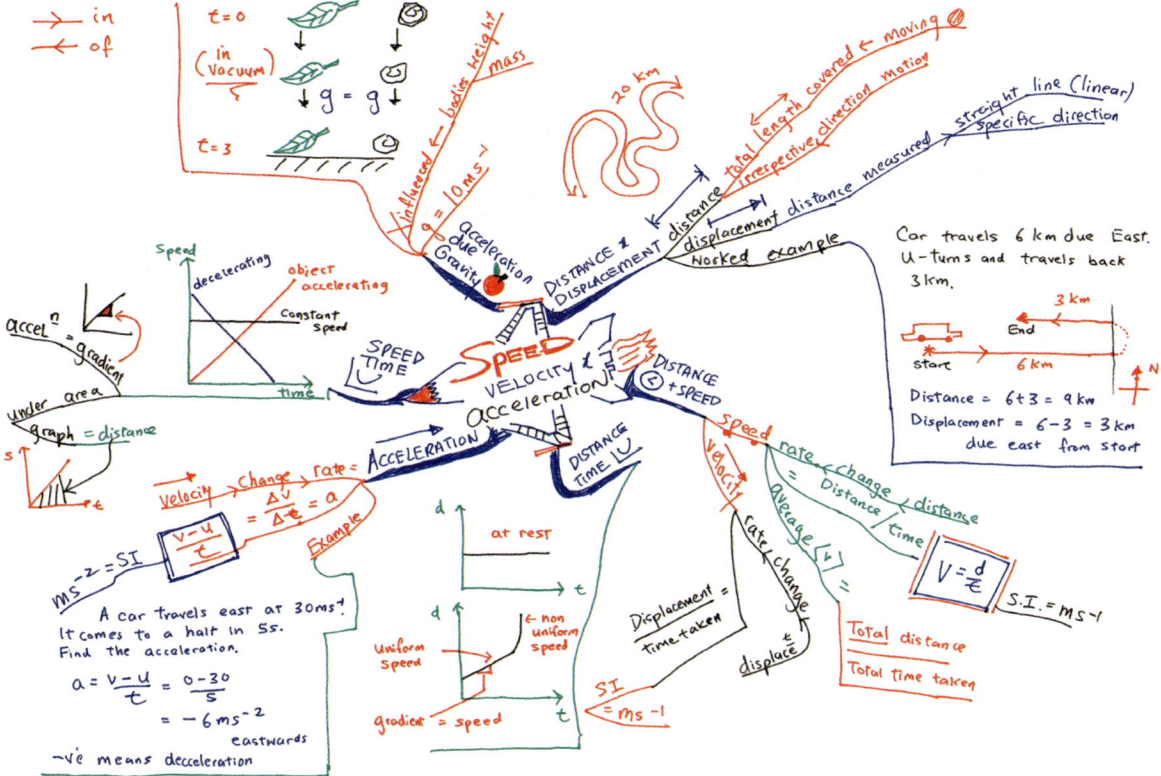

3. Paragraph Mind Maps®

An alternative to drawing Chapter Mind Maps® would be to do small paragraph Mind Maps® within your textbook. Each Mind Map® will summarize a paragraph or a section.

When there is a need to revise a particular chapter, there is no need to waste time reading the text. Instead, the Paragraph Mind Map® by the side will give you the information you need, allowing you to save time. An example is given below. These paragraph Mind Maps® can also be drawn on sticky notes that can be pasted in your text books.

The Impact of Fishing on Our Lives

The world's population is expected to reach over 8 billion by the year 2030. The amount of agricultural land for the cultivation of food crops may not be sufficient to feed this large number of people. Besides increasing the amount of agricultural land through methods such as irrigation and land reclamation, the best alternative food source would be from the sea.

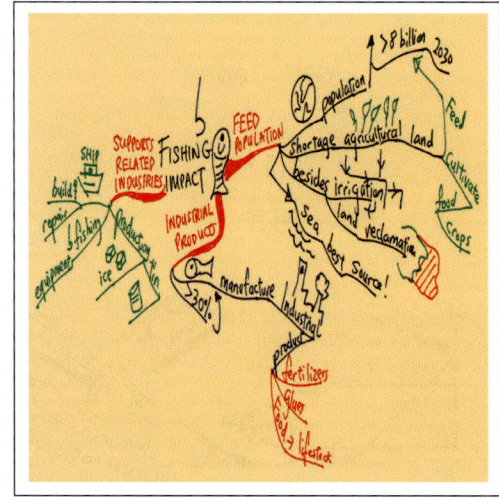

Besides being an important food source, fish is used to manufacture industrial products such as fertilizers, glues and food for life stock. In fact, more than 30% of the world's fish catch is used for such purposes.

The fishing industry also supports the existence of related industries such as shipbuilding and repair, manufacturing and retailing of fishing equipment as well as the production of ice and tin cans.

Physical Factors that Affect Fishing

Water Depth

The first physical factor that affects fishing is the depth of the water. In shallow waters, sunlight penetrates onto the ocean floor. This sunlight stimulates the growth of plankton which fish feed on. As a result, plankton abundant shallow waters attract a lot of fish. This is why shallow waters make excellent fishing grounds.

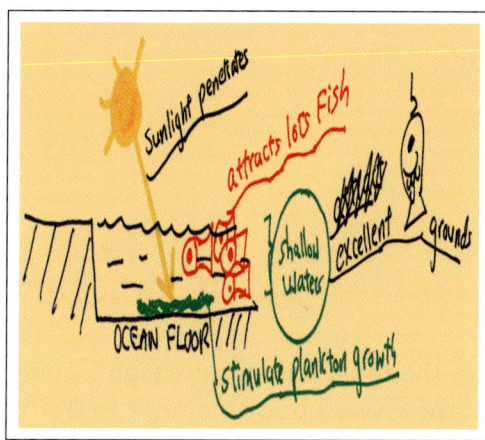

Temperature of Waters

Cold temperate waters tend to be better fishing grounds as compared to warm tropical seas. This is because in cold waters, bacteria, which compete with plankton for food, are less active. This allows the plankton to grow and attract more fish. In winter, the warm bottom waters replace the surface water, bringing with it nutrient salts required by the plankton.

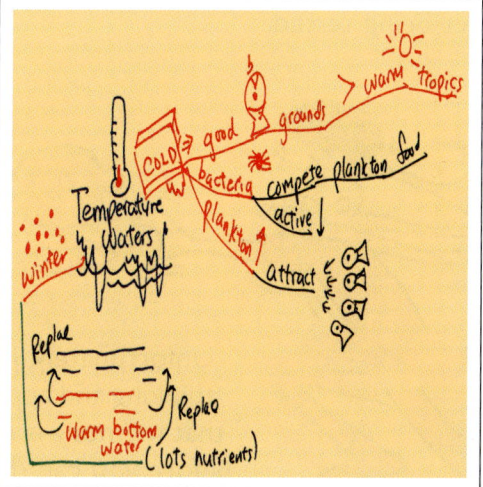

This concludes the chapter on Mind Mapping®. In the next chapter, you will learn how to unleash your brain's natural super memory to remember all the necessary points and facts easily and effortlessly.

Chapter 8

Super Memory For Words

IS YOUR MEMORY HOLDING YOU BACK?

One of the most common reasons students give for not doing well in school is that they have a poor memory. In fact, many students often fully understand the subject matter they are being tested on, but their minds just go blank when they have to produce an answer within a short period of time in the examination. As a result, their grades do not reflect their true ability in the subject being tested.

Fortunately, many educational systems around the world are moving away from examining students purely on content (what they remember) and more on their ability to think and apply what they have learnt. Unfortunately, just because more exams are more thinking and application orientated, it does not mean that memory is no longer important. This is because before you can think and apply what you have learnt, you must first remember what you have learnt! Before you can think logically, critically and creatively, you first need to have a broad base knowledge of the subject. And knowledge comes from memory.

Often, 'open book' exams where textbooks and notes are allowed give a very false sense of security. Most students think that for such exams, they do not need to remember facts since they can refer to it in the exam. The reality is that you will have no time to refer in the exam! Having the ability to memorise all the facts without having to refer will give you that added edge over everyone else.

THE GIFT OF MEMORY

Many students have the misconception that the ability to remember well is a gift or a talent that some have and others do not. People who think they do not have a good memory give up trying to remember things completely because they expect to forget them. Sure enough, having a poor memory becomes an excuse for failing and they will continue to produce bad results.

YOU CAN HAVE A SUPER MEMORY, TOO!

The first thing you have to understand is that there is no such thing as a good or bad memory. There is however a difference between a trained memory and an untrained one. Studies have shown that people who have an extraordinary capacity to remember things — a fact often mentioned by memory expert, Harry Lorayne — do not have brains different from ours. Rather, they know the correct keys to tap and so access their natural memory.

So, remember, memory is not a gift. We already have a natural super-memory, which we only need to learn to access. Before you learn just how to do that, let's explore the notions of 'retention' and 'recall'.

PERFECT RETENTION IMPERFECT RECALL

The process of memory includes retention, registration and recall. Retention involves storing information which we are exposed to. 'Recall' refers to the ability to retrieve that information after it has been registered.

There is now increasing evidence to show that our ability to retain information is perfect and does not deteriorate over time. This means every word, picture or sound you have ever registered in your mind, since the time you were born, lies perfectly intact somewhere in your brain. The only problem is that most of the time we have problems recalling or retrieving the information.

A LIBRARY METAPHOR

So, if we can retain everything, then why can't we recall it as effectively? To understand this, you must understand that your mind is like a massive library which contains a huge amount of information in hundreds of thousands of books.

If I were to ask you to look for a particular library book, you would be able to do it easily by using the library's index system of arrangement, as the books would be classified according to details such as subject matter and author's name. But imagine, if all the books were haphazardly placed and no index system were maintained, it could take you months to find the particular book. Well, your ability to recall works in the same way.

Most of the time, the information we have consciously and subconsciously been taking in has not been stored in an orderly way for retrieval. Therefore, we find that we cannot recall it easily, although it is there. So, one of the keys to developing a super memory is to develop a well-arranged index system in our minds. The way to do this is by using memory systems which will help you retrieve information quickly during examinations.

THE DEFINITION OF MEMORY

All memory involves linking one piece of information to another. More specifically, remembering anything new involves linking that piece of information to something we know already.

For most people who have not been trained in memory techniques, this linking process is a purely subconscious one. Sometimes, our subconscious mind makes strong links and sometimes weak ones. When the links are strong, we find that we can remember the information easily. What makes the links strong are the principles of memory.

THE PRINCIPLES OF MEMORY

You can probably cite me a hundred and one instances of you having forgotten something that happened very recently, like what you had for breakfast this morning. Yet, you also remember some things that happened many years ago, which you have not forgotten, and probably never will. In fact, you probably remember these experiences vividly, with all the associated pictures, feelings and sounds. One or two of these might have been traumatic or particularly memorable, such as an aeroplane trip or a first date. The funny thing is the more you try to forget these experiences, the more you will be able to remember them.

But why do you have the power to recall in one instance and not the other? We certainly had the same brain on both occasions. The difference was that when we were in a state of super-memory, certain principles of memory were present that helped us remember. If you can identify what these principles are, you can apply them all the time, you will be able to access your super-memory at will!

By studying people with hypernesia (photographic memory), researchers have discovered that they too use these same principles to perform fantastic memory feats! The most powerful principles of memory are listed on the following pages.

1. Visualisation

Visualisation is one of the two most powerful principles in memory. Our mind thinks in pictures. We therefore tend to remember pictures more easily than words. The more detailed and vivid the picture in our minds, the stronger our memory of it will be.

The reason why most students forget easily is because we try to remember words, while our mind thinks in pictures. The secret is to therefore convert study material into pictures that our brain can absorb very fast. In the exam, we will recall the pictures and translate them into words which we give as our answer!

2. Association

The second most powerful principle of memory is association or creating links between things we need to remember. Association forms the links between ideas we talked about earlier. This in turn creates an ordered index in our minds for quick recall. Linking pictures (visualisation and association) in our minds is the basic principle behind super memory.

3. Making Things Outstanding

If I were to ask you what you had for lunch on your last birthday, would you remember? I doubt it. What if for your last birthday, you were forced to eat fried cockroaches by your friends? Would you remember now? Of course you would. In fact, I bet you will remember what you ate when you are 80 years old. You see, the brain tends to remember things that are very outstanding. And one of the best ways to make things outstanding is to use humour and absurdity.

We hardly remember what we study because conventional notes tend to be boring and monotonous. We will increase our memory power by creating notes that make information really stand out! We also tend to remember things that are ridiculous, funny and out of the ordinary.

4. Imagination

We tend to remember things that we create out of our own imagination. This is especially so when we imagine experiences using as many of our senses as possible. In other words, instead of just imagining what a banana looks like, we should imagine the smell, the texture and the taste of it.

We should also use our imagination to create strong emotions within us. This is because we also tend to remember experiences that arouse strong emotions such as fear, laughter, anger, love, pain and hate.

5. Colour

Colour is also a powerful trigger of memory. This is why we should use multiple colours in note-taking. This can improve our memory by up to 50%.

6. Rhythm

Rhythm increases our ability to remember because it activates our right brain, a hemisphere usually dormant during study. For example, have you ever wondered how effortless learning the words of a song are compared to memorising the same number of words in a history textbook? Ask yourself how you can still remember the alphabet song, despite learning it in kindergarten. We can use rhythm in our learning by playing music in the background or creating rhyming phrases for facts we need to remember.

7. Holism

Finally, holism also helps you to remember. Holism (from the word 'whole') is learning things by seeing how it fits into the whole picture. Learning facts by seeing how it relates to the whole concept helps you remember better than learning facts in isolation.

MEMORY SYSTEMS

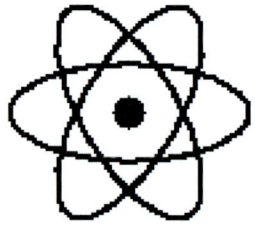

Memory systems are techniques that will enable you to create strong links between new information that you want to remember and information that you already know. Different memory systems are designed to help you remember different types of information. This is achieved through making use of the principles of memory. The two most common memory systems are the link system and the number system.

THE LINK SYSTEM

What Is It Used For?

It is used to remember a list of words or main points and it is especially useful for studying subjects with a lot of hard facts such as in physics, history, literature and geography.

The Process

The Link System involves the use of your imagination to associate visual images of the (key) facts you would like to remember. You will, in the process, use colour, movement, absurdity and humour and all other principles of memory. Therefore, the Link System involves two steps: visualisation and association.

1 Visualize

The first step is to create a picture of the words or objects you want to remember. For each word or fact, assign a detailed and vivid visual image. For example, if one of the words you want to remember is 'car', then see in your mind's eye, the picture of a car in detail. See the colour, shape, model, design and all the specific features. If you have a list of ten words you need to remember, create ten mental images in your mind.

**2
Associate**

The next step is to link all the ten pictures together to form a story. It is very important to make these associations strong. The way to do this is to use all the principles of memory in creating the story. In your story, there should be a lot of movement, many colours, music and rhythm and, most importantly, the story has to be absurd, humorous and memorable.

A SIMPLE EXAMPLE: REMEMBERING A SHOPPING LIST

Now let's take a very simple example of how you can use the Link System to remember a shopping list of 12 items. Imagine that your shopping list comprises the following:

1.	egg	7.	glasses
2.	beef	8.	orange juice
3.	fork & spoon	9.	soap
4.	bikini	10.	toothbrush
5.	perfume	11.	paint
6.	banana	12.	nail polish

Using the Link System, visualise yourself holding a smooth, hot egg as you leave your house. As you feel the smoothness, you make a hole in the shell. Out of this hole pops a cow's head (reminds you of beef steak) with two horns. The left horn is in the shape of a silver spoon while the right is in the form of a fork. You accidentally wave the fork which jabs a girl in a polka dotted bikini reeking of strong, sweet smelling perfume sprayed all over her. The pain makes her drop a long yellow banana she is holding on the floor.

Not looking, you trip on the banana and go crashing into a row of crystal glasses filled to the brim with orange juice. The entire floor is dirty and the manager orders you to clean it up with soap but using only a toothbrush. However, as you clean the floor, you accidentally scrape off the red paint. Later, you cover up the paint scratches with red nail polish.

If you had used your mind to visualise the events that were described, you should remember the shopping list easily. In the space below, jot down as many items as you can remember. Now you have a go!

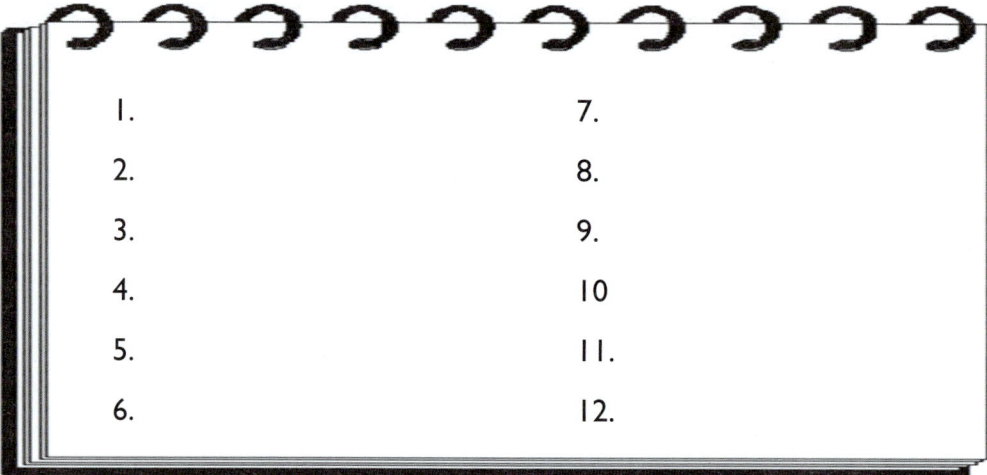

1.
2.
3.
4.
5.
6.
7.
8.
9.
10
11.
12.

How many items could you recall? You may have missed one or two, but I'm sure that you managed to recall much more that you normally would have been able to. If you couldn't remember an item, it is probably because you did not create the image clearly in your mind's eye while listening to the story.

> **Notice that in creating the story that linked all the words, we used :**
>
> 1. movement ('drop the banana', 'out pops a cow's head')
> 2. humour ('jabs the girl')
> 3. absurdity ('cow's horns in the shape of a fork or a spoon')
> 4. our five senses ('strong-smelling perfume'; 'hot smooth egg')

I Am Gifted, So Are You!

Again, it is very important that you use these memory principles to create strong links between the images. If you find that you cannot remember, it is because the links you have created did not have sufficient movement, absurdity, humour or sense of impressions.

IMAGING ABSTRACT WORDS

In most study materials, there will be many abstract words that you may find impossible to visualise. Under these circumstances, you must convert the abstract word into a visual image through the process of imaging. Only then can you use the Link System to associate the words. There are two methods you can use, the Similar Sound Technique and the Trigger Technique.

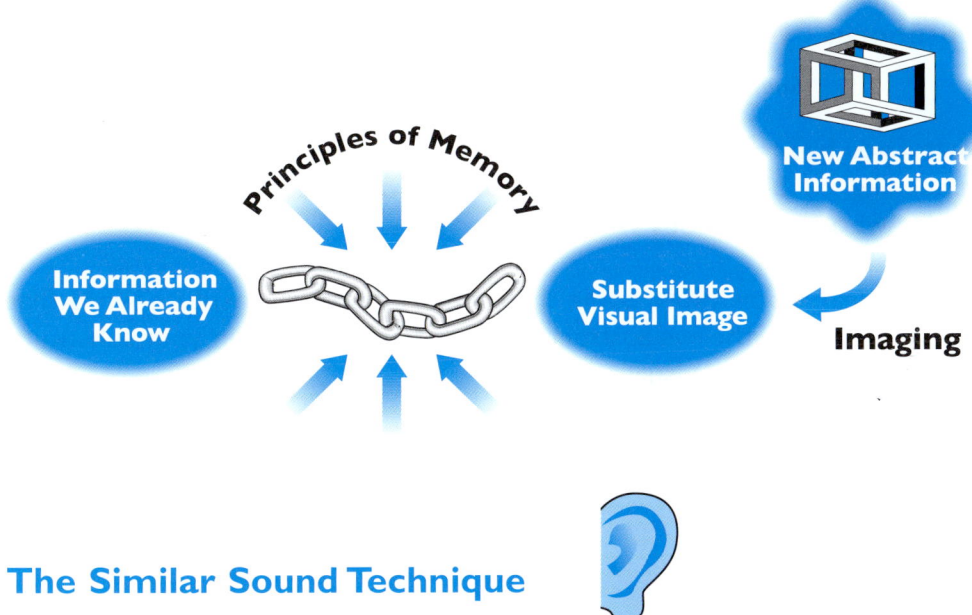

The Similar Sound Technique

To recall an abstract word, it must first be broken down into syllables, and a substitute word or words which rhyme with the syllables of the abstract word are used instead. The substitute word(s) should be easy to visualise.

For example, the chemical compound 'chlorine' is abstract, but it can be replaced by the word 'crawling' which rhymes with 'chlorine'. So, we can form a mental picture of a person 'crawling' on the floor. When we think of the visual image, it would remind us of 'chlorine'.

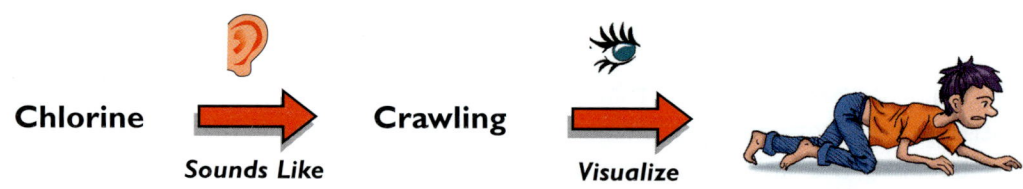

Next, think of the biological term 'colon', which means large intestine. Since 'colon' sounds like 'cologne', simply visualise a bottle of cologne to remind you of the 'colon'.

How about 'phosphorus'? What substitute word could sound like 'phosphorus'? The word can be broken down into three syllables: 'phos', 'pho', 'rus'. This could sound like 'frost forest'. So you could visualise a forest covered with frost.

What if you had to remember a chemical compound copper oxide? 'copper' sounds like 'cobbler' and 'oxide' sounds like 'ox hide' So simply visualise a cobbler who mends shoes with ox hide.

Got the idea? Good. Now, come up with at least one substitute word that sounds like each of the five abstract words listed below. Again, your substitute word must be easy to visualise.

Abstract Word	Your Substitute Word
1. gravity	
2. fluorine (chemical)	
3. glucose	
4. hydrogen	
5. oesophagus	

I Am Gifted, So Are You!

> **Possible Substitute Words**
> 1. 'gravity' sounds like 'gravy' and 'tea'
> 2. 'fluorine' sounds like 'flower' and 'urine'
> 3. 'glucose' sounds like 'glue' and 'ghost'
> 4. 'hydrogen' sounds like 'high Trojan' (horse)
> 5. 'oesophagus' sounds like 'Esso for gas'

Notice where all of the abstract words I have listed come from? If you are studying subjects like history, literature and geography, there is rarely a need to use substitute words because most of the facts are tangible and easy to visualise. The only time you may need to substitute a word is when you have to remember names and places.

For example, let's say you wanted to remember the historical character 'Nikita Krushchev'. Can you create an image of it? 'Nikita' could remind you of the famous 'female spy named Nikita'. 'Krushchev' sounds like 'crush the chef'. So, simply imagine Nikita crushing the chef.

If you need to remember that Napoleon was defeated in the Battle of Waterloo. ' Napoleon' (a name) can be broken up into the syllables 'nap', 'pole', and 'lean'. So, you could visualise Napoleon as someone who took a nap on a pole that was very lean. 'Waterloo' (a place), and when the word is broken up into syllables, it sounds like 'water' and 'loo'. To remember, you could visualise a loo (toilet) submerged in water.

To remember that Napoleon was defeated in the Battle of Waterloo, simply link the two images together using an absurd story. You could imagine the man taking a nap on a lean pole when he was shot down and fell into a loo (toilet) that was submerged in water.

THE TRIGGER TECHNIQUE

This technique can be used when you cannot find a substitute rhyming word. Basically it involves arriving at an image that leaps into your mind when you think of the abstract word. This is highly subjective and different people may see different things, but be consistent. Once you have chosen an image to represent the word, stick to it.

For example what comes first to your mind when you think of the word 'politics'? You may think of 'President Obama' or 'people in parliament. The more specific the image is the better. How about the word 'aluminium'? It could trigger the common image of 'aluminium foil'.

How about 'oxygenated blood'? Again, you could imagine each small red blood cell wearing an oxygen mask.

What about 'population'? Does it remind you of many new born babies, crowded places and people of different nationalities? Again, use whatever image that first comes to mind.

APPLYING THE LINK SYSTEM

Now, let's explore some examples of how the Link System can be used to memorise the facts presented below.

Subject 1: Elementary Physics

For the first example, let's consider something very simple. Let's say you want to learn the desirable features of an effective thermometer.

An effective thermometer is:

1. **easy** to read
2. **safe** to use
3. **inexpensive**
4. **sensitive** to temperature changes
5. has a **big range** of temperatures

1. Identify Keywords

The first thing we need to do is to identify the keyword or words in each of the five features listed above. Remember, not all the words are important and need to be memorised. We only need to remember one or two keywords that will give us the entire meaning of each feature. The keywords are highlighted on the previous page.

2. Visualize

The next step is to create a visual image for 'thermometer' (the main subject we are learning about) and for each of the five features listed above. Remember if the features are abstract, we have to use either the Similar Sound Technique or the Trigger Technique to create the visual image for them.

The first thing we need to visualise is the main subject, thermometer. See in your mind's eye a gigantic, glass thermometer with a bulb of mercury at one end and tiny black markings over the length of its body.

Now, let us form images for all the five features. The first feature is 'easy to read'. So you could visualise someone reading a thick blue book (remember to add colour) very quickly, flipping the pages to and fro (remember to have a lot of movement).

Triggers

EASY to READ ➡ **READING A BOOK QUICKLY**

The next keyword is 'safe'. Since you cannot see the word 'safe' (in the context, it means 'protected from danger'), we will use the Similar Sound Technique. Notice that it sounds like 'safe' (meaning a security vault). Therefore, to remember 'safe', we visualise a large, black, metal safe with a combination lock on it.

SOUNDS LIKE

SAFE ➡ **SAFE**
(protected from danger)   (vault)

For the next keyword, 'inexpensive', we can use the Trigger Technique (ask yourself what is the first image that comes to mind) to create a visual image that represents it. In this case, perhaps you could imagine a bag of 1¢ coins to represent 'inexpensive'.

The next keyword is 'sensitive'. Again, using the Trigger Technique, we can picture someone crying because he or she is very hypersensitive.

As for the last set of keywords, 'big range', we can use Similar Sound Technique to visualise a shooting range with many targets.

3. Associate

Now that we have created a visual image for each point, we can link them all up using a nonsensical story with a lot of movement, humour, colour and other principles of memory.

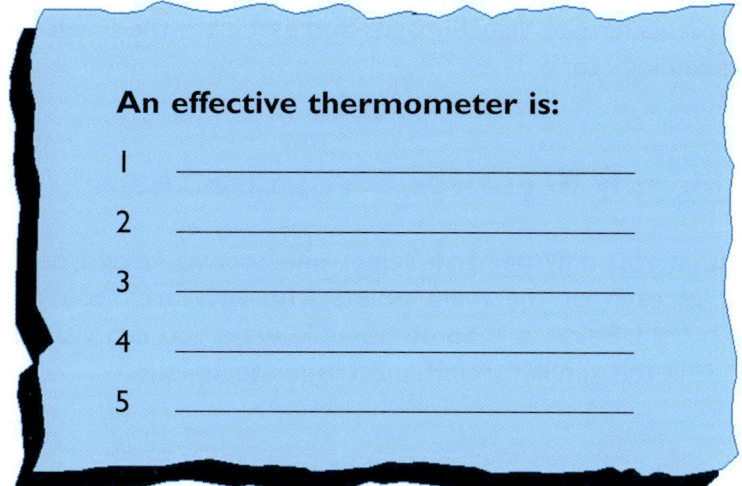

I suggest you picture a gigantic glass thermometer with a bulb of mercury at one end and markings on its body. This thermometer is reading a thick blue book, flipping through the pages very quickly (reminds you of 'easy to read'). To his surprise, he finds a black, metal safe with a combination lock (reminds you of 'safe to use') between the pages of the book. Getting very excited, he opens the safe only to find a bag of one-cent coins (remember 'inexpensive').

Disappointed, the thermometer starts crying (remember 'sensitive to changes in temperature') the tears dripping down its long body. To cheer him up, he decides to go to the shooting range and shoot at the biggest targets (remember 'big range of temperature'). See the story in the mind's eye and test yourself! Recall the five points discussed in this section.

So, what makes an effective thermometer?

Test your Memory

An effective thermometer is:

1 _____
2 _____
3 _____
4 _____
5 _____

Subject 2: History of Singapore

Suppose you needed to remember the seven effects of the Japanese Occupation on Singapore as shown below.

> The **Effects** of the **Japanese Occupation**
> 1. There was no **law** and order
> 2. There were **racial hostilities** and riots
> 3. The emergence of the **Malayan Communist Party (MCP)**
> 4. There was social and public **health disorder**
> 5. There were many **economic problems**
> 6. Demand for Malayan **rubber fell**
> 7. The prestige of the **British** forces was **lowered**
>
> * In bold are the possible keywords you can use to remind you of each point.

The principle is exactly the same. Identify the keywords in each of the main points, create visual images and associate the images into an outstanding story.

STEP 1: Identify Keywords & Visualize Them

Remember that you only need to select one or two keywords that would remind you of each of the main points. The keywords you can use are highlighted in bold. Below are some possible ways you can visualise each of the points using the similar sound and trigger technique.

122   I Am Gifted, So Are You!

STEP 2: Associate

Now, associate all the images you have created into an absurd and humorous story.

For example, you can visualise a fat Japanese looking for a job (reminds you of '**effects** of the **Japanese Occupation**'). Finally, he finds a job as a lawyer (reminds you of no **law** and order).

As a lawyer, he has to defend a racist horse (reminds you of '**racial hostilities**') whose owner is a male chauvinist pig (reminds you of the 'emergence of the **MCP**').

Suddenly, the horse lets out a disgusting fart that causes everybody to become sick ('social and public **health disorder**') and the offices to collapse ('**economic problems**'). Thousands of rubber balls come crashing down from the offices ('**fall** in demand for **rubber**') and hit the British, who are lowered into the ground ('**British** prestige **lowered**').

STEP 3: Test your Memory

Now, having gone through the exercise using the link system, write down the seven effects of the Japanese Occupation.

The Seven Effects of the Japanese Occupation

1. _____
2. _____
3. _____
4. _____
5. _____
6. _____
7. _____

Subject 3: Basic Economics

This is a popular pre-university or college course, so let's spend some time on the next section. Suppose you have to remember all the factors that influence the quantity demanded for a commodity. These factors are:

1. Price of the commodity
2. Price of related commodities
3. Taste and preferences
4. Income distribution
5. Population size

To remember these factors, imagine 'quantity demanded' as a child demanding sweets from his mother. To please the child, mother goes to the shop and finds the price of sweets ('price of the commodity') too high.

So, she buys chocolate candy which is cheaper (price of related commodities). The child tastes it and likes it even more (taste and preferences). In fact, he gets so excited that he spills a bottle of ink on the carpet, and the stain distributes throughout the fabric (income distribution sounds like 'ink' and 'distribution').

As the ink comes into contact with the fabric, it creates a 'pop' sound (sounds like population) that reverberates everywhere. Create the images in your mind and test yourself when you are done.

Subject 4: Elementary Geography

Let's say you are taking a course on physical geography and need to remember the following points on soil conservation.

The Seven Methods of **Soil Conservation**

1. **Contour** ploughing
2. **Terracing** of hills
3. Creating **shelter belts**
4. Crop **rotation**
5. Performing **strip** cropping
6. Planting of **cover crops**
7. Replenishing the soil using **fertilisers**

Once again, follow the steps of identifying the keywords (highlighted in bold) that will remind you of each point, create visual images and associate the images into a story.

Here is one way you can remember the 7 methods of soil conservation very easily. Imagine that the pieces of soil on the ground are having a *conversation* (reminds you of **soil conservation**). They discuss and decide to go on a *tour* to see *corn* (sounds like contour, reminds you of **contour ploughing**). Instead of staying at a hotel, they wind up in a *terrace* house (reminds you of **terracing of hills**). In the house, they are asked to put on safety belts (reminds you of **shelter belts**). Suddenly, the house starts *rotating* very fast (reminds you of **crop rotation**), causing all their clothes to be *stripped* off (sounds like **strip cropping**). Feeling very embarrassed, they start *covering* their bodies with *crops* (reminds you of **planting of cover crops**). Unfortunately, they start to itch from all the *fertiliser* on the crop (reminds you of **using fertilisers**).

THE FIVE STEPS OF REMEMBERING FACTS

You have seen how easy it is to remember a list of main points. To summarise, for optimal results, you should follow five basic steps.

> 1. Identify the keyword(s) that will remind you of each of the main points, including the title.
> 2. Convert each of the keywords into visual images.
> 3. Associate all the visual images into an absurd and humorous story.
> 4. Draw images of the story in your notes.
> 5. Review the images and the story at least three times.

With practice, you will find the link system to be a very powerful aid in learning. It impresses the facts very strongly in your memory and, as a result, allows you to retain information much faster. Instead of having to commit facts to memory using repetition, this system requires you to go through the facts only once. It also makes the process of learning a lot more enjoyable and interesting.

FURTHER APPLICATIONS OF THE SIMILAR SOUND TECHNIQUE:
LEARNING NEW VOCABULARY

This technique is especially helpful if you are learning a new language or studying a subject that requires you to learn the definitions of many complex words.

The Idea

Use the Similar Sound Technique to find substitute word(s) which sound like an abstract word you want to learn. The substitute word(s) should be easily visualised. You then use a story to link the visual image of the substitute word(s) to the true meaning of the abstract word.

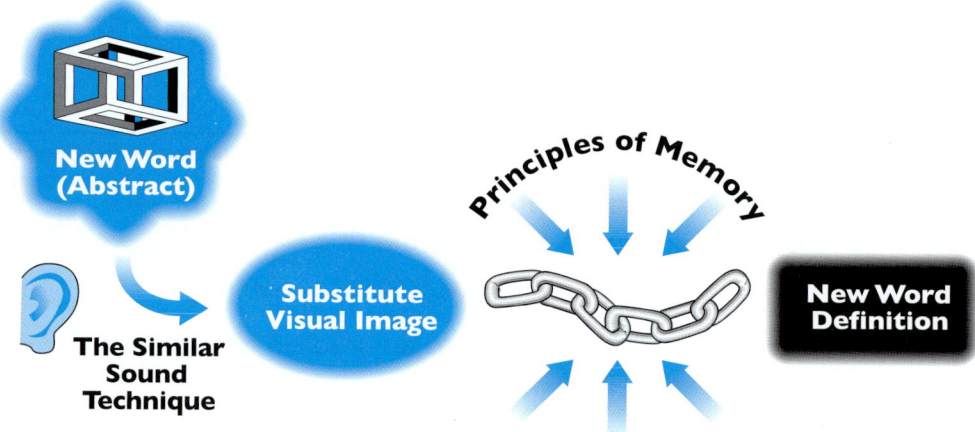

Some Examples
Consider the following new words and their meaning which you may have to learn:

1. Poignant — A sharp pain

How to do it!
First break down the abstract word into its syllables, if necessary. In this case, we get 'poig' and 'nant'. 'Poig' sounds like 'point' and 'nant' sounds like 'nun'. So imagine that a sharp point pierced a nun and caused an intense pain. So, whenever you think of 'poignant' it reminds you of 'sharp pain'.

2. Exhort — To advise

How to do it!
Again, break down the word into 'ex' and 'hort'. 'Ex' sounds like 'axe' and 'hort' sounds like 'hot'. Imagine that every time your father gives you advice, he holds a sharp axe with a blade threateningly, so you will heed him. When you are asked the meaning of 'exhort', you will remember its meaning i.e. to advise strongly.

3. Pumice — Volcanic Stone

How to do it!
'Pumice' sounds like 'pool' and 'mice'. To link the substitute word to the meaning, you could imagine the crater of a volcano filled with water (pool) and mice swimming in the pool.

4. Prodigy — Genius

How to do it!
You can imagine a (pro)fessional who went (dig)ging for a special mineral which, when he ate, turned him into a genius!

5. Salient — Most prominent

How to do it!
'Salient' sound like 'sail' and 'ant'. Imagine an ant who excels in sailing and becomes the most prominent ant around. So when you think of 'salient', you will immediately think of 'prominent' (prominant).

6. Forebear — Ancestor

How to do it!
Imagine that your ancestor was a circus trainer. His most famous act was training four bears (sounds like 'forebears') to play mixed doubles in tennis. Again, 'forebears' will remind you of 'ancestor'.

7. Amoeba — A one-celled organism

How to do it!
'Amoeba' sounds like 'amy' and 'baa'(the sound made by a sheep). You could imagine that a girl, Amy, suddenly starts to bleat ('baa') like a sheep because she is unable to speak like a normal person. Because of the strange behaviour, Amy has to be locked up in a prison with one-cell! (a one-celled organism).

Go through all the material once, seeing the images in your mind. Then write down the meaning of all the new words you have learnt.

Test Your Memory

Next to each word listed on the right, write down the meaning or definition.

New Word	Meaning
1. poignant	_____
2. exhort	_____
3. pumice	_____
4. prodigy	_____
5. salient	_____
6. forebears	_____
7. amoeba	_____

MORE EXAMPLES FOR YOU

Below are more new words you can practise with. Apply the same method and have fun doing it. Go through the words once, then visualise them being part of a ridiculous story. When you are done, test yourself and you'll be amazed at the results!

1.	emanate	– to come or flow from
2.	monolith	– a large block of stone
3.	equipoise	– balance between competing forces
4.	herculean	– very difficult
5.	mayhem	– confusion
6.	mitochondria	– a cell part that produces energy
7.	humerus	– a bone in the arm

This concludes the chapter on developing an excellent memory for words. We will now look at how memory can be applied to numbers.

Chapter 9

Super Memory For Numbers

THE NUMBER SYSTEM

Unlike words, numbers are abstract. They cannot be visualised and hence associated with each other or with other items. The number system overcomes this obstacle by using phonetic sounds to assign a key visual image to represent each number. Once numbers can be visualised as images, they can be easily remembered. This technique is especially useful for remembering dates, formulae and chemical equations.

HOW IT WORKS

Every number from 0 to 9 has got a phonetic sound associated with it. Once you have committed these sounds to memory, you can convert any number (even numbers with more than four digits) into a visual image which you can see in your mind and register in your memory. The ten basic numbers with their corresponding phonetic sounds are as follows:

Number	Phonetic Sound
1	d, t, th
2	n
3	m
4	r
5	l
6	j, soft g, sh, ch
7	hard g, k, c
8	ph, f, v
9	b, p
10	z, ce, s

Notice the 1 has the sounds 'd', 't' and 'th' which sound similar. 8 generates the 'ph', 'v' and 'f' sounds. You can use any memory aid to remember these sounds, but let me share with you the most common methods used.

REMEMBERING THE PHONETIC SOUNDS

The number 1 is made up of the vertical downward stroke. Similarly, the letters, 'd', 't' and 'th' are made up of that same downward stroke.

2 could remind you of the letter 'n' and 'n' has two downward strokes.

3 could remind you of 'm' because 'm' has 3 downward strokes. Alternatively, if you turn the number 3 ninety degrees in an anti-clockwise, you get 'm'.

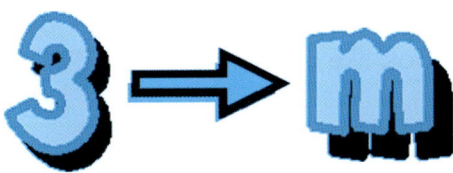

Chapter 9 • Super Memory For Numbers

The number 4 is spelt 'four'. The last letter of 'four' is 'r'. Therefore, 4 will remind you of 'r'.

How about 5? Take a look at your right hand and your five fingers. Notice that the space between your index finger and your thumb forms an L shape. Thus, 5 will remind you of the letter 'l'.

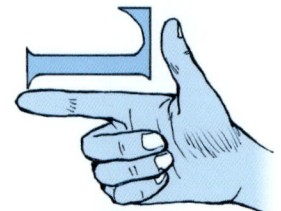

As for 6, its mirror image looks like 'j'. The sound of j is similar to the sounds of soft 'g', 'sh' and 'ch', or you could remember the phrase '<u>J</u>ack <u>ch</u>eats <u>sh</u>ort <u>g</u>iraffe'.

If you take the mirror image of 7 and look at it together with the original letter you will see the letter k facing downwards. Again, by remembering the phrase '<u>g</u>irl <u>k</u>icks <u>c</u>ow', you will remember that the sound hard 'g', 'k' and 'c' relate to 7.

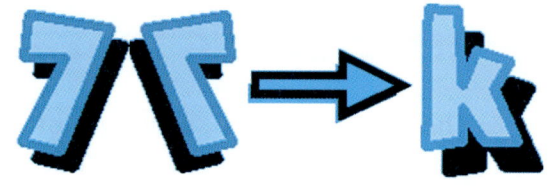

If you look closely, at the number 8, it looks like two 'f's facing one another. Therefore, 8 will remind you of 'f'. Using the phrase, '<u>Ph</u>ilip <u>f</u>ools <u>v</u>ampire', you will remember that 8 reminds you of the phonetic sounds 'ph', 'f' and 'v'.

9, when seen upside down, looks like a 'b' while the mirror image of 9 will look like a 'p'.

I Am Gifted, So Are You!

Lastly, 0 is spelled **Z**ero. The 'z' in the word will remind you of the sound of 'z'. This in turn has the same phonetic sounds as 's' and 'ce'. To remember this think of the phrase 'zebra sees cellophane'.

A QUICK TEST

Have you committed the sound to memory yet? Great! Now try a simple test for yourself. Next to each of the ten numbers given, write down in the blank spaces provided, their phonetic sounds. Please read the next section only after you have committed the phonetic sounds to memory.

Number	Phonetic Sound/Sounds	Number	Phonetic Sound/Sounds
1.	_____	6.	_____
2.	_____	7.	_____
3.	_____	8.	_____
4.	_____	9.	_____
5.	_____	10.	_____

USING PHONETIC SOUNDS

Now what do we do with all these phonetic sounds that we have just learnt? We will use them to create visual words from each set of numbers we are given. We do this by inserting vowels like 'a', 'e', 'i', 'o', 'u' as well as 'w', 'h' and 'y' (notice that it spells 'why') into the phonetic sounds of numbers.

Let's look at a simple example. The number 21 is made up of the numbers 2 and 1. We learnt that 2 has the sound 'n' (pronounced 'ne') and 1 has the sound of 't' (pronounced 'te'). Note that we could also use 'th' and 'd'. So 21 yields the sounds 'n' and 't' (sounds like 'ne' and 'te'). Notice that we create a visual word 'net' if we add a vowel 'e' in between the two phonetic sounds. Therefore, the number '21' is represented by the image of a 'net'!

Let's try another example. The number 94 is made up of 9 and 4. 9 has the sound of 'b' and 4 is represented by the sound of 'r'. Thus, 94 has the sounds 'b' and 'r'. Can you think of any word you can form by inserting vowels into the phonetic sounds for 'b' and 'r'? Of course we can get the image of a bear by inserting the vowels 'e' and 'a'. Therefore, the number 94 is represented by the visual image of a 'bear'.

Notice that what we have been doing all along is to convert abstract numbers into images we can see in our mind!

136   I Am Gifted, So Are You!

WE ARE ONLY INTERESTED IN PHONETIC SOUNDS

Take a look at the word 'ball'. If I were to ask you to do the reverse and convert that word to numbers based on the phonetic system, what would it be represented by? Many would say 955. Because the word 'ball' has one b (represented by 9) and two ls (l is represented by 5). Note that the letter 'a' in 'ball' is not represented by any number since it is a vowel.

This is however a mistake! 'Ball' is represented, instead, by 95 (not 955) because in pronouncing 'ball', we used the sounds 'b' and 'l' only once each! Having two letter 'ls' in 'ball' is irrelevant to generating the corresponding numbers because the second 'l' is silent.

Here's another example. What about the word 'knife'? Again, many people think that 'knife' contains phonetic sounds 'k', 'n', 'f' ('i' and 'e' are vowels so they are not taken into consideration). Thus, it is represented by the number 728. This, too, is a mistake. 'K' is not included here because it is silent (you don't say 'k' in 'knife'). Hence 'knife' is represented by 28.

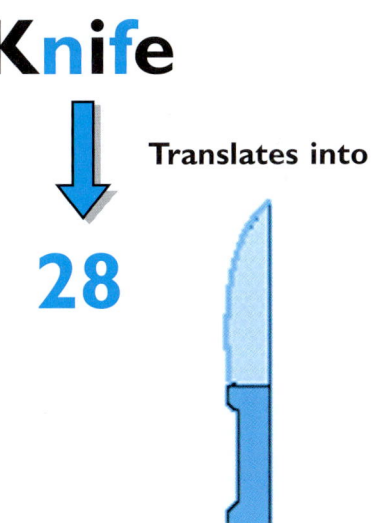

TEST YOURSELF

Now that you understand the concept, work on the following:

Exercise 1

Use the Number System to convert each number into a visual word.

Number	Visual Image
53	_____
21	_____
30	_____
541	_____
471	_____

Exercise 2

Convert the following words into the numbers represented by them.

Visual Image	Number
Dad	_____
Love	_____
Daze	_____
Mafia	_____
Check	_____

I Am Gifted, So Are You!

Possible Answers to the Exercises

Have you done the exercise? Great! Here are some of my answers to the exercises.

They may be different from yours, but it does not matter. You should learn to create your own unique word for each number and you will be alright as long as you follow the rules of the system. The numbers with the phonetic sounds are underlined for you.

Number	Visual Image
1. 53	li_me_
2. 21	_net_, _nod_
3. 30	_maize_, _mace_
4. 541	_lard_
5. 471	_rocket_, _racket_ (the 'k' is silent)

Visual Image	Number
1. _dad_	11
2. _love_	58
3. _daze_	10
4. _mafia_	38
5. _check_	67 (the 'k' is silent)

100 READY-TO-USE NUMBER PEGS

Now that you have learnt the phonetic sound of the numbers, you can easily translate any number into visual images (called pegs) which can be pictured and easily remembered.

To facilitate the use of the number system, create your own standard key visual images (pegs) for the first one hundred numbers. This way, every time you encounter a number between zero and one hundred, you will immediately know what visual image you can use to represent it. I have included below, the standard visual images I use for the first hundred numbers. You can follow them, modify them and create your own!

1. Tie	21. Net	41. Rat	61. Jet	81. Fat
2. Noah	22. Nun	42. Rain	62. Chin	82. Fan
3. Ma	23. Name	43. Ram	63. Jam	83. Foam
4. Ray	24. Nero	44. Rear	64. Chair	84. Fur
5. Law	25. Nail	45. Rail	65. Jail	85. File
6. Jaw	26. Notch	46. Rash	66. Cha-cha	86. Fish
7. Key	27. Neck	47. Rock	67. Jack	87. Fog
8. Ivy	28. Navy	48. Rafia	68. Chef	88. Fife
9. Bee	29. Knob	49. Rope	69. Chip	89. Fab
10. Toes	30. Mice	50. Lace	70. Case	90. Base
11. Dad	31. Mat	51. Lad	71. Cat	91. Bat
12. Tin	32. Man	52. Lion	72. Can	92. Bin
13. Dam	33. Mummy	53. Lime	73. Comb	93. Bomb
14. Deer	34. Mower	54. Lair	74. Car	94. Bar
15. Tail	35. Mail	55. Lily	75. Coal	95. Ball
16. Dish	36. Match	56. Leech	76. Cage	96. Beach
17. Deck	37. Mic(rophone)	57. Lake	77. Coco	97. Bike
18. Dive	38. Mafia	58. Lava	78. Café	98. Puff
19. Tap	39. Map	59. Lip	79. Cap	99. Baby
20. Nose	40. Rice	60. Jazz	80. Face	100. Daisies

Note that the letters in black are either vowels, letters that are silent (their sounds are not pronounced in their respective words) or letters that have been defined as phonetic sounds of any numbers (i.e. such as 'w', 'h' and 'y')

APPLICATION OF THE NUMBER SYSTEM

As mentioned earlier, the Number System is a powerful tool which can be used to learn any subject that has anything relating to numbers. In this section, you will learn how to remember dates from history, memorise atomic numbers of elements and numerical values of any kind.

REMEMBERING DATES

Studying History often requires students to remember when a particular event occurred. There is thus a need to associate the event with the date (which is a series of numbers) when it occurred.

How It Works

In order to remember dates and events, you must

1. form a visual image of the event that you want to remember

2. use the Number System to translate the date, which consists of numbers, to an appropriate key visual image

3. use an absurd story to link the visual image of the event to the key visual image of the date

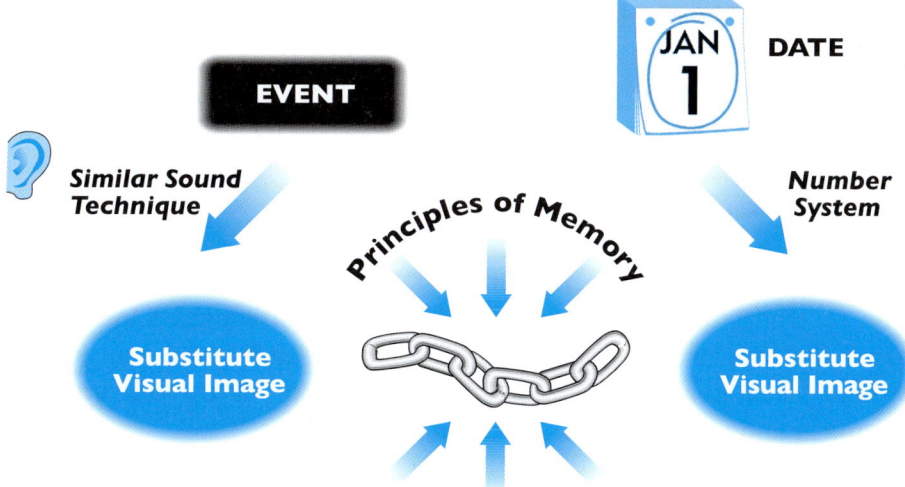

Example 1: Atomic Bomb

Say you need to remember that the first atomic bomb was dropped on 6 August 1945. As the event is the dropping of the first atomic bomb, the first step you need to take is to create a visual image of an atomic bomb in your mind.

Next, convert the date into its numerical equivalent, which is 6-8-45. Notice that we ignore the century (1900's), because you should be able to deduce the century through sheer logic. This leaves you to convert 6845 into visual images, based on the Number System you learnt earlier. One way is to pair the numbers into 68 and 45. As you know, 68 can be translated into 'chef' and 45 into 'rail'.

The last step is to make an absurd link between 'atomic bomb', 'chef' and 'rail'. So let's imagine that the first atomic bomb was built by a famous French chef who used old train rails as the main ingredient.

So every time you think of the first atomic bomb, you will be reminded of 'chef' and 'rail' which you can immediately translate 6-8-45, which is 6 August 1945.

Example 2: Pearl Harbour

Suppose you wanted to remember that Pearl Harbour was bombed by the Japanese on 7 December 1941. Again, you can create a visual image of the event, which is the bombing of Pearl Harbour, by simply visualising a string of pearls exploding.

Next, convert the date 7 December 1941 into 7-12-41 and use the Number System to translate the numbers 71241 into visual images. One way is to separate the numbers into three groups of 71, 24 and 1 and translate them into three visual images. This way, you will need to link up four images, the event image and three images for the date.

A faster way is to separate the numbers into 712 and 41. 712 translated into 'kitten' (one 't' is silent) and 41 can be translated into 'rat'. Finally, link the images 'pearls exploding', 'kitten' and 'rat' together. Imagine that a string of pearls exploded and one of the beads hit the kitten which subsequently choked on a rat it was eating.

Now, every time you think of the bombing of Pearl Harbour, you will remember 71241 which translates into 7 December 1941.

Dates In History To Practise On

This technique of remembering dates is not only a lot of fun, but also has lasting results. The explanation seems laborious but once you start, you will find that actual process takes only a few seconds to execute in your mind.

Let's commit to memory the dates listed below using the technique you have just learnt. Have a go!

	Event	Date
1.	Adolf Hitler's birth	20 April 1889
2.	Collapse of the Soviet Union	8 December 1991
3.	Franklin Roosevelt's election	1936
4.	The Great Depression	1929-1933

When you come across names of people or countries, convert them into visual image using the Similar Sound Technique or the Trigger Technique. For example, 'Adolf' sounds like a 'dwarf'. So, Adolf Hitler can be represented by the visual image of a fierce dwarf with pointed ears. Similarly, 'Roosevelt' sounds like 'rooster belt'. So think of a rooster wearing a belt if you want to remember Franklin Roosevelt.

How about the Soviet Union? How do you visualise this country? One way is to use the Trigger Technique to represent the country using the images of a hammer and a sickle (a symbol found on the flag).

Test Yourself

In the space below, write down the dates of the events which you have just remembered and be sure to check if you have got them correct.

Event	Date
1. Adolf Hitler's birth	_____
2. Collapse of the Soviet Union	_____
3. Franklin Roosevelt's election	_____
4. The Great Depression	_____

REMEMBERING THE ATOMIC NUMBERS IN CHEMISTRY

Now let's see how we can remember the atomic numbers of elements in chemistry. Let's say you had to remember the following elements and their atomic numbers:

Element	Atomic Number
sodium	11
rubidium	37
tungsten	74
phosphorous	15

How It Works

What you need to do is to create a visual image for each element, using the Similar Sound Technique and a visual image or the corresponding atomic number using the Number System. You can then use the Link System to associate the image of the element with the image of the corresponding atomic number.

 ## STEP 1: Visualize the Elements

Since the elements are abstract (we cannot see 'sodium'), we must use the Similar Sound Technique to come up with a visual word that sounds like the element to be remembered.

For example, 'sodium' sounds like 'sew dium'. (We can ignore 'dium' since most of the elements ends up with a 'dium'). So, as a visual image, you can imagine yourself sewing with a needle and thread. This will remind you of the word 'sodium'.

Similarly, ' rubidium' sounds like 'ruby'. So you can imagine a big red sparkling ruby. How about 'tungsten'? It sounds like 'tongue stern'. You can imagine a tongue with a stern face. As for 'phosphorous', it sounds like 'frost forest'. So you could imagine a forest made of frost.

Element	Visual Image
Sodium	sew
Rubidium	ruby
Tungsten	stern tongue
Phosphorus	frost forest

 ## STEP 2: Visualize the Atomic Numbers

Next, convert the corresponding atomic numbers to visual images (words) using the Number System. In doing this, we get the following:

Atomic Number	Visual Image
11	Dad
37	Mic
74	car
15	tail

Chapter 9 • Super Memory For Numbers

 **STEP 3: Link the Visual Images**

Finally we link the visual image of the element with the visual image of the corresponding atomic number like this:

Image of element	Link	Image of Number
sew	⟷	Dad
ruby		mic
stern tongue		car
forest		tail

To link 'sew' and 'dad', you could imagine yourself taking a needle and sewing your dad's feet to the ground so he can't go to work. So every time you think of 'sodium' (sew), you think of the atomic number 11 (represented by 'dad').

To link 'ruby' and 'mic', imagine a million-dollar microphone made up of sparkling red rubies. So every time you think of 'rubidium', you will remember the atomic number 37.

Now, come up with your own absurd story to link the next two elements to their atomic numbers. When you are done, test your memory by filling in the table below.
Have a go!

Test Your Memory

Element	Atomic Number
sodium	_____
rubidium	_____
tungsten	_____
phosphorous	_____

I Am Gifted, So Are You!

REMEMBERING NUMERICAL VALUES

The Number System can be used to remember numerical values of any kind.

How It Works

The method is similar to the way we remember dates in history and atomic numbers in chemistry. Simply link the visual image(s) of the keywords to the visual image(s) of the numbers involved.

EXAMPLE 1: HOW FAR IS THE MOON?

Suppose you have to remember that the Moon is 384 630 km from the earth, the first step is to create a visual image of the moon, since 'moon' is the key word.

The second step is to translate the number 384 630 into visual images. One way is to separate them into 38, 46 and 30. The three numbers translate into the images 'mafia', 'rash' and 'mice' respectively.

Finally, use a ridiculous story to link up the images for 'moon', 'mafia', 'rash' and 'mice'. Imagine that in order for you to go to the moon, you have to engage the services of a mafia chief with a rash, caused by mice that can fly you to the moon.

Remembering this story will remind you that the distance of the moon from the earth is 384 630 kilometres.

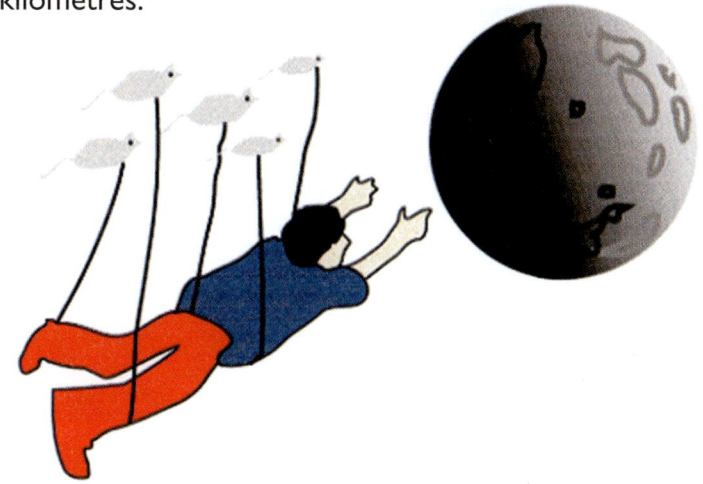

Example 2: What is the Speed of Light?

To remember that the speed of light is 3×10^8 metres per second, form a visual image of light travelling very fast.

Next, translate 3108 into visual images. One way is to separate it into the numbers 310 and 8, which translate into 'mats', and 'ivy' respectively.

Finally link the images of 'light', 'mats' and 'ivy' together. To do this, imagine a beam of light travelling very fast on long mats made of ivy.

Numerical Values To Practise On

You are now ready for some practice. Look at the list below and use the Number System to remember the numerical values given.

1. The boiling point of liquid is 78 degrees Celsius.
2. The value of pi is approximately 3.142.
3. The density of oxygen is 1.43 kilogramme metre cube.
4. The average rainfall in Singapore is 2 413 millilitres a year.
5. The area of the African continent is 30 320 000 square kilometres.

Tips

Notice that it would be impractical to form a visual image of the last four zeros found in 30 320 000 sq km (the last practice example) using the Number System. In such instances, where a number (normally zeros) is repeated many times, you have to be flexible and creative in forming your own visual images. You could, for example, represent the last four zeros as four eggs (zeros look like eggs).

Test your Memory

Are you ready to test your ability to remember numerical values? Good, here is your chance. In the spaces provided, write down the appropriate numerical values and be sure to check your answers when you are done.

The boiling point of liquid is _____ degrees Celsius.

The value of π is approximately _____ .

The density of oxygen is _____ kilogramme metre cube.

The average rainfall in Singapore is _____ millilitres a year.

The area of the African continent is _____ square kilometres.

A FINAL WORD ON MEMORY SYSTEMS

The usefulness of the Link System and the Number System is by no means limited to the examples you have seen here. They can be used to remember any subject matter. It is up to you to be creative and experiment with the different ways of modifying and applying the memory systems. Remember, as long as you follow the principles of visualisation and association through absurdity, you will develop super memory! Now, discover more about your memory in the chapter on memory patterns.

Chapter 10

The Pattern of Memory

Do you know that your memory follows a certain cyclical pattern? Knowing this, you will understand why there are times when you are able to learn so easily and effectively, while there are other times when you feel as though your memory is saturated and no matter how long you stare at the book, nothing seems to be going in. By understanding your memory pattern, you will be able to make efficient use of your study time.

DISCOVERING YOUR MEMORY PATTERN

Let me take you through a short experiment that will allow you to discover your own memory pattern. Read through the list of words given below only once and without using any memory principles and systems, do your best to remember as many of them as possible.

right	may	to
from	is	far
five	why	for
him	the	is
cute	if	left
the	is	the
soar	been	maize
is	the	ring
the	Santa Claus	baby
row	can	goal
the	the	ruler

Now, without looking back at the list, write down as many items as you can remember in the blank spaces provided. You do not have to recall them in sequence.

1. _____	12. _____	23. _____
2. _____	13. _____	24. _____
3. _____	14. _____	25. _____
4. _____	15. _____	26. _____
5. _____	16. _____	27. _____
6. _____	17. _____	28. _____
7. _____	18. _____	29. _____
8. _____	19. _____	30. _____
9. _____	20. _____	31. _____
10. _____	21. _____	32. _____
11. _____	22. _____	33. _____

Look at the list you have just made. If you did not use any memory systems, you would probably have left out a number of words. But look at the words you remembered. Why did you tend to remember those words and not the others? If you look closely, you will find a pattern to the way you remember. In general, in any period of learning, you will tend to :

Remember things at the beginning of a learning period.
So you probably would have remembered the first three to five words.

Remember things that appear toward the end of a learning period.
You probably wrote down the last three to five words.

Remember things that are repeated.
Such as 'is' and 'the'.

Remember things that stand out.
You would probably have easily recalled 'Santa Claus'.

 Remember things that are associated or related.
You would probably have recalled 'left' and 'right'.

Therefore if we were to plot a graph of 'percentage recalled against time', it would yield the following graph.

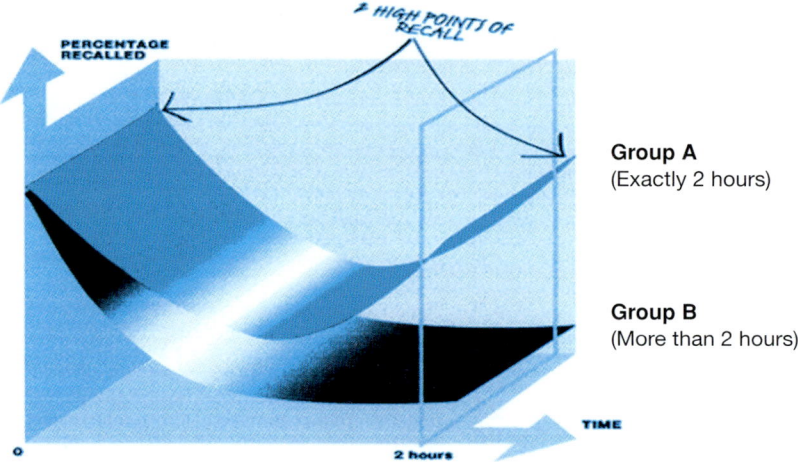

Group A
(Exactly 2 hours)

Group B
(More than 2 hours)

We can see from the above graph that in any period of study of up to two hours (see Group A), there will be only two high points of recall: at the beginning and at the end. During the middle of a study period, there is a dip in the percentage of the content recalled. So, in any period of study, a lot of what you are learning in the middle would probably be forgotten. The longer the study period, the larger the dip.

If you were to study for more than two hours continuously (see Group B), there would only be one significant high point of recall, and you would be wasting your time. This is why many students experience reaching a point where they feel that their mind is saturated and incapable of absorbing anything else.

AN OPTIMAL STUDY SESSION

Research has shown that the ideal length of study of an entire session should be no more than two hours. This session should be broken into four periods of twenty-five minutes or thirty minutes. In between each period, you should take a break of about two and five minutes.

During these short breaks, you should do some relaxation exercises. After each study session of two hours, you should relax for at least thirty minutes before starting again.

In this way (as shown in the diagram below), you will have eight high points of recall and the dip in percentage of recall for each learning period would be much less. The result would be a greater ability to recall, and a more efficient use of your study time.

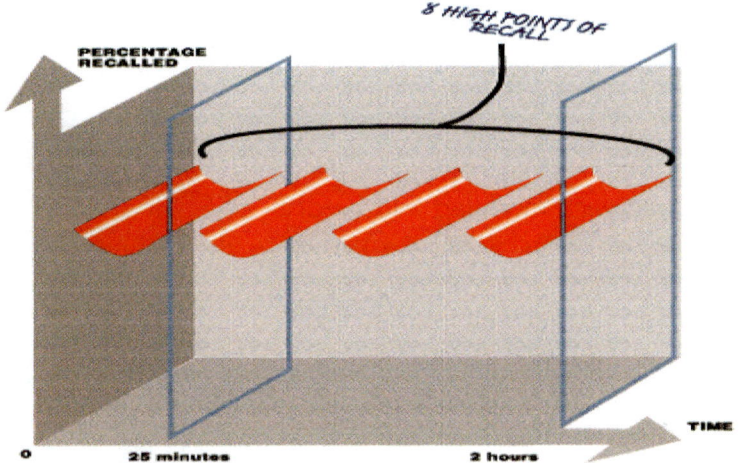

Study for two hours each time.

Take four five-minute breaks in between.

Relax during breaks.

After each two-hour session, relax for half an hour.

Chapter 10 • The Pattern of Memory

'CRAMMING' DOES NOT WORK

Many students I have come to know believe that it is useless to start studying early, because they would simply forget everything well before the examinations and would therefore have to study everything all over again. These students believe that they should only study about five days before each paper and, if they are lucky, they would have time for one revision, before the examination. As such, they often do badly or go blank during the exam, getting their facts confused and making very careless (and unnecessary) mistakes.

To me, this is a suicidal way of studying because it goes against all the principles of effective learning. Studying at the last minute would probably involve long hours, without the luxury of being able to take breaks, and will result in low recall ability.

In addition, the students' knowledge of facts would probably be very muddled and before their minds have had the chance to organise and integrate what they have already learnt, this new information could well interfere with existing information, causing greater havoc!

Furthermore, as a result of the last-minute studying, they are not as relaxed, and are therefore unable to learn well.

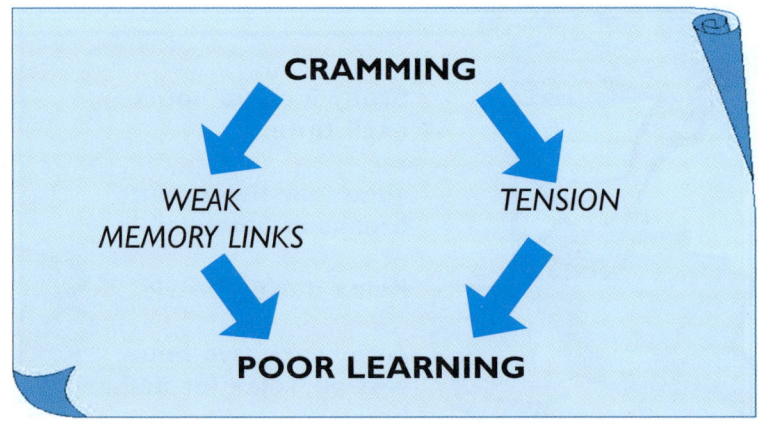

154 I Am Gifted, So Are You!

So, if you were to start preparation early and spread out your study time, how do you keep your memory at its peak until the examination day? The answer is through revision.

Many students think that revision is a waste of time, but done strategically, with Mind Maps®, it should save you more time than your normal method of studying. Not only that, the more revision you do, the greater your understanding, the stronger your memory links and the greater your skill in the subject.

Very often, we may know a concept, or how to solve a problem, but during the examinations, we become confused and make all sorts of mistakes. The reason for this is insufficient mastery of the skills to a level of unconscious competence. The only way to achieve this level of mastery is through thorough revision.

YOU FORGET 80% WITHIN 24 HOURS

Studies have shown that if revision is not done within the next twenty-four hours of initial study, 80% of what has been learned will be forgotten.

This is the reason why many students who study early but do not revise within the next twenty-four hours complain that they have forgotten almost everything before the examination. Any attempt to revise just before the examination is like starting all over again. Revision would take almost as much time as it did in the original period of study because most of what was supposedly learned would have been forgotten.

This does not mean that we should not start learning early. What it means is that we should revise at the right time, while our memory is still at its peak. In this way, revision would take a very short time and it would further strengthen the memory links put in place earlier. In fact, revision should take five to ten minutes for every hour of initial study time.

STRATEGIC REVISION

Revision should take place at specific times after a learning period. The first revision should begin ten minutes after initial learning. This is because research has shown that recall tends to peak ten minutes after learning, before declining steadily. The next revision should be within twenty-four hours, a week, a month and after the six month, respectively, if necessary. This schedule will keep the memory at its peak. The graph below provides a summary of the optimum revision schedule.

Ideally, you should start preparing for an examination about a month before it. This means you will go through about four revision periods. You should time your revision such that the last revision period falls on the day before the examination. However, much depends on your revision schedule and the number of subjects you are studying.

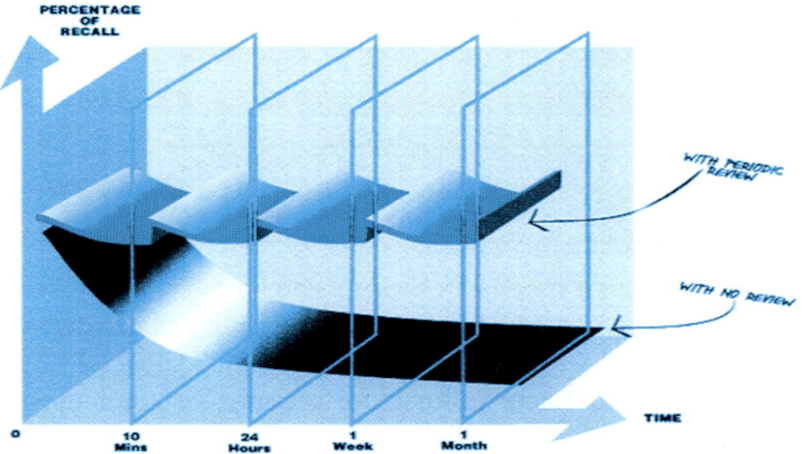

REVISION SAVES YOU TIME

You are probably thinking to yourself, 'If I follow this method of revising four times before the examination, wouldn't it take up a lot more time than the normal method of revising just once before?' The answer is 'No'.

Remember, if you were to follow the conventional way of studying once and then once more before the examination, more than eighty percent of the facts would have been forgotten. This means your revision time would be just as long as your initial study time. Not only that, but because you did not revise while everything is still fresh in your mind, the revision would be quite useless in reinforcing what was studied.

So, if you originally took two hours to study a chapter, you would probably take at least one-and-a-half hours to go over it. Thus, you would take a total of three-and-a half hours to complete a chapter.

If you were to revise four times, your initial study period would still take two hours, but your first revision (within ten minutes) would take only ten minutes. This is because the facts should be still very fresh in your mind. Your second revision (within twenty-four hours) should take you another fifteen minutes.

The third revision which should be done one week later, should again take you less than fifteen minutes. The final revision, on the day before the examination, should take you less than ten minutes.

If you add up all four revision time periods, you would take a total of two hours and fifty minutes which is forty minutes less than a conventional method. But, more importantly, because each revision was done at the time when all the facts were still fresh in your mind, your comprehension of the material is four times better than revision done according to the conventional method.

	Revising Four Times	**Revising Once**
Number Of Revisions	4 times	1 time
Total Time	2 hours 50 minutes	3.5 hours
Comprehension	4 times better	

Congratulations! You have just learned two of the most powerful learning techniques around, the Mind Map and the Memory Systems. Master them and you can expect to yield the results you desire.

Chapter 11

Mastering The Art Of Application

With the full arsenal of super memory techniques, you would have taken care of the first criteria of excelling in exams. You would have the ability to recall all the facts and figures in a short period of time.

But having content intelligence is not enough to get you that 'A'! The second test of exams is perhaps even more important. It is the ability to apply your content knowledge to the different combinations of questions that the examiners can throw at you.

In order to master the ability to apply what you have learnt, you must develop a range of core thinking skills that include creative, analytical and critical thinking. The thinking skills you must master include:

- Comparing data for similarities and differences
- Analysing information and relationships
- Identifying cause and effect
- Selecting and organising relevant information
- Making inferences
- Creative problem solving
- Explaining and elaborating
- Evaluating information for reliability and relevance
- Distinguishing facts, non-facts and opinions
- Drawing conclusions from evidence

Although all these application skills may seem intimidating, they are easily mastered once you know the strategy to use. Remember that students who are able to perform all these skills effectively do so because they use certain strategies. Once you learn and use these same strategies, you will be able to produce the same outstanding results!

THE STRATEGY OF GREAT THINKERS

The first thing you must understand is that the process of thinking involves asking questions (to yourself) to form links between new information and information that you already know. If you are 'thinking' about what I just said, then you are probably asking a question to yourself such as, 'Is that so? Do I think by asking questions?'

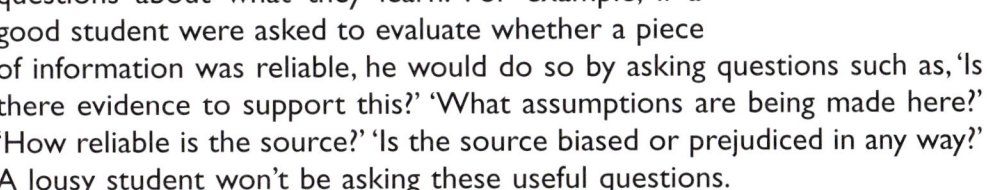

Students who possess great thinking skills ask themselves useful questions. Lousy thinkers do not ask themselves questions about what they learn. For example, if a good student were asked to evaluate whether a piece of information was reliable, he would do so by asking questions such as, 'Is there evidence to support this?' 'What assumptions are being made here?' 'How reliable is the source?' 'Is the source biased or prejudiced in any way?' A lousy student won't be asking these useful questions.

The second strategy of great thinkers is that they make use of pictures and visual tools such as Mind Maps, flow charts, diagrams, graphs and tables to help them to understand, analyse and manipulate information. On the other hand, poor thinkers do not make use of pictures and visual tools.

MASTERING THE ART OF APPLICATION

In any subject you are studying, be it history, literature, geography, physics or mathematics, there is always a common number of ways, patterns or styles in which questions can be asked.

> **THERE IS ALWAYS A COMMON NUMBER OF WAYS, PATTERNS AND STYLES IN WHICH QUESTIONS ARE ASKED IN THE EXAM**

Keeping this in mind, there are four steps you must use to master the application of any subject. For each chapter of every subject;

Step 1: Identify All Common Possible Question Types

The first step would be to go through all the different sources of questions such as past year questions, textbook questions, past test papers and class assignments. From there, record in a notebook, the different types of questions that are normally asked. You will discover that there is always a fixed pattern of question types. For example, in History, the common types of questions would include the following:

Samples of Secondary School History Common Patterns of Questions

1. **Essay-type questions**

   a. '*How far <u>do you agree</u> that...?*'
   - e.g. How far <u>do you agree</u> that Hitler maintained himself in power after 1933 solely because he crushed any opposition?
   - e.g. 'A superb leader'. How far <u>do you agree</u> with this summary of Mao ZeDong?
   - e.g. <u>Do you agree</u> that 'the Allies produced a constitution in Japan that everyone would be happy with?'

   b. '*<u>Do you think</u> that...?*'
   - e.g. <u>Do you think</u> that Japan would have surrendered if the atomic bomb had not been dropped?

c. **'Is it fair...?'**

e.g. <u>Is it fair</u> to call the Nazi state a totalitarian one? Explain your answer.

d. **'Describe and give examples'**

e.g. <u>Describe and give examples</u> of the methods used by the Nazis to maintain political control.

e. **'Why...'**

e.g. <u>Why</u> was reform needed in the Soviet Union after 1985?

e.g. <u>Why</u> did relations between the Japanese and Americans deteriorate in the 1930s?

e.g. <u>Why</u> did Mao introduce the Great Leap Forward?

f. **'What...'**

e.g. <u>What</u> policies did Gorbachev use to reform the Soviet Union?

e.g. <u>What</u> arrangements were made for the government of Japan after World War II?

e.g. <u>What</u> problems did Mao face in trying to implement his policies in China?

2. Source-Based Questions

a. **'Why do you think he said this?' or 'What do you think he meant...?'**

e.g. <u>Why do you think</u> Winston Churchill said what he said in his speech in Jan 1946 to the American people?

e.g. <u>What do you think the Soviets meant</u> when they said that the crisis in Berlin was 'planned in Washington'?

b. **'How similar are these two sources...?'**

e.g. <u>How similar are these two sources</u> in what they say about Lenin? Explain your answer.

e.g. <u>How similar are these two sources</u> as evidence about the treaty of Versailles?

- c. **'How does the author/speaker feel about...?'**
    - e.g. <u>How does the speaker of the source feel</u> about the treaty of Versailles? Explain your answer.
    - e.g. <u>Who does the author of this extract blame</u> for the supposed injustice of the treaty of Versailles?
    - e.g. <u>What does this source tell you about Japan's attitude</u> towards China in 1931?

- d. **'How useful is this source as evidence/proof about...'**
    - e.g. <u>How useful is this source as evidence</u> about events in the Soviet Union at that time?
    - e.g. <u>Does this source prove</u> that the United Nations was a success? Give reasons.
    - e.g. <u>How far does this source show</u> that militarism was on the rise in Japan in the 1930s?

- e. **'What is the opinion of the author about...'**
    - e.g. <u>What is the opinion</u> of the author about Gorbachev's failure?

- f. **The source is a cartoon**
    - e.g. What point is the cartoonist making?
    - e.g. What can a historian learn from this source?

- g. **'This source suggests....do you agree?'**
    - e.g. <u>This source suggests</u> that economic factors was solely responsible for the fall of the Soviet Union. <u>Do you agree</u>?

So, as you can see, if you go through all the sample examination questions, they always fall into these common groups or question types.

Step 2: Identify the Thinking Skills Tested

You will find that for each type of question such as 'How useful is this source as evidence that...' or 'How far do you agree that...', specific thinking skills are being tested. So, for each type of question, identify which thinking skill they are testing you on.

For example, for all question type **'how far do you agree that…'**, they are testing you on the following thinking skills:

a. The ability to *select relevant information* to show data where this is true and where this is not.

b. The ability to *present two points of view*.

c. The ability to make your own *judgement based on evidence* presented.

Step 3: Learn the Strategy to get Full Marks for Each Question Type

Each type or category of question requires a particular strategy in order for you to get full marks. So the next step is to learn what kind of answers you must give in order to receive full marks. You can learn this from your teacher or through studying sample questions and answers.

Example: The strategy to get full marks for source based questions of the type 'Why do you think…?'

Let's look at the strategy or the type of answers you must give in order to get full marks for 'why do you think…?' questions. An example of this could be 'Why do you think Churchill said the things he said in his speech?' from the source below.

> *From Stettin in the Baltic to Trieste in the Adriatic, an Iron Curtain has descended across the continent. Behind that line lie all the capitals of the ancient states of central and eastern Europe. All these famous cities and the populations around them lie in the Soviet sphere of influence and are all subject, in one way or another, to a very high and increasing measure of control from Moscow. The growth of communist parties in these countries poses a growing challenge to Christian civilisation.*
>
> *– Winston Churchill addressing the Americans in January 1946.*

In order to get full marks, you must give <u>three parts</u> in your answer:

1. Give your answer to the question
2. Use details in the source to support your answer
3. Use historical knowledge outside of the source to further support the answer.

Most students fail to get top marks because they give only one or two parts. They may just give a general answer such as, 'Churchill said those things in his speech because he doesn't like Communists'.

However, you can see that to get top marks, you must also support your answer with details from the source (i.e. because he thought there was a growing challenge to Christian civilisation and that the famous cities are subject to a lot of control from Moscow). In addition, you must also use historical knowledge outside of the source to further support your answer (i.e. because Churchill was talking to Americans which hated Communists... because Churchill was British and did not trust Stalin...)

In summary, note down all the common types of questions for each subject. For each type of question, learn what thinking skills they are testing you on and what level of answers (strategies) is required to get full marks. Finally, practise a few examples of each type of question.

MASTERING THE APPLICATION FOR MATHS AND SCIENCE BASED SUBJECTS

I find mastering the ability to answer and apply knowledge to science and mathematics subjects a lot more straightforward. This is because there is normally only one specific correct answer.

Many students train themselves in application by constantly practising past years examination questions found in assessment books. Yet, how many times have you heard of instances where students (maybe even yourself) practise doing hundreds of possible types of questions from assessment books, yet at the exam, they still get stumped by difficult questions which the examiner gives a new twist or slant to?

How do you prepare yourself in such a way that when you go for the exam, you would be able to tackle and answer any possible type of question that is set? No matter how much the examiner slants and twists the question, you would be able to handle it?

Well, the way to achieve this is not simply practising past year questions until your hands drop off. There is a systematic way of doing it.

N WAYS A QUESTION CAN BE ASKED

In the case of science-based subjects like mathematics, physics and chemistry, I believe that for every chapter or every concept that you are taught, there is always a fixed number of ways (combinations) in which questions can be asked! Let's call this fixed number N.

Let's demonstrate this in a very simple way. Say you are taught the Physics concept that Force = Mass x Acceleration or $F = MA$. There are only a fixed number of ways in which you can be tested on this! There are only three possible combinations. They are:

Possible question type 1: Given Mass & Acceleration, calculate the Force
Possible question type 2: Given Mass & Force, calculate the Acceleration
Possible question type 3: Given Force & Acceleration, calculate the Mass

This should be great news for any student! What must be done is that for every chapter, you must find all the different combinations of questions. For each type of question, you then find out the steps needed to solve it! Once you have learnt the steps to solve each type of question, the next step to internalise it is to practise doing each type of question at least three times! Let's elaborate on these three steps.

Step 1: Collect

Collect all the possible different types (combinations) of questions for each chapter. There are a fixed number, so find them all!

You search for all these possible questions from a variety of sources. They include ten-year series books (a compilation of examination questions over the last ten years), assessment books, homework from school, past test papers and the test papers of other schools (especially the elite ones).

You know you have found every possible combination when you can confidently go through the entire list of sources and not find any new combination that you may have missed out!

Step 2: Learn the Steps to Solve

For each of the question types you have collected, find out the steps needed to solve each one. You will find that for a particular type of question, the steps involved are the same, even though the numerical numbers may vary.

Step 3: Practise to Internalise

Finally, you must practise doing each type of question at least three times, using the steps needed to solve each one.

Now, why is it that there are many students who diligently go through hundreds of question types and practise solving them, yet still run into new question types that stump them during the exam? This is because they fail to use the technique I have just explained and instead, just practise on questions at random.

Let me explain this using an illustrative example. In a chapter (let's call this chapter X), you will find that there are a fixed number (N) of possible question types. They are X1, X2, X3, X4…Xn. This is illustrated below. Every question type requires a different set of steps or skills to solve. For example, in the case of elementary maths (solving equations), $y = x$, $y = x^2$, $y = x^3$, $y = x^4$…are all different types of questions which require different steps or formulas to solve!

Chapter: X

X1
X2
X3
X4
X5 } N different types of questions in Chapter X
X6
X7
.
.
.Xn

However, you will find that for each type of question (let's say X1), there are many possible variations that could appear in the exam. This will be X1a, X1b, X1c, X1d, X1e…etc. Many variations of a particular type of question are generated by changing the numerical values involved. For example, $y = 2x$, $y = 2x+1$, $y = 3x$, $2y = 10x$…are all different variations of $y = x$ (a linear equation). How many possible variations can there be? The answer is infinite! However, all the different variations of the same type of question can be solved using the same formula or steps. If you can solve one (i.e. X1a), you should be able to solve the rest (i.e. X1b, X1c, X1d…etc.)

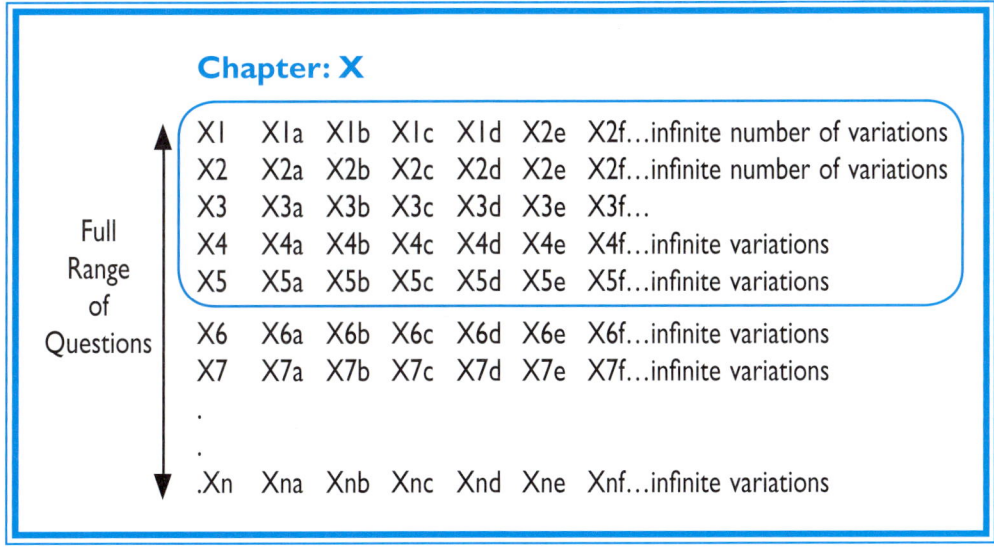

Chapter 11 • *Mastering The Art Of Application*

Add Range & Variations

Given a limited period of time to revise thoroughly for the exams, what is the best way to ensure that you can master any question that comes out? The answer is to make sure that you practise at least one of each type of question. In other words, just learn and practise X1, X2, X3....Xn. This is because if you can do X1, you should be able to do the many variations such as X1a, X1b, X1c and so on. For example, if you can solve y = x+3, you should be able to solve y = x +10, y = 2x +4, y = 3x +3, y = x +22 etc...

The trouble with most students is that they waste their time going through and practising hundreds of questions that are just variations of the same few questions. They may practise all those circled in red in the above illustration. However, because of all the time spent, they are unable to cover the full range of questions up to Xn. They may fail to learn the steps needed to solve X6 to Xn. If any of these questions come out, they will be stumped! So remember, it is not the number of questions that you go through, rather it is the range of question types you must master!

A PHYSICS EXAMPLE: SPEED, VELOCITY & ACCELERATION

Let's take an example from secondary school physics. If you study the chapter on speed, velocity and acceleration, you will discover that there are only 20 possible combinations of question types.

Below, I have listed all the 20 possible question types and categorised them into formula-based and graph-based questions.

Chapter: Speed, Velocity & Acceleration

From the formula: V = d/t (v is velocity, d is displacement and t is time)
1. Given d & t, calculate V
2. Given V & t, calculate d
3. Given V & d, calculate t

From the formula: a = v-u/t (v & u are final and initial velocity, a is acceleration and t is time)
4. Given v, u & t, calculate a
5. Given v, u & a, calculate t
6. Given a, t & u, calculate v
7. Given a, t & v, calculate u

From the displacement-time graph
8. Given t, calculate d
9. Given d, calculate t
10. Given t, calculate v (the gradient of the slope)
11. Given v (the gradient of the slope), calculate t

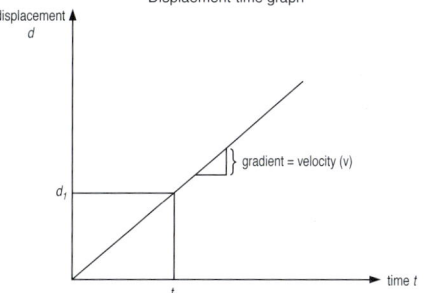

From the velocity-time graph
12. Given t, calculate v
13. Given v, calculate t
14. Given t, calculate a (the gradient of the slope)
15. Given a (the gradient of the slope), calculate t
16. Given v_1, v_2, t_1, t_2, calculate d (area under the graph)
17. Given v_1, d (area under the graph), t_1, t_2, calculate v_2
18. Given, d (area under the graph) v_2, t_1, t_2, calculate v_1
19. Given v_1, v_2, d (area under the graph), t_2, calculate t_1
20. Given v_1, v_2, t_1, d (area under the graph), calculate t_2

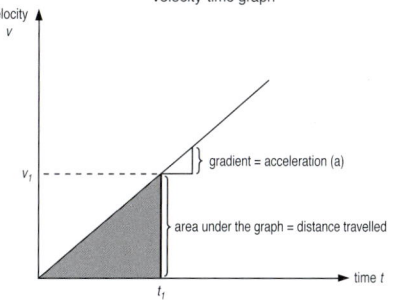

The next step is to find out the steps to solve each of the 20 possible question types. Finally, practise at least one of each of the 20 question types.

Congratulations! You have just completed the section on Super Learning Strategies. By adopting and mastering the tools I have just covered, you will have the full arsenal of weapons to blow away any difficult questions that come your way in the exam. Now let's move on to my favourite topic…

Chapter 12

Dare To Dream: The Power Of Goals

SUCCESS HAPPENS NOT BY CHANCE, BUT BY DESIGN

Welcome to my favourite chapter. Although this is arranged as the 12th chapter, setting goals is the first and most important step you must take in the whole process of succeeding both in school and in life. It truly excites me to talk about the power of daring to dream because I have witnessed first hand the impact it has had on my own life.

I want to tell you that everything I have achieved and accomplished did not happen by chance. Instead, it happened because I dreamed it and designed it clearly in my goals. In chapter one, I said that the first thing I did to turn my whole life around was to set three big goals! To top my secondary school, to enter Victoria Junior College (the top junior college in Singapore at the time) and to enter and top the National University of Singapore. Within eight years, everything I had set my mind on had materialised. It had come true exactly the way I had envisioned.

As I began to start achieving, it really excited me and further encouraged me to set bigger and bigger goals. I set clear visions about what I wanted to achieve in my life, beyond my studies. I wrote down that I wanted to be a best-selling author, an owner of several companies and yes…a millionaire.

I set all these exciting goals when I was just 15 years old. At that time, I was not sure exactly how I was going to pull it off but the thought of living the life that I had designed really excited and drove me to work really hard.

At the age of 21, the first edition of *I Am Gifted, So Are You!* became a number one bestseller. And at 26, I had achieved my dream of owning four different businesses and making over a million dollars. I wanted to start off this chapter by sharing this with you not to show off or to impress you. But I truly hope that I have given you the message that you must dare to dream and that goals are the driving force behind every success.

YALE 1952: FIRST LESSONS ON THE POWER OF GOALS

What first made me realise the power of goals was what I had learnt about a study that was done in Yale University in 1952. In that year, the graduating batch of students was asked if they had clear goals about what they wanted to achieve after they graduated.

Surprisingly, out of the entire cohort, only three percent of the students had their goals written down. They were very clear about the kind of job they were going for, the amount of money they wanted to earn and achievements they wanted to accomplish. They had truly designed the next 15 to 20 years of their life. However, 97% of the students had no goals at all. They did not know what they wanted. They left everything up to chance and had the attitude of 'whatever will be will be'.

Twenty years later, in 1972, a follow up study was done on the surviving members of this group of students. What they found was astounding. The combined income of the three percent of the students who had set their goals was three times greater than the combined income of the 97% of the students who had not set any goals!

What accounted for this huge difference in success? It certainly was not their level of intelligence or ability. After all, they all came from the same ivy-league college. The difference was in the power of goals.

WHAT DO TIGER WOODS, STEVEN SPIELBERG AND BILL CLINTON HAVE IN COMMON?

If you look at many of the most famous people around, you will also notice that their success came because they had dared to dream about it at an early stage. They too understand that everything happens by design.

Tiger Woods is one of the most successful golf professionals in the world. At his age, he has accomplished more in golf than anyone else in history. Did you know that he achieved all this because at the age of 8, he set his goals to beat all the top golfers and be number one?

At the age of 12, Steven Spielberg set his goal to be a top movie director when he grew up. At the age of 36, he became one of the most successful filmmakers in history. He directed four out of the ten highest grossing films in history, winning numerous academy awards. What allowed him to achieve such phenomenal success at such a young age? Again, it was because he had understood the power of goals.

Bill Clinton, the former President of the United States had, as a young boy growing up as the son of a poor widow in a small farm estate, set his ambition of becoming the President of the United States when he grew up. His teachers, relatives and friends said, 'Get real kid!' But like Woods and Spielberg, he dared envisage the future in his mind and made it into a reality.

WHY DOESN'T EVERYBODY SET GOALS?

You may be wondering to yourself, 'Wow, if setting goals is so powerful in helping you succeed, then why doesn't everybody set goals?'

When we were young, we all had big dreams and goals about our future. We dreamed about being doctors, firemen, movie stars and heroes. Unfortunately, as we grew up many of us gave up continuing to think about our goals and we stopped setting new ones. There are three main reasons why people do not set goals.

1. They Have Low Self Esteem

The main reason that people do not set goals is because they have low self-esteem. Self-esteem is a feeling of confidence and self worth. Often I would ask my students to aim for the best results and the best colleges. Some would say that they could never achieve those results or enter those top colleges. Others would say that it was not for them, that those great results were only reserved for 'other students'. It could be because in the past, we were told by our parents, teachers or friends that we were lousy or not good enough. All this may have caused us to have low self-esteem.

Remember that all this is not true. In fact, you have tremendous potential within you and that if others can, so can you! You deserve to have the very best in life. Once you understand this, you will begin to set high goals for yourself.

2. They Do Not Believe in Goals

Many students do not set goals because they do not believe in it. They do not believe in the power of goals. They give many examples of how they have set many goals in the past, but it never worked for them. We have also heard of many people with big goals who failed to achieve them. The reason all these people did not achieve their goals is not because setting goals did not work. It could be because they did not work hard enough towards their goals or because they used the wrong strategy and gave up halfway.

Setting goals by itself will not bring you success. It must be backed up with lots of action and undying determination.

3. They Fear Failure and Embarrassment

Another big reason why students dare not set goals is because they fear failure and embarrassment. They are afraid that if they aim for seven 'A's and they do not achieve it, they would feel like a failure. So in order to avoid failure, they never set goals. If you do not set goals, you can never fail, right? But at the same time, if you never set goals, you can never succeed and have big accomplishments.

Successful students dare to set high goals because they do not believe in failure. When they do not achieve their goals, they do not look at it as failure. Instead, they look at it as an outcome they can learn from. As a result, they do not feel bad about it. They know that as long as they learn something and keep taking action, they will eventually reach their goals. We will talk more about this in the chapter on 'The Ultimate Formula for Scoring 'A's'.

Many students I know are also afraid to set goals for fear that other people would laugh at them! 'Are you crazy? You will never achieve seven 'A's'. Instead of feeling demoralised when others laugh at you or look down on you, I want you to use their ridicule to empower and motivate yourself even more!

In fact, a big driving force for my motivation as a student was the fact that I wanted to prove all my teachers and friends wrong. The more they laughed at me and said that I couldn't make it, the more excited and motivated I was to work hard, achieve my goals and show them! So, do not let the fear of embarrassment discourage you, let it empower you instead!

GOALS EMPOWER US TO SUCCEED

Why are goals so powerful? What is it about setting a goal that puts in motion the process that allows us to achieve what we want? Goals have three powerful characteristics that help us succeed.

1. Goals Direct Our Choices and Actions

The goals you have direct how you live your life at every moment. They direct the choices you make and the actions you take. If your goal is to be the top student of your school, what kind of choices will you make? What kind of actions will you take? Chances are, you will make choices and take actions that will lead you to your goal. You will make the choice of paying attention in class, making good notes, preparing early for exams. When friends ask you to hang out and go to the mall after school, you would probably say no as you know it will not help you reach your goal.

On the other hand, if your goal is to be a professional golf player like Tiger Woods, would you make different decisions and take different actions? Of course! Besides focusing on good grades, you will make the choice of practising your golf swing and spend hours playing golf. Similarly, if your goal is to be a national swimmer, you would make the choice of going swimming instead. So you see, your goals determine what you do. They determine the choices you make.

What's dangerous is when we have no goals. When you have no goals, you have nothing to focus on and you will tend to move towards anything that gets your attention. You will move in all directions and go nowhere. You will just follow the crowd and become nothing more than a sheep.

The other danger with having no clearly designed goals is that your mind will subconsciously develop self-sabotaging goals. Before I learnt how to set goals after SuperTeen, I used to have self-sabotaging goals like 'watch as much TV as I can', 'avoid studying', 'make trouble for teachers' 'sleep whenever I can' and 'just avoid failing the examinations'. No wonder I was getting such terrible results, my goals were directing me away from success and towards failure. So remember, if you do not decide and design what you want, your sub-conscious mind will decide for you!

> **YOU MUST CONSCIOUSLY DESIGN GOALS THAT WILL DRIVE YOU AND DIRECT YOU TO SUCCESS**

Alice:	Which road should I take?
Cheshire Cat:	Where do you want to go?
Alice:	Anywhere
Cheshire Cat:	Then, it does not matter which road you take.

From Alice in Wonderland

2. Goals Drive Us

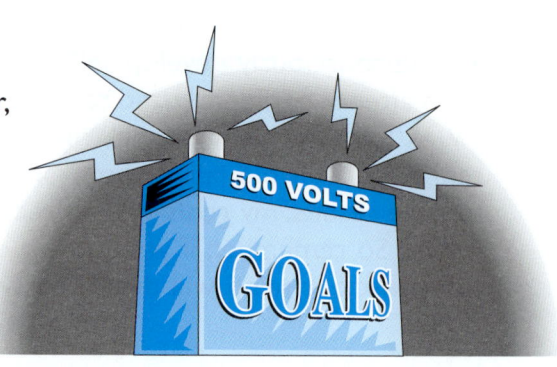

During my days as an underachiever, I always wondered how and where my successful classmates found the energy and drive to finish their homework, or to study thoroughly for a test. How could they study for long hours, even on weekends, giving up TV, computer games and fun? What was their secret? How could they have so much drive and motivation while I felt lazy and tired all of the time? I found out that the secret is in the goals we have. Goals energise and empower us. Without goals, we will feel lazy and tired.

> **THERE IS NO SUCH THING AS A LAZY STUDENT, ONLY ONE WHO DOES NOT HAVE A CLEAR GOAL!**

Have you ever experienced a time when you had to study a chapter and felt very sleepy and lazy? But the moment you started playing your favourite computer game, you felt the surge of energy come back and you would find yourself playing for hours without feeling lazy at all? Then, the minute you go back to your books, you would start to yawn and feel sleepy again? Why is this so? Well, when we are playing a computer game, we have a very clear goal, to win! That gives us the energy and motivation to play on. The trouble is when we study, most of us do not have a clear goal of scoring 'A's or achieving top honours, and so our mind shuts down and saps our energy! The minute you set exciting goals for yourself in your studies, you will find that you will have the energy that will drive you and overcome laziness.

3. Goals Stretch Our Potential

Another reason for setting goals is because they stretch us beyond our normal potential and help us attain results above our usual average. Let's say for example that you have been always getting a 'D' for mathematics. This is your usual average grade. And you decide to set a goal to score an 'A' for your upcoming exams. By setting that 'A', you will probably begin to study differently. You will take better notes, clarify doubtful concepts and spend more time practising tough maths problems. As a result, even if you do not eventually get that 'A', you would probably get a 'B', much higher than your average 'D'.

SET GOALS IN ALL AREAS OF YOUR LIFE

All of us know that houses are built by construction workers. But before they can start the construction work, they would first need the architect to draw the blueprints or the design plans. Why? Because the design plans would tell the workers how high the roof is, how many doors there are, the number of pillars, the number of doors, the height of the roof etc. The workers would follow these plans as they lay the bricks and erect the structures. Finally the house will be shaped until it resembles the design plans.

Would it be possible for the workers to build the house without any design plans? That would sound ridiculous. The workers would just lay one brick at a time until they run out of bricks, all the time not knowing what the final house should look like. What would eventually happen? They may end up with a wall or a funny looking structure that nobody would expect.

You may think this sounds absurd but do you realise that living our life is like building a house? Yet, many people live their lives without first designing a plan so they will know what their lives would be like when it is finally complete. Living each day is the same as laying a brick on your house. If you keep laying bricks without knowing what you are creating, you will end up with a life that you do not want. Unfortunately, many people do not realise this until they suffer from a mid-life crisis and discover that they would rather have lived their lives in a more successful way.

When you build a house, you must design all the different areas that make up the house. You must design the bedrooms, the bathrooms, the dining room and so on. Similarly, when you set goals for your life, you must focus on all the different areas that will give you a successful life. For example, it is no use being very successful in your studies when you have very poor health. It is also of no use if you had a great career, good health but were dead broke.

In total, you must design and set goals in four main areas of your life. They are:

1. Study and career goals
2. Health and sports goals
3. Financial and lifestyle goals
4. Family and social goals

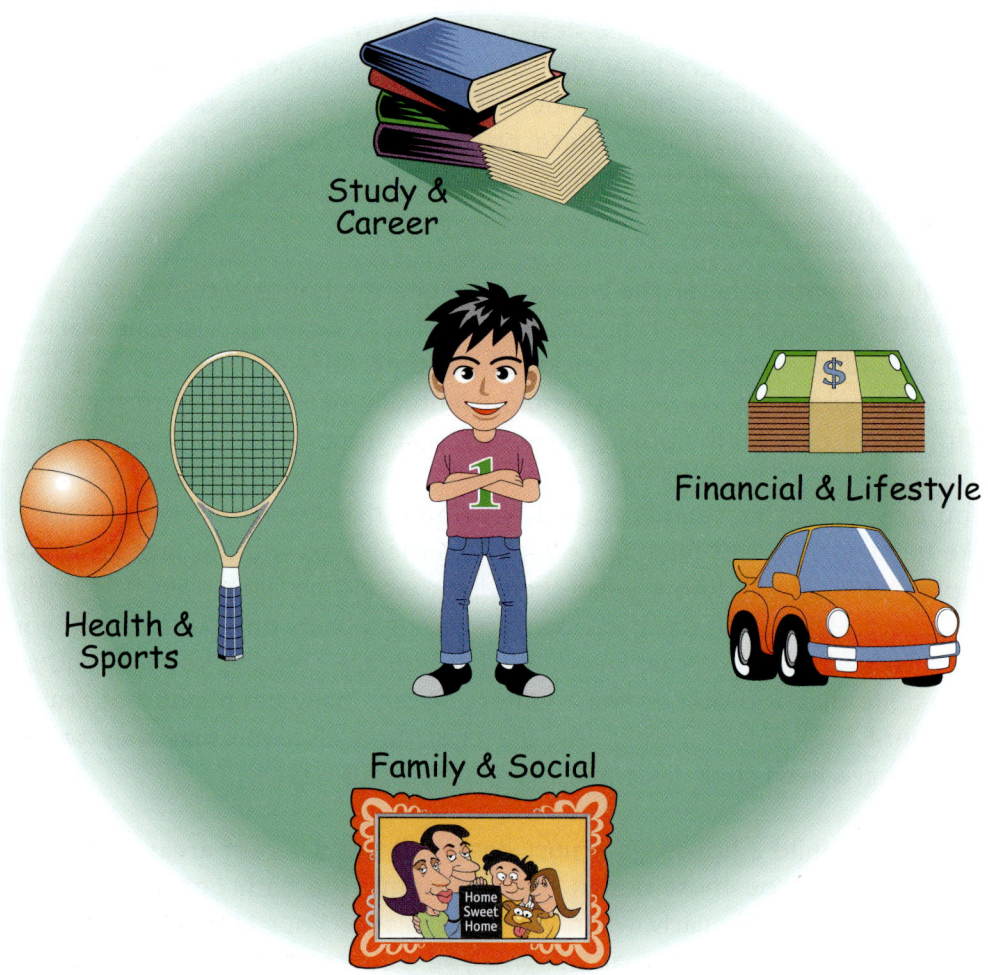

CREATE BIG AND EXCITING GOALS

Many people tell me that they still do not feel very motivated even after setting their goals. They still do not feel driven to take action. The reason is because the goals they set are not exciting enough.

In order for your goals to really excite you and drive you to take action, you must set big goals. Big goals are goals that may be way beyond your current level of ability or skill. These are the kind of goals that seem very difficult or even impossible at first, but the thought of achieving them really excites you!

When I set my goal to top the school (a really big goal), the thought of achieving it was really exciting, especially since I was at the bottom at the time. That excitement drove me to work very hard throughout the night. The other big goal I set of making a million dollars excited me so much that it drove me to start my first business at 15 years old and to hold two jobs while I was still in school.

Instead, many people tend to set easy, puny goals thinking that they will be a lot easier to achieve. The trouble is that these goals will not excite you or drive you. If I set a goal to be in the top 50 in my school, it would not have excited me as much as wanting to be number one.

You must have heard friends or teachers say, 'It is better not to be too ambitious. You must be realistic'. Most people who say this are fearful of big challenges because they are fearful of failure. Such people lead mediocre and boring lives.

Great people and super achievers are rarely 'realistic' or 'down to earth' according to most people's standards. They tend to have dreams and goals that other people think are unrealistic, but they get excited by the possibility of achieving their goals and this drives them to achieve them. When the Wright brothers first conceived the idea of creating a flying machine, people thought they were crazy. When John F Kennedy, the former US president set the goal of sending a man to the moon and back, people thought he was unrealistic. But today, we have achieved all those things and more! Why? Because all it took was for these leaders to dare to dream the supposed impossible.

SIX STEPS TO CREATE POWERFUL GOALS

Now that you understand the power and importance of setting goals, you must learn how to create goals in such a way that they empower and motivate you to see them through. Many new-year resolutions are seldom followed through simply because they were not set in an empowering way. They were nothing more than weak wishes or desires. For our goals to empower us, you must follow six key steps.

1. Write Down What You Want Specifically

The first step is to write down your goal as specifically as possible. When you make your goal specific, your mind is better able to focus on achieving it. When your goal is too general or not clear, your mind will find it difficult to get what you really want. For example, goals like 'I want to improve my maths', 'I want to do well for my exams', 'I want to save more money' or 'I want to have a stable career' are unclear goals.

Improving your mathematics could mean improving by 5 marks, by 10 marks or 30 marks. It is a huge difference. Doing well for your exams could simply mean passing with a 'C' or it could be getting straight 'A's. A good career could mean being a trash collector or it could mean being a scientist. They are both stable jobs.

Instead, your goals should be specific like 'I want to increase my maths grade from 45% to 85%', 'I want to score 6 'A's and a 'B' for my exams', 'I want to save $7 a week and $2000 by the time I reach 17' or 'I want to be a nuclear physicist specialising in researching alternative forms of energy'.

2. List all the Benefits & Reasons for Achieving that Goal

The reason why a lot of people do not consistently work towards their goals is because they are not clear why they want that goal. We are rarely motivated to do something unless we know the reason or benefit from it. So after you have set a goal, write down at least five reasons why you must achieve it. Write down how you will benefit from achieving this goal. Unless you can come up with good and compelling reasons, setting goals will not motivate you.

3. Write Down a Strategy and A Plan of Action

Write down the strategies you intend to use and a detailed plan of how you are going to carry out those strategies. A personal organiser with a calendar is ideal for planning.

Example:
a) My strategy is to make Mind Maps®, for my History textbook and use memory techniques to remember the information.

b) My plan of action is to make two Mind Maps®, a day for the next two weeks. I will then spend three hours a day memorising the information for another week.

4. Set a Deadline

Next, you must set a specific deadline for achieving your goals because without one, you will tend to procrastinate till the goal is forgotten. Setting a specific date means writing down the date, month and the year of accomplishment.

5. Emotionally Charge Your Goal

At the end of the day, most of our actions are driven not by our logic but by our emotions. Intellectually, we may want to achieve a goal and know all the reasons why we should but what really drives us is our emotions. So, this step is one of the most important. You must close your eyes and imagine yourself achieving the goal and enjoying all the benefits that come with it.

I want you to fantasize about achieving your dreams until it becomes very real in your mind. Doing so will give you the emotions to consistently act on your goal.

6. Create Momentum by Taking Action Now

Very often, people set goals and action plans only to put it off to the next day. Pretty soon, they will procrastinate and never get started on realising their goals. What you must do to avoid this is to immediately get momentum by taking some action the minute you finish writing the goal. You should do something straight away that will move you towards your goal, even if it is 1:00 a.m. in the morning! The minute you set a goal to increase your maths grades, you should pick up your maths books and start reading at least one page! The minute you set the goal of buying a new car, you should go to the showroom and get a brochure. There is great power in creating immediate momentum.

AN EXAMPLE OF EFFECTIVE GOAL SETTING

Let's look at a few examples of effective goals you can set. What you can do is to write them down in your diary, journal or organiser.

An Example of A Study Goal

I am committed to score 86% in mathematics for the final year examination

Benefits and Reasons:
- *To qualify for the science course in junior college*
- *To achieve my aim of studying medicine in Oxford and becoming a doctor*
- *I want to prove to all my friends that I can score an 'A' in maths*

Strategy & Plan of Action:
My strategy is to work on examination papers from the past six years until I can score 90% on each one. I will practise this twice a week (Monday and Thursday). In addition, I will spend two hours a day revising each chapter in the textbook.

The date of accomplishment will be 26 November 2015.

An Example of A Health Goal

I am committed to achieve a gold in my Annual Physical Fitness test.

Benefits and Reasons:
- To be an all-rounder in school
- To have a high energy level
- To prove to myself that I can do it

Strategy & Plan of Action:
Run two kilometres every Tuesday and Thursday evening.
Do 50 push-ups and 100 sit-ups every morning

The date of accomplishment will be 14 October 2015.

A GOAL POSTER

A goal is not something you set and put aside, only checking up on it one year later. Goals are something you must look at and be reminded of everyday. A good routine to start will be to start your day by reading your goals in your personal organiser. Another good strategy would be to summarise your study goals on a goal poster that you can paste on your wall. That way, you will be reminded of it the minute you wake up and get home from school. Below is an example of a goal poster you can draw for your upcoming examinations.

> **Final Year Examination results 2015**
>
> | | |
> |---|---|
> | English | 85% |
> | Mathematics | 95% |
> | Physics | 90% |
> | Chemistry | 90% |
> | Geography | 96% |
> | Second language | 79% |
> | History | 88% |
>
> My reasons for achieving these results are to get into the science stream in Victoria Junior College. I want to prove to myself and my friends that I am indeed intelligent, and can accomplish anything I want.
>
> The date of accomplishment is 26 November 2015.

DESIGNING A LIFE PLAN

Besides setting goals on the four main areas of your life (i.e. study/career health/sports, financial/lifestyle and family/social), you must also set long term goals as well as short term goals. Long term goals are goals that you aim to achieve anywhere between 2 and 15 years. Short term goals are goals you want to achieve within two years.

Many students do not feel motivated even after setting all their study goals of scoring 'A's because they do not know what they want to do in the long term. I always tell my students that they will never get motivated about learning unless they know what they want to do with their lives in the long term. If you have no clear vision of what your life will be like 10 to 15 years from now, then, scoring 'A's or learning a particular subject will hardly have any meaning and motivation for you.

On the other hand, if you have the long term goal of being a politician or even a President, then you will be motivated to learn history, economics and politics. You will be motivated into going to top colleges. If you have the long term vision of being an actor, then you will be motivated to learn literature, human psychology, mass media and history. You will see the relevance in aiming to go into a top college of the Arts.

So, it is time you begin to dream and decide what you want to do 15 years from now. What career to dream of having? Is there a dream company you want to be working for or do you have dreams of creating your own business? How much money would you like to earn? What kind of lifestyle do you want to have? What kind of people would you like to be mixing with? What is your dream house? Your dream car? What kind of things would you like to be able to do? Vacation in exotic places twice a year? What else would you like to be able to do?

It is having all these wonderful long term dreams and goals that will give us the meaning, passion and desire to excel in what we do now, get good grades and get into prestigious colleges. As you think about all your own dreams, let your imagination run wild. Remember to dream big and that you are limited only by your imagination. You can create anything you desire. The idea is to get emotionally charged up. This is because as people, we tend to do things not so much out of logic but out of emotions.

Once you have jotted down all these long term goals of yours, I want you draw them in a flow chart on a piece of poster paper. This will act as a design plan for your life. Once you have completed it, paste it on your wall where you can get inspired everyday. An example is shown below. There is no limit to what you can put on your Life Design Plan. However, it is important that you include the following:

1. Write down what you want to achieve specifically
2. Write down the date of accomplishment
3. Write down your age at each stage.

MY LIFE PLAN

Ping Yi Secondary School
- Score 7As
- 6 points (LIRS) for O levels

Age 16

Victoria Junior College
- Score 4As for A levels
- Physics/Economics/Maths C F Maths

age 16–18

National University of Singapore
- Achieve top 1% & Dean's List
- Graduate with First Class Honours Degree in Business Administration

age 21–24

 Army National Service
- Go to Officer Cadet School
- Achieve rank of Lieutenant
- Get Gold for Fitness Test

age 18–21

Full Time Motivational Trainer, Business Consultant & Best-selling Author
- Sell 100,000 books in 1 year
- Target $20,000/month salary

age 24–26

 Be A Business Owner of at least 5 Companies in Event Management, Education and Consulting

age 26–28
- Achieve total sales of $20m per year
- Achieve total profit of $5m per year

* Buy my dream car BMW/Mercedes Sports Convertible. age 25
* Marry an Intelligent Beautiful, Caring Wife and have 2 Children. age 29
* Buy my Dream House
  – 15,000 sq. ft bungalow
  – swimming pool
  – 6 bedrooms
  – video/music room
  age 30
* Travel annually to exotic destinations for vacations with my family. age 31 onwards

Take Companies to Public Listing

age 31

Retire Financially with $100m

age 35

Play Golf & Do Charity Work, Travel

age 36 onwards

I Am Gifted, So Are You!

Design Your Life Plan

Are you ready to begin designing the kind of results you want and the life you will ultimately lead? Good. Remember that you have all the potential and resources to produce exceptional results. So design your life with passion and absolute faith! To get you started, I want you to design a similar life plan to the one you have just seen. Have fun!

YOUR MOVE: DESIGN YOUR INDIVIDUAL GOALS

When you have finished, you can then proceed to use the four steps of goal setting to set individual goals in your journal or diary. Remember to include all the different areas of your life as you have outlined in your life plan. Follow the format below.

1. Define your goals specifically.

   _____

   _____

2. List the benefits & reasons for achieving them.

   _____

   _____

3. Write down the strategy & plan of action.

   _____

   _____

4. Write down the date of accomplishment.

   _____

   _____

Design Your Goal Poster

Have you finished setting your goals? Great! Now, I want you to design a goal poster for your upcoming examination. Follow the guidelines given below, then redraw them on a big piece of poster paper with a lot of colours and images. Stick it up in your room when it is complete.

Step 1:

Write down the name of your upcoming examination below.

_____

Next, list the subjects you are taking and your expected grades.

	SUBJECT	GRADE
1.	_____	_____
2.	_____	_____
3.	_____	_____
4.	_____	_____
5.	_____	_____
6.	_____	_____
7.	_____	_____

Step 2:

Write down the reasons for & benefits of scoring those grades.

1. _____
2. _____
3. _____
4. _____
5. _____

Step 3:

Write down when you will accomplish them.

_____

SET A GOAL, AND YOUR MIND WILL FIND A WAY!

In goal setting, one of the most important beliefs you must have is that whatever you can conceive and believe, you will be able to achieve. As you plan your life, do so with absolute faith and expectation.

Even if at this point in time you are unsure of how you are going to be able to achieve the goal, it does not matter! Set it anyway! If you can find enough reasons why you want to achieve it, your mind will eventually lead you towards deciding how to do it. Goals actually make our mind alert and receptive to opportunities all around us. Without goals, we tend to let such opportunities in life slip by.

So, if all these goals are in place, does this mean that we will definitely succeed? You cannot be absolutely certain of it. If our goals are not followed up by concrete action, they will forever remain dreams. But if you act on them, they will become your destiny. So how do we get ourselves to act? Find out in the next chapter on how you can spur yourself on.

Chapter 13

Motivation – Moving Beyond Procrastination

MOVING BEYOND PROCRASTINATION

How many times have you made a goal, a resolution, but never got started achieving it? Or how many times have you got started on something only to lose stamina by the end of the first day?

We all know what we should do in life, like studying for that big examination, but somehow, we never get round to doing it, until it is too late. This habit of procrastination affects just about everybody. It is simply paralysis in taking action that we know will benefit us.

Procrastination is the main saboteur of all success. You can set the most inspiring goals and plan the perfect timetable but if you fail to act when you are supposed to, then you would have already failed.

When you procrastinate, do you not also get this feeling that your life is being controlled rather than you having control over it? Your sense of fear tells you to stop watching TV and to get started on that school project, but a compelling force drives you to watch one more programme. In order to overcome procrastination, you must learn how to control it, instead of letting it control you.

THE FORCES OF PAIN AND PLEASURE

The forces that drive any behaviour are those of pain and pleasure. We always behave in a way that will move us away from what we think is painful and towards what we think will be pleasurable. Why do we keep putting off doing a project till the last minute even though we know we should start early? Well, because most of us have been conditioned to link massive pain with doing the project now (the pain of stress, frustration and giving up our favourite TV programmes) and link pleasure with doing something else, such as watching TV.

How do we eventually get around to doing it? Normally, we start taking action when the project is due the next day or when we suddenly face pressure from peers who have finished it. But why are we able to act now and not earlier? Again it is because we now perceive that not doing our project now will bring us more pain (the pain of not being able to finish on time and producing a bad report) and this overrides the short term pain of doing the project now.

Instead of being a slave to pain and pleasure, take charge of your life and use the same forces to drive you to take the action that you want, such as to start studying consistently, to watch your diet and to finish your project well before the due date! The quality of your behaviour depends on what you have consciously or subconsciously linked pain and pleasure to. Nothing is, by itself, pleasurable or painful but it is what we link it to that makes it so. Successful students have learned to link pleasure with studying and pain with not studying. These people never procrastinate and always score 'A's.

Others have, instead, been conditioned to link a lot of pain with studying and a lot of pleasure with avoiding studying. These people always procrastinate and are never able to follow through on their plans and goals. In trying to overcome their procrastination, they try all sorts of methods, but these methods do not address the root of the problem. In their mind, they still link pain with studying and pleasure with avoiding it. This is why, no matter how hard they try, they always end up procrastinating again.

So, the key to changing any behaviour, whether it is to stop smoking or to overcome procrastination, is to change what you link pain and pleasure with. You have to learn to link pleasure with studying now and pain with putting it off. So right now, let's see how we do that.

REWIRE YOUR MIND

First identify what present behaviour you would like to change and what new behaviour or action you want to replace it with. For example, you may want to change your present behaviour of putting off studying till the last minute (procrastinating) with a new behaviour of doing it immediately.

In the next exercise, you will learn how to link massive amounts of pain to procrastinating and great pleasure to taking immediate action.

Reconditioning your mind to act now

 ### Step 1

Write down in the space given, all the pain you will possibly experience if you continue putting off studying for a test or examination. For example, you may eventually feel the pain of failing and being retained or being ridiculed by your teachers, relatives and friends. Write down as many of these painful outcomes as you can, making sure that they are enough to upset you.

All the pain that I will feel if I continue with my old behaviour (e.g. procrastinating)

1.
2.
3.
4.
5.
6.
7.

 ## Step 2

Use your imagination and actually see in your mind's eye, all the pain you would eventually experience as a result of procrastinating and studying only at the last minute using the ideas you jotted down earlier. In your imagined experience, I want you to actually see what you would see, hear what you would hear and feel what you would feel, going through all that pain.

This exercise is intended to create enough emotion to drive you to change your behaviour. For example, imagine yourself having scored low grades. See your friends with their high grades. Feel the regret, anger and frustration of not having studied earlier. Feel the agony of not being able to get into the school or course of your choice. Visualise yourself being reprimanded by

parents and teachers and despised by classmates whom you admire. Create as many painful feelings as possible and make the pain seem as real as possible to you.

 Take three minutes and do it now

Next, I want you to imagine what your life will be like five years from now as a result of your procrastination. I want you to imagine the worst possible scenario. You could see yourself as a dropout, with no friends and no job, regretting your past behaviour. Again, use sight, sound and feelings to create experiences that seem real.

 Take three minutes and do it now

As you begin to feel compelled to overcome procrastination, you can now imagine what your life will be like ten years from now as a result of procrastination. Again, imagine the worst scenario and make it as real as possible. For example, you could see yourself in a lowly paid job and with few friends.

 Take three minutes and do it now

Why are you doing this? Because you'd only start to regret and wish you could change things when it is too late. It's only when you have no education, no money and no prospects that you begin to say, 'If only I had…'. Unfortunately at this stage, it is too late. So, before this happens, create the painful consequences for yourself so you can take immediate action instead of wishing you could.

 Step 3

The next step is to link as much pleasure as possible to the new behaviour that you want. First, write down all the pleasurable feelings or experiences you will enjoy if you studied consistently. Do this in the following chart.

▶▶ 198   *I Am Gifted, So Are You!*

All the pleasure that I will have with my new behaviour

1.
2.
3.
4.
5.
6.
7.

Step 4

Again, this is a very important step in the process of reconditioning yourself. Use your imagination and see yourself as if you are already feeling and experiencing all that wonderful pleasure that comes with studying early. Imagine yourself receiving a report card with all the results that you want. It's your passport to success and happiness.

Feel the satisfaction and joy of holding your well deserved results and seeing them before your very own eyes. See yourself being congratulated and praised by your parents, friends and teachers. Make the experience as real as possible for yourself!

Take three minutes and do it now

When you think about studying now, it should evoke a more positive response than it did before. Now, I want you to imagine your life five years from the date you begin to start studying consistently. You can see yourself in a prestigious university enjoying all the benefits that you desire.

Take three minutes and do it now

Lastly, see yourself ten years from now in a respectable job which you particularly enjoy. Make the experience, together with all these wonderful sensations, as real as possible.

 Take three minutes and do it now

 ## Step 5

In the final step, you need to break your old habit of doing things and condition yourself towards accepting your new behaviour. Starting right now, make it a point to do things that you normally would not do, or change your sequence of doing things. Instead of vegetating in front of the television or taking a nap straight after school, do a quick review of the day's work or read a book. You may even consider going for a quick jog or working out with weights.

We are all creatures of habit and need to break whatever behavioural pattern is limiting our success. Finally, repeat the two imagination exercises regularly (at least twice a week) until you have conditioned your new behaviour and made it a part of your new pattern of behaviour.

LESSONS FROM LIFE: HOW CATHERINE OVERCAME PROCRASTINATION

One of my friends, Catherine, shared with me her way of overcoming procrastination. Catherine was the top commerce student in a top junior college in Singapore for two years. She valued both her sleep and her time for going out.

She was aware that if she kept putting off doing her work, it would mean less sleep later on, and less time for going out. In actual fact, she was subconsciously linking massive pain with putting off her work and pleasure with starting it immediately. This simple process drove her to make an optimal use of her time and it earned her a top position in the National University of Singapore.

MORE TIPS ON TAKING ACTION...NOW!

Besides the mind conditioning exercises, here are a few other things you can do to get moving beyond procrastination. All these tips are based on the same principle: linking pain with procrastination and linking pleasure with taking action.

1. Make a Commitment to Yourself

The best way to compel yourself to take action is to make a personal commitment that you will take action to achieve your goals. Everybody wants straight 'A's, but not many are committed to working towards getting them. The difference between wanting something and being committed to it is that commitment involves doing whatever it takes to achieve it. It means that it takes precedence over anything else and is your priority. If you want to realise your goals, you must first be sure that you are committed to achieving them and not merely wanting them.

You must put down your commitment in writing in the same way you set your goals. Sign this statement and get your best friend or your parents to endorse the statement as witness. Next, put up the contract you have just made on your mirror, so you can be reminded of it everyday.

2. Publicize Your Commitment

Making a personal commitment is powerful, but it is not enough. This is because most people manage to find excuses to break promises they have made to themselves. So, make a public commitment.

Tell your friends, teachers, parent and even your relatives that you will score seven 'A's in your examinations. Will they laugh at you?

If they do, instead of feeling bad about it, use their mockery to drive yourself. In fact, the more they laugh, the better! By putting your reputation on the line, you have no choice but to act.

3. Constantly Review Your Goals

Review your goals daily, especially your specific wants and your reasons, and the benefits of achieving them. This will keep your mind focused and give you direction. Very often, external forces may misdirect you so reviewing your goals keeps you on track.

4. Reward Yourself Along the Way

It is important to give yourself small rewards as you achieve each milestone goal. Even when you achieve something as small as doing well in a class test or finishing an assignment on time, reward yourself. Take a break by going to the beach or by watching TV.

Similarly, punish yourself whenever you procrastinate. If you procrastinate and do not finish a tutorial by the deadline, make yourself stay up the next night to finish it. In fact, forgo your favourite television programme if you have to.

Chapter 14

Formulas For Scoring 'A's

I have always believed that when a student produces excellent results, there is always a formula or a strategy behind it. In other words, success leaves behind clues. If we can learn from these clues, we can produce the same results too.

Have you ever wondered how some of your friends seem to hardly spend much time studying and yet score 'A's effortlessly? While you on the other hand spend many late nights before the examination mugging up tons of pages and get a 'C' in return? In this section, I want to share with you  some of these secret formulas that all successful students use to minimise their study time but maximise their results.

FORMULA 1: BE CONSISTENT

The first thing I found common to all 'A' students was that they were consistent in learning their schoolwork throughout the entire school year. This means that at any point in time, they were prepared to answer any question, on any topic that has been taught.

The way these students maintained their consistency was to ensure that they fully understood a topic that was taught, before the teacher moved on to the next topic. If they were not sure about anything, they would ask and find it out straight away. As a result, when the exams drew near, they would have learnt almost everything! They would only need to spend minimal time doing some extra practice and preparation before the big day. That is why they hardly need to spend much time studying for exams. They have in fact spread out their learning time throughout the 12 months!

> **SMALL ACTIONS OVER TIME BRING HUGE RESULTS!**

On the other hand, most students are not consistent at all! During the school year, they hardly learn or understand anything that is going on. When the exams approach, they start panicking and study very hard, burning the midnight oil, hoping to learn the entire year's schoolwork in two months! As a result, they often get lousy results although appearing to study very hard for the exam.

Tips on Being Consistent

Here are some useful tips you can take to ensure that you keep up during the school year. I have found that they are used instinctively by all successful students.

1. Read Ahead of Your Teacher

Do you find it difficult to follow and understand whatever your teacher is teaching in class? Do not worry. You are not alone! I have discovered that after 20 minutes of listening to a lesson, most students tend to drift off or switch off. By the time they walk out of the class, they would have understood only 30% of the lesson and remembered only 10%! By the next day, they would have remembered 2% or less. What a terrible waste of time in school.

I Am Gifted, So Are You!

'A' students on the other hand, walk out of the classroom understanding 100% and remembering 100%! How do they do this? The answer is that before the lesson, they find out which chapter the teacher is going to teach. They then read the chapter ahead of the teacher and make Mind Maps®. As they have already read through the chapter and done the Mind Maps®, the teacher's lesson will be very easy to follow.

2. Be Attentive & Ask Questions

You may ask, 'if I have already read the chapter, then what is the purpose of going to class and have the teacher teach what I already know?' Well, I believe that the teacher's job is not to teach you facts, but to clarify what you do not understand.

So, make use of the teacher's lesson to clarify facts you do not understand and also create memory systems to remember the facts! If you do this, you will indeed walk out of every class with 100% understanding and 100% recall.

3. Do Quick 24-Hour Revisions

On the way home in the school bus, do a quick revision of the day's learning. As a result, you will retain your memory of it for much longer! By the time the exam comes, you will be able to relax as you would have learnt everything during the school year!

4. Always Complete Your Homework Before Class

By doing your homework before it is discussed in class, you will make the best use of your time. You will find out where your weakness in your subject lies, and be able to address the problems early. In addition, your homework will help you find out if you have understood the concepts taught.

5. Always Clarify Mistakes in Your Homework

If you make a mistake in your homework, do not just leave it at that. Find out where you went wrong straight away. If you do not, you are very likely to repeat it in your examinations.

FORMULA 2:
LEARN EARLY FROM YOUR MISTAKES

Contrary to what most students think, good students do not make fewer mistakes than poor students. In fact, they make more mistakes than anybody else! The only difference is that they make their mistakes during their self-practice sessions and learn from their mistakes before the examinations.

Mistakes are the Best Teachers

When you make mistakes in your homework, assignments and class tests, it does not mean that you are condemned to a life of failure and will never do well. Making mistakes simply means discovering that your understanding of ideas and how to apply them is not perfect yet. More importantly, address the mistakes and learn from them.

Let Mistakes Help, Not Destroy

Change your beliefs about making mistakes. Successful students treat mistakes as signals that the strategies they used are not appropriate. As a result, they consistently keep changing their learning strategies until they reach a point of total preparation for the exams.

Students Do Not Fail, They Just Give Up Trying

As long as you learn from your mistakes and failures and continually align your strategies, you will ultimately succeed. However, if you give up trying because of your mistakes, then you would indeed have failed.

LESSONS FROM LIFE: A MAN WHO KNEW NO FAILURES

Almost every great man or fabulously wealthy business person has reached where he or she is after setbacks that would have knocked out most other ordinary people. But the person whose life story inspired me the most was a man who…

> Was born in a log cabin to illiterate parents
> Had no formal education
> Had no positive role models
> Lost his mother at age 9
> Failed in business at age 22
> Was defeated in an attempt to become a legislator at age 32
> Went bankrupt again in business at age 25
> Overcame the death of his companion at age 26
> Was overcome with depression at age 32
> Ran for congress and was defeated at age 37
> Failed in an effort to become vice president at age 47
> Lost a senatorial race at age 49
> Was elected the 16th President of the United States at age 51

This man was Abraham Lincoln, one of the most respected US presidents that ever lived. Despite repeated failures, he believed that he was worthy of greatness. To him, failure simply served as an indication that he must keep on changing his strategies and work harder until he finally reached his greatest goal of all. So every time you make a mistake and think it is the end of the world, think of Abraham Lincoln.

FORMULA 3:
MAKE FULL USE OF TESTS AND ASSIGNMENTS

Many students do not realise the importance of tests and assignments and consider them burdensome. Tests are in fact vital indicators of where you are now and in realising your goals.

If you have failed every test very badly, then it is unlikely that you will get an 'A' in the finals. If you have consistently understood what you are studying and perform well at every milestone, then you can be quite sure you will do well. Before we can make full use of these tests to improve ourselves, we must do two things, i.e. give the test our best shot and do a post-mortem on each test.

1. Do Your Best in Each Test

It is only when we study for a test that we can analyse the results to reveal real weaknesses or confirm our strengths. Many students do not bother studying for tests, so when they get poor results, they cannot tell if their dismal performance was due to a wrong learning strategy or simply because they did not put in any effort. As a result, you will not know which areas of your learning to improve.

2. Do a Post-mortem After Each Test

Sitting for tests and examinations is only useful if you do a post-mortem on the results that you get back. A post-mortem is analysing why you made the mistakes you did. Once you know this, you can then correct your areas of weakness and make sure that if the same question appears, you will not make the same mistake. By the time you sit for the final exams, you will be sure that there will be no more mistakes.

STEP 1: Identify the Types of Mistakes Made

The first thing you must do when you get your marked test or exam papers back is to identify the types of mistakes you have made. There are altogether four categories of mistakes or four reasons why you may get a question wrong.

Category 1: Did not Study (S)

The first category of mistakes occurs because you did not study or cover that particular chapter or section. As a result, you have no idea how to answer the question. This is caused by the student not having the time to study or thinking that the particular chapter or section will not be tested.

Category 2: Cannot Remember (R)

The second category of mistakes occurs because you cannot remember the facts, although you may have taken the time to study and understand the relevant chapters.

Category 3: Unable to Apply (A)

The third type of mistake made is when you may have studied the relevant chapter and can remember the facts, but you do not know how to apply what you have learnt to the question. This is especially so for questions that require you to think rather than list what you remember.

For example, you may have studied and remembered the formulas for calculating speed, velocity and acceleration. However, you are unable to answer the physics problem as it requires you to manipulate the formulas in a way that you do not understand.

You may also make these mistakes when you simply list the facts when you are actually asked to discuss, compare and contrast or to illustrate.

Category 4: Careless (C)

This is the most common type of mistakes made by students who may have studied hard, made an effort to remember and are able to apply what they have learnt. However, they still get their answers wrong simply because they made a careless oversight. These are also known as stupid mistakes. These are mistakes you make in the exam. However, when you go home and try answering the questions again, you can get the correct answers. This often happens with mathematics and physics.

So the first thing you must do is to go through all the mistakes you have made in your test and identify which category of mistakes they are in. If it is a careless mistake, draw a 'C' next to it. If it was because you did not study, draw an 'S'. Similarly, draw an 'A' for questions you did not understand how to apply and an 'R' for questions where you could not remember what you have studied.

Why Must We Categorise Our Mistakes?

You must identify the kinds of mistakes you make in order to know how good you really are. Unless you really analyse the mistakes you make in your tests, you will not know your true standard.

Let me give you an example. Let's say Peter and Susan both score 50% on the chemistry test. Now, at first it seems that they are both equally good at the subject. However, what if you found out that all Peter's mistakes were careless mistakes (C) and that Susan's mistakes were caused by her truly not understanding how to apply what she had learnt, i.e. unable to apply (A). Then you will know that actually Peter is a lot better at chemistry. He just needs to find a way to stop his carelessness, whereas Susan has a lot more learning to do.

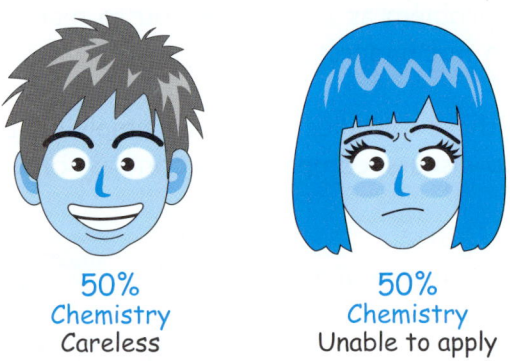

50%
Chemistry
Careless

50%
Chemistry
Unable to apply

Once you categorise your mistakes, the next step is to…

 ## Step 2: Find A Solution to Your Mistakes

You must make sure that if you keep making careless mistakes (C), you find a way to solve the problem. If you have trouble applying what you have learnt (A mistakes), you must find a way to improve in this area too. Following are solutions and steps to take to solve the four different types of mistakes.

Category 1: Did not Study (S)

This first category of mistakes is the easiest to solve. If you keep failing exams because you did not study the relevant chapters, then the solution is to make sure you plan enough time to cover everything that is relevant for the exam. The examination syllabus which can be obtained from your school will tell you exactly what is examinable.

Category 2: Cannot Remember (R)

If your main reason for not doing well is because you forget easily, then it is because you are using the wrong method to remember facts, i.e. rote memory. Instead, you must apply the Super-memory principles and memory systems you have learnt in Chapters 8, 9 and 10!

Another reason why you may forget what you have learnt is because you have not sufficiently revised what you have learnt. In Chapters 10 and 17, you will learn that you should revise a particular topic at least three times before the exams.

Category 3: Unable to Apply (A)

If you find that you are unable to apply what you have read and remembered, then it is because you have not spent the time to practise all the possible types of questions that can be asked. You have not exposed yourself to all the possible types of questions. You may be practising a few sample questions before the exam, but it is not enough! You must practise all types of questions, both easy and difficult ones.

In Chapter 11, you learnt that you must go through your textbooks, assessment papers, homework and past year examination papers to compile all the different possible questions and subsequently learn the required steps to solve them.

Category 4: Careless (C)

Before you can solve the problem of making careless mistakes, you must understand why you make them in the first place. Careless mistakes are the results of not paying enough attention in reading the question or giving your answers. This is because of the limited time you have in the exam. There are three ways to solve this problem.

1. Budget Time for Checking Back

Always budget for half an hour of time to double check your answers. If the exam paper is three hours, aim to answer all the questions in $2\frac{1}{2}$ hours and use the remaining half hour to re-check the answers in detail. Notice the most common careless mistakes made in your homework and look out for these.

2. Read the Questions and Answers

In order to focus your attention more, try mouthing the words when you read the questions and as you write down your answers.

3. Practise Answering Questions More

Before the exam, practise doing possible questions over and over again until you become very familiar with the steps in solving them. During the exam, you will be able to answer these questions accurately.

FORMULA 4:
THE ULTIMATE FORMULA FOR SCORING 'A'S

All the first three formulas along with what we have talked about so far can be summarised into an ultimate formula for academic success that you must apply in order to score 'A's.

The formula can be summarised into the flow chart that you see on page 212. The first step is to set a clear, specific goal on the results that you aim to achieve. We discussed this in Chapter 12. Setting goals is of no use unless you develop a strategy and a plan of action for achieving the goals. This book is packed with loads of super learning strategies that you can use.

The third step is to take action consistently, to consistently work your plan. In Chapters 13 and 16, I outline ways for you to consistently empower and motivate yourself to take action.

When you take action, two things can happen. The first possibility is that you achieve good results and move towards your goals. You start scoring 'A's for your assessments and tests. This is the 'success' arrow in blue.

Often times, we may not get good results right away. We may still get results below our expectations. Despite putting in lots of effort in our maths, we may still get a 'D'. We do not get any closer to our goals. A lot of people refer to this as failure.

Well, it is not what happens to you but rather how you respond to this that will determine whether you will eventually succeed. There are three ways you can respond to such 'failure'.

LOSER'S RESPONSE 'I'M LOUSY! ITS TOO DIFFICULT'

A first group of students will respond by saying that they have failed. They tell themselves that they have failed because they are not good enough or that it is just too difficult. They start making lots of excuses and start blaming the teachers or the tests. They eventually give up and stop trying, saying that it is of no use. This first way to respond is the losers' way.

AVERAGE STUDENT'S RESPONSE
'I DID NOT TRY HARD ENOUGH!'

A second group will respond by saying that they failed because they did not study hard enough. As a result, they will continue taking more and more action. They will spend more time and effort studying for the next round of tests. Although they will definitely show some improvement, they will never get the great results they have set as their goals. After a while, they will start to get frustrated and give up, too. You see, although they are working harder, they are studying the same old way! Same old ineffective methods will get you the same old lousy results.

WINNER'S RESPONSE: CHANGE MY STRATEGY & TAKE ACTION UNTIL I SUCCEED!

The third group responds in a way that will lead them to success. When they do not achieve their goal, they do not see it as failure. They see it as just an outcome. They understand that they got the undesirable outcome because they used an ineffective strategy or plan of action. As a result, they have the flexibility to change their strategy and take action again. If they still do not achieve their goal, they will re-look their strategy again and make even more changes and take even more action. They will keep changing their strategy and take action until they achieve their goals. In other words, they will do whatever it takes to succeed.

This is the path I want you to take. If all along you have been getting lousy results, see it as an outcome. Then have the open mind to use the new strategies you have learnt in this book and continually take action. If you do this, you will eventually reach your goals.

Chapter 15

The Time Of Your Life

HE WHO MASTERS HIS TIME, MASTERS HIS LIFE

I have always admired those students who not only excelled academically, but found the time to be very involved in extra curricular activities, often holding important positions in school clubs, teams and societies. They would score straight 'A's, play basketball for the school, be vice-president of the Science Club and to top it off, they would be on the Student Council Committee. 'Where do they find all the time to do so much?', I always wondered.

On the other hand, many below average students complain that the reason they do not do well in their exams is because they have no time. Yet, these students are often not as active in extra curricular activities as their straight 'A' counterparts.

How can this be? After all, everybody has 24 hours a day. Time is a resource that everybody has equal share of. Whether you are an 'A' student, a lousy student, the President of the United States or a janitor, you will have the same amount of time given to you. Time is the only thing that cannot be bought. Yet, how is it someone like the President of the US can find the time to run an entire country while a janitor complains that he never found the time to study? The difference is that people who succeed in life have learnt to master their time. We cannot control how much time we have, but we can control how we use it. If you can master your time, you will master your life.

HOW WELL DO YOU USE YOUR TIME?

Successful people appear to have a lot of time to achieve many of their goals because they know how to use their time. On the other hand, average people unknowingly waste a lot of their precious time every day.

Time is like money. Every minute that passes by is a minute you have spent. If you use it wisely, you would get something in return. If you spent that minute reading, you would have exchanged that one minute for knowledge! If you spent that minute idling then you would have received nothing in exchange for it. It would be the same as throwing good money away. So be careful how you use your time.

So, do you know how well you use your time? Do you use your time to achieve your goals or do you waste it? Do the exercise below to find out.

In the time grid on the next page, fill in the activity you would normally be performing and the corresponding time slots given. For example, you may write down 'travelling home' as your activity from 5–6pm. In column 'time wasted', write down the amount of time you waste under each of the activities you listed.

When is Time Wasted?

An activity is considered a waste of time when it is not goal directed. In other words, it does not help you to achieve your goals such as study goals, financial goals, health goals, sports goals, etc. For example, if your goal is to score seven 'A's in your upcoming exams and you spend four hours a day playing soccer with your friends, it is considered a waste of time. However, if your goal was to be a national soccer player, then training four hours a day may not be a waste of time.

If you had written 'class lesson' from 9–10am, does it mean that no time was wasted? It depends. If you tend to spend your time in class talking, not paying attention and you do not learn anything, then you would have wasted that hour. Activities like sleeping or visiting the bathroom may be considered a waste of time if excessive time is spent. For example, if you sleep for 12 hours a day, then I would say you would have wasted five hours, since seven hours of sleep is sufficient.

Have you got a clear idea now? Great! Fill in the time sheet below before you turn to the next page.

TIME GRID

Time	Activity	Time Wasted
6 am – 7 am		
7 am – 8 am		
8 am – 9 am		
9 am – 10 am		
10 am – 11 am		
11 am – 12 pm		
12 pm – 1 pm		
1 pm – 2 pm		
2 pm – 3 pm		
3 pm – 4 pm		
4 pm – 5 pm		
5 pm – 6 pm		
6 pm – 7 pm		
7 pm – 8 pm		
8 pm – 9 pm		
9 pm – 10 pm		
10 pm – 11 pm		
11 pm – 12 am		
12 am – 1 am		
1 am – 2 pm		
2 am – 3 am		

A SHOCKING CALCULATION

Now, add up the total time (in hours) you would normally waste in a day. Take this figure, assuming this figure is six hours, and multiply it by 365 days. This will give you the total number of hours you waste in a year.

Next, multiply this figure by 80 years (assuming that your life expectancy is 80) and you will arrive at the total number of hours you could waste in your whole lifetime.

Time wasted in a day = 6 hours

Time wasted in a year = Time wasted a day × 365 days
= 6 hours × 365 days
= 2190 hours

Time wasted in your lifetime = Time wasted in a year × 80 years
= 2190 hours × 80 years
= 175200 hours

Next, convert this figure (i.e. 175200 hours) into years by dividing it by 24 and then dividing it again by 365.

Time wasted in your lifetime = 175200 ÷ 24 = 7300 days
= 7300 ÷ 365 = **20 years**

Assuming that you waste six hours a day on average (which is the norm), you will have wasted 20 years of your life in your whole lifetime. Think of how much you could achieve with 20 years if that time was used properly.

THE POWER OF PRIORITY

Successful people master their time by learning the power of priority. Since all of us have 24 hours in a day, you must give priority to goal directed activities. These are activities that will help you achieve your goals and make you more successful in every area of your life.

Average people do not know this so they give priority to doing things that get them nowhere. They spend their 24 hours doing all the wrong activities. They major in minor things like hanging out, going to the mall or idling.

To understand the different ways we use our time every day, I want you to look at the four quadrants below.

How We Use Our Time

	Urgent	Non-Urgent
Goal Directed	**P1** Do homework Study for surprise test Last minute doing of project	**P2** Reading in advance Doing Mind Maps® Early exam preparation Daily exercise Training for marathon
Non-Goal Directed	**P3** Interruptions Answer phone calls, SMS Catch TV programme Answering emails	**P4** Hours of surfing net, TV Lazing around Hanging out Chatting on the phone

On the vertical axis are goal-directed activities and non goal-directed activities. Goal directed activities are things we do that move us towards our goals and make us successful. Non-goal directed activities do not help us achieve our goals. However, doing some of this is necessary as we will burn out if we only do things that are goal directed. There are times when we just need to 'veg out' and watch TV, to control our stress and have fun. However, too much time spent on non-goal directed activities is considered a waste of time.

On the horizontal axis, I have divided the things we do into urgent things that require our immediate attention and non-urgent things that we can put off till later. From the two axes, you can see that there are four ways in which we can spend our time. (P1) Goal-Directed & Urgent Activities, (P2) Goal Directed & Non-Urgent Activities, (P3) Non Goal Directed & Urgent Activities and, finally, (P4) Non Goal-Directed & Non-Urgent. Let's explore each of them.

(P1) GOAL-DIRECTED & URGENT

All of us spend time doing goal-directed and urgent activities. These are activities that are important in achieving our goals and need immediate attention. They include doing our homework for the next day, rushing to finish a class project, cramming for a test or helping our brother with his homework. This category is labelled Priority 1 (P1) because, since it is important and urgent, it is the first thing we should spend our time doing everyday.

Some of these activities are necessarily urgent, such as looking after a sick parent or having to prepare for a surprise test the next day. However, many Goal-Directed & Urgent Activities are caused by our own procrastination. When we keep putting off assignments, projects and exam preparations to the last minute, we end up having to urgently do them. If they were done early, they would not have to be urgent.

P1 Activities lead to stress & low performance

The trouble with Goal-Directed & Urgent Activities is that they give us a lot of stress and often lead to low performance and average results. Cramming for a test would give you worse results than if you had started to prepare early!

If you find that you spend a lot of your time doing these activities, you are likely to be a procrastinator or a 'last minute' kind of person. We should aim to reduce our time spent in this quadrant by planning and preparing early. We should spend more time doing these Goal-Directed Activities when they are non-urgent (i.e. the P2 quadrant).

I Am Gifted, So Are You!

(P2) GOAL-DIRECTED & NON-URGENT

Although this is the way successful people spend most of their time, many of us hardly do it. Goal directed & Non-Urgent Activities are activities that are important in achieving our goals, but they do not require our immediate attention. This includes preparing early for the final exams, starting our project assignment straight away, Mind Mapping® chapters ahead of our teacher, planning our time, exercising in the morning, etc.

This category is labelled Priority 2 (P2). Once you have cleared all your P1 activities, you must then spend time doing P2 activities. Although they are not urgent, we must still do them now! This is because they lead to high performance and success. Unfortunately, most students skip these activities as they do not appear urgent and spend their time doing P3 activities instead. P3 activities as you will see are urgent but a waste of our time!

P2 Activities lead to high performance.

Students who spend most of their time doing these P2 activities are called 'investors' or people who plan ahead. Like people who invest money, they invest their time to do things which are very important for them in the long term. As a result, they will reap the benefits of high achievements. You must plan to spend a lot more time on these.

(P3) NON GOAL-DIRECTED & URGENT

Non Goal-Directed & Urgent Activities are activities that seem to be very important, they need to be done now. However, they are actually not important at all as they do not help you to achieve your goals and be successful. They include answering phone calls from friends, going off to see the latest blockbuster movies, catching your favourite TV show, sending urgent emails and SMSes, joining your friends for bowling, etc. These P3 activities should only be done when you have finished all your P1 and P2 activities.

Many students find themselves doing a lot of P3 activities and so they feel that they do a lot but never get good results. P3 activities lead to high stress and no achievements. These people who take part in a lot of P3 activities are what I call people who are 'easily distracted' by the things around them.

P3 Activities lead to high stress & no achievement

You must aim to spend less time on these activities by learning to avoid peer pressure and saying 'no' to activities that do not help you to achieve your goals. Although some friends may feel that you are anti-social, they will respect you in the long term.

(P4) NON GOAL-DIRECTED & NON-URGENT

This final activity is the activity of the bum. Bums spend a lot of their time doing activities that are not goal-directed and not urgent. These include excessive sleeping, excessive watching of TV, excessive surfing of the Internet, lazing about and hanging out for no reason. These are the people who kill time.

Although it is fun to do some P4 activities sometimes, they should be our last priority (P4). They should only be done after we have completed P1, P2 and P3 activities.

If you find that you spend a lot of this time on P4 activities, you have to start changing your lifestyle or you will be headed for disaster.

P4 Activities lead to no stress & no achievements

HOW TO PRIORITISE OUR TIME

Now that we know of the three different ways in which people spend their time, how much time should we give to each activity?

Most average students who do not plan their time will tend to focus on doing the urgent and immediate activities first. They will do the P1 and P3 activities. Whatever time they have left, which is normally very little, they will use for the less urgent activities such as P2 and P4.

The Average Student does the following in this order of priority.

Priority	Time spent	Activity
P1:	50%	Doing urgent homework, last minute
P3:	40%	Checking emails, answering phone calls, SMSing, etc.
P4:	15%	Lazing about, watching TV, surfing the Internet, etc.
P2:	5%	Early preparation for exams, doing Mind Maps®, etc.

The result is high stress, low performance and poor achievements.

You should instead prioritise your time the following way. First, plan to do all your P1 activities. Through proper planning, you can keep this to a minimum. Next, plan to spend the bulk of your time to do P2 activities. Although they are not urgent, you must force yourself to do them every day.

Whatever time you have left can be spent on non goal-directed activities like P3 and P4. The table is shown below.

The successful student does the following in this order of priority.

Priority	Time spent	Activity
P1:	20%	Doing urgent homework, last minute
P2:	60%	Early preparation for exams, doing Mind Maps etc.
P3:	15%	Checking emails, answering phone calls, SMSing etc.
P4:	5%	Lazing about, watching TV, surfing the Internet etc.

HOW TO PLAN OUR TIME

Now that you know what activities to do in terms of priority (P1, P2, P3 and P4), we must learn how to put it into a plan and schedule it into our daily activities.

Human nature is such that if we do not plan to do something important like P2 activities, we will always procrastinate and never do them. This is because we will end up spending our time on things that get our attention and distract us from what we are supposed to do. How many times have you said, 'When I have time, I will...', but end up never doing it?

> WHEN WE SET A GOAL, WE HAVE A DREAM
> WHEN WE START TO PLAN, OUR DREAM BECOMES POSSIBLE
> WHEN WE SCHEDULE IT AND DO IT,
> OUR DREAM BECOMES REAL

Are you ready to start mastering your time? Great! The first thing you need to get is a diary or a personal organiser with a

a. monthly planner, and a
b. weekly planner.

The monthly planner is used for you to come up with a one-year plan. The weekly planner is used for planning your week and days ahead.

A One-year Plan

At the beginning of the year, you should always spend a day designing your one-year plan. For this, you will need a monthly planner. A monthly planner shows all the days of a month on one or two pages.

Step 1: Mark Major Events

The first thing is to mark all the major activities for the year in your monthly planner. These include examination dates, test dates, project completion dates, birthdays etc.

Step 2: Define Your Syllabus

The next thing you need to do is to find out how many chapters you will need to learn for every subject within the year. For example, there may be 24 chapters of mathematics, 30 chapters of geography and so on. Add them up to find out the total number of chapters you will need to learn for the year. For example, if you have an average of 20 chapters per subject and seven subjects, then you will have a total of 140 chapters to learn.

Subject	No. of Chapters
Maths	24
Geog	30
History	10
Chem	15
Physics	16

Chapter 15 • The Time Of Your Life

Step 3: Plan When to Cover All the Chapters During the Year

Now, roughly plan when to cover each chapter throughout the year. You should ideally plan to finish studying all the chapters two months before the final exams. So for example, if you have 24 chapters of history and 10 months to your final exams, then you must plan to study three chapters of history a month. Maybe you could plan to do a chapter on history every first, second and third Tuesday of the month. Each study session should include Power Reading, Mind Mapping® and the other learning techniques we have talked about.

Realise that for your one-year plan, you are actually planning only P2 activities. These are your goal directed and non-urgent activities. Once you have completed your one-year plan, then you should follow up with more specific weekly plans below.

Monthly Planner

July 2013

Sun	Mon	Tue	Wed	Thu	Fri	Sat
	1 * Geography 1	2 * Geography test today! * Literature 4	3 * Physics 1	4 * Biology 2 * National holiday	5 * History 1	6 * Maths 6 * History test
7 * Biology 4	8 Tennis championship finals	9	10 * Chem 1	11	12	13
14	15 * Geography 2	16	17 * Maths quiz today	18 * Fitness test	19 * History 2	20 * Maths 7
21 * Susan's birthday	22	23 * Geography project due!	24 * Physics 2	25	26	27
28 * Biology 5	29	30 Physics 3	31			

Note: Physics 1 refers to Reading, Mind Mapping® & application strategies for Physics chapter 1

A WEEKLY PLAN

Every Sunday of the week, you should spend some time planning the next week (seven days) ahead using your weekly planner. Your weekly planner shows you a week on one or two pages. This is much more specific as compared to your one-year plan.

Your weekly plan should consist of all the activities to be done each day. In your weekly plan, you must list all the activities to be done for each of the seven days. Your monthly planner only gives you the P2 activities (reading ahead, Mind Mapping®, etc.), so you must add in the P1 activities as well (doing homework, projects, etc.). Finally, add in the P3 and P4 activities. Remember that most of your time should be spent on P1 (20%) and P2 (60%) activities. Whatever time is left can then be spent on unimportant P3 and P4 activities.

A Weekly Plan

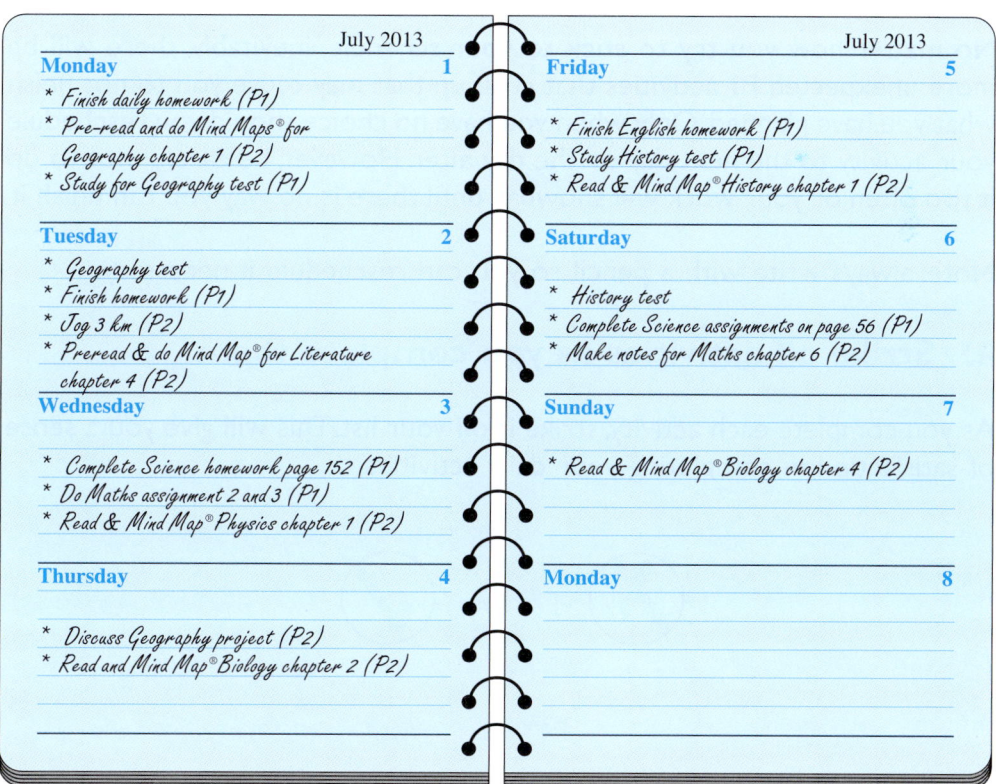

Chapter 15 • The Time Of Your Life

CHECK THE NEXT DAY'S ACTIVITIES EVERY NIGHT

1. Specific times allocated to each activity

Every night, go through your daily activities for the next day and allocate specific times for each activity. Setting a specific time frame prevents you from procrastinating and saying, 'I will do it later.'

2. Stick to your schedule

No matter what, you must discipline yourself to finish up the day's planned activities before you go to bed even if it means sleeping a bit less or giving up your favourite TV programmes. Self-denial will teach you the price you have to pay for wasting time and delaying your work.

3. Plan for rescheduling

No matter how you try to stick to your schedule, inevitably, there will be more unexpected P1 activities that crop up that may cause you to not finish what you have planned. Only when you have no choice should you reschedule your activity to the next day or the day after. However, be careful not to do it too often or your work will snowball until there is no way you can finish it.

Note: always write with a pencil so you can reschedule if necessary.

4. Strike off activities as you complete them

As you complete each activity, strike it off your list. This will give you a sense of satisfaction in completing your daily activities.

Chapter 16

Getting Empowered… In An Instant

YOUR EMOTIONAL STATES CONTROL YOUR LIFE

At this stage, you have learnt many strategies and techniques on how to learn more effectively and score 'A's. You have also learnt how to design inspiring goals and plan your time. Now, does this mean that you will definitely go ahead and take action?

In fact, you may be saying to yourself right now, 'Yes, I know that I must start planning my time, Power Read and create Mind Maps®, but you know what? I just do not feel like doing it! I feel bored, tired, lazy and depressed.'

As human beings, do we do things more out of logic or emotions? The answer is emotions. Emotions always override our logic. There are a lot of things which we know we should do but we still do not do it, because of how we feel. Many times, we know we should stop watching TV and start doing our work, but we just do not feel like doing it. Although many people know that smoking is bad and that it will kill them, they still continue smoking. Why? Because they feel good about smoking.

When you feel bored, lazy or depressed, chances are you will not feel like doing anything. You will probably throw your books aside and flop down on your bed and laze about. However, when you feel motivated, energised or excited you will get things done straight away.

So you see that how we feel determines what we do. If we can learn to control how we feel (i.e. our emotional state), then we can control our actions and therefore our results!

> **HOW WE FEEL DETERMINES WHAT WE DO!**

WE CAN TAKE CHARGE OF OUR EMOTIONAL STATES

Unfortunately, many students feel powerless because they think that they cannot control the way they feel. To them, other people control their emotional states and so they helplessly move from one state to another. They accept the states they get into and let them rule their behaviour and their lives.

For example, if their teacher scolds them or if their girlfriend dumps them, they will get into a state of depression and end up not being able to study. If they receive praise or do well on a test, they will feel motivated and happy. On some days, when they wake up, they just feel bored and lazy. On other days, they wake up feeling energised and motivated.

The truth is that we are solely in control of our emotional states at any one point in time. What you must understand is that emotional states are not like viruses that we catch from someone. We alone create our own emotional states. If you feel bored and lazy, it is because you have created it. If you feel motivated and energised, it is because you have created it. So if we create our states, then we can change them in an instant.

So, even if your parents reprimand you, your girlfriend leaves you or you fail your exams miserably, you can always put yourself into a totally energised, excited state to take positive action. Before we can learn how to control and change our states, let's learn how we create them in the first place.

HOW ARE EMOTIONAL STATES CREATED?

What determines how we feel at any given moment in time? Our emotional state is determined by our thoughts and how we use our body. Again, our emotional state (how we feel) will affect the kind of actions we take and therefore our results. When we are in empowering states like motivation, excitement and happiness, we will take positive action and yield positive results. When we are in negative states like depression, boredom and laziness, we will take negative actions and produce lousy results. So in order to change our actions and our results, we must learn to control our thoughts and how we use our body.

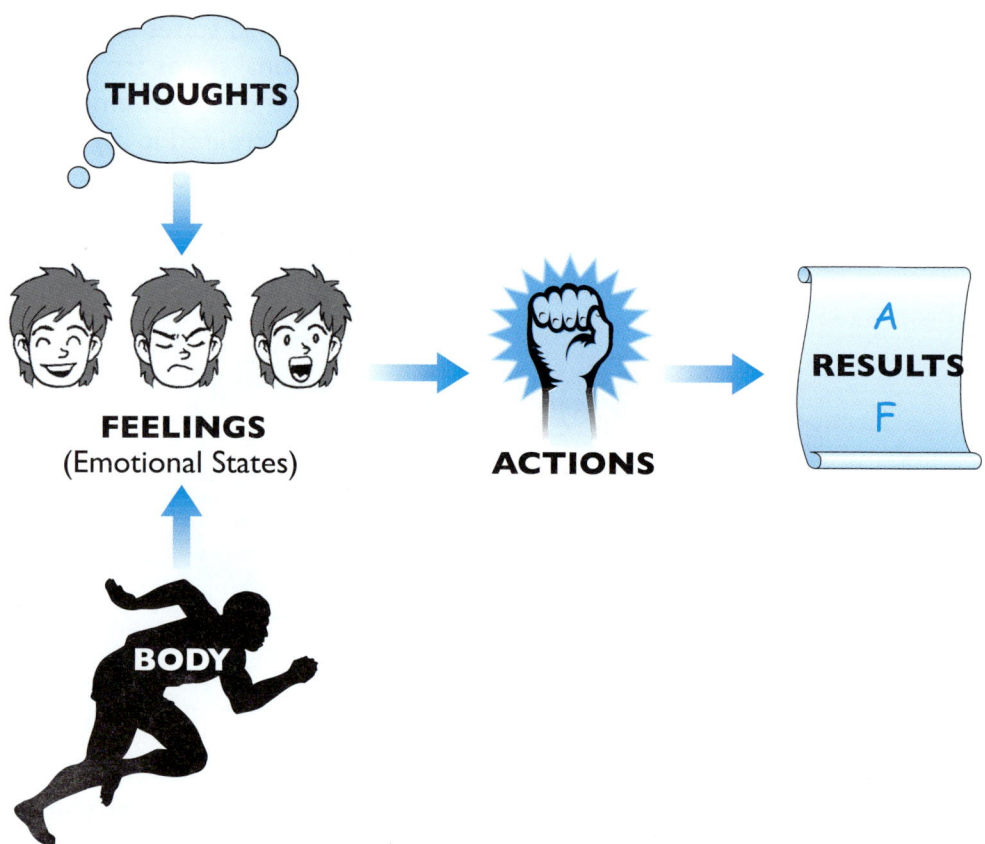

THE WAY YOU USE YOUR BODY AFFECTS YOUR STATE

The first thing that affects how you feel is the way you use your body. The emotional state you are in right now is affected by:

- Your posture, whether you are slouching or throwing your shoulders back.
- Your facial expression, whether you are smiling or frowning.
- Your breathing pattern, whether deep or shallow, slow or fast.
- The muscular tension in your body and your face.
- The tone, pitch and volume of your voice.

In fact, the expression that you are putting on your face right now, along with the way you are breathing and sitting, is affecting the way you are feeling now. What I would like you to do is to play along with me and join in the next few exercises I will ask you to do. These exercises are aimed at getting you to note how your facial expression, body posture, tone of voice and breathing can affect how you feel.

Exercise 1

Sit the way you would be sitting, breathe the way you would be breathing and put an expression on your face as if you were totally bored and tired. Now, in this position, I want you to observe your shoulder posture. Is your breathing deep or shallow? What is the rest of your posture like? Are the muscles in your face tense or slack?

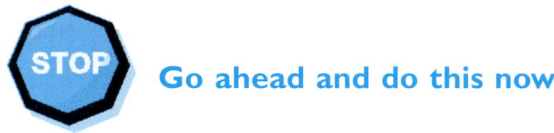

Go ahead and do this now

Welcome back. Most of you would agree with me that your shoulders are drooping and that you are slouching and your breathing is shallow and slow. Also, your facial muscles would probably be slack and your eyes looking down. Isn't that interesting? Before we can actually feel bored and tired, we must first position our bodies in a certain way. If we did not change our body posture in that way, it would be impossible to feel bored and tired.

Exercise 2

Let's try another experiment. I want you to put this book down and stand the way you normally stand, breathe the way you normally breathe and change your facial expression to one that's totally energised and excited.

Now, while your body is in this totally powerful and energised state, I want you to try to feel depressed. Do not drop your shoulders and do not wipe off that smile! Do not cheat! Just breathe deeply, keep that big smile on your face, stand straight with shoulders back and eyes up. In this position, can you feel bored and tired?

STOP Go ahead and do this now

Welcome back. Notice that if you did not change your expression or your body posture at all, there was no way you could have felt depressed. In order to feel a certain way, you must work your body in certain ways.

So, whenever you feel lazy and bored and cannot get down to doing your schoolwork, simply stand up straight and snap yourself into an empowering state by breathing deeply, throwing your shoulders back and putting a big wide grin on your face. Shout in an energetic tone, 'I feel energised!' It will instantly change the way you feel and the way you behave. If your friends or family members see you doing this, they may think you have gone crazy. Do not bother about them. Successful people do things that the failures would not.

This is a simple but an extremely powerful concept. Practise snapping yourself into a powerful, energised, motivated state by changing your body posture whenever you feel bored or lazy. The more you practise this, the more automatic it will become. Pretty soon, every time you feel bored or tired, your mind will snap itself back into a state of motivation.

LESSONS FROM LIFE

A piece of research was done in the University of California in the early 1980s, involving a study on a group of people who were habitually depressed. These people had gone through all kinds of therapy but nothing could be done to change their depressed state. However, when the researchers got these people to smile and to breathe more deeply, many of them who had been depressed for years saw improvements in their mental health and states.

YOUR THOUGHTS AFFECT YOUR STATE

You have seen how the way you use your body can affect your state. The second thing that affects how we feel is our thoughts. If we can learn to control our thoughts, we can control how we feel.

Have You Ever Thought How You Think?

Before you can learn how to control your thoughts, you must first understand how you think. So think about this. How do you think?
For example, think of your favourite school teacher.

 **Stop and think about your favourite school teacher now**

Now, as you thought about your favourite school teacher, what went on inside your mind? Did you see an image of your school teacher? Did you talk to yourself in some way such as, 'Let's see. I wonder which teacher is my favourite?' If you are like most people, you would have seen an image in your mind and you would have some internal conversation with yourself.

So you see, we think by:

a. Seeing images in our mind
b. Talking to ourselves

Again, the way you feel at any point in time depends on the images you make in your mind and the way you talk to yourself. If you are in a lousy emotional state like depression, it is simply because you are creating depressing images in your mind, such as seeing images of your parents shouting at you or seeing how you have been betrayed by your friend. It is also because you are talking to yourself in a negative way such as, 'Life sucks', 'I do not know why I am so stupid', 'I feel lousy'.

Whenever you find yourself in a motivated state, it is because you make inspiring images in your mind about how you will succeed and benefit. It is also because you say things to yourself like, 'I can do it!' 'This is easy' and 'I feel great'.

Now, let's learn exactly how we can control the images we make and the way that we talk to ourselves.

CONTROL YOUR THOUGHTS THROUGH YOUR WORDS

The first thing you have to learn to consciously control is the words that you say to yourself. On average, we talk to ourselves over 60,000 times a day. Unfortunately, 80% of what we usually say to ourselves is negative.

There are some positive words that we say to ourselves that will put us into an empowering state where we will be motivated to act and produce good results. At the same time, when we use certain negative words, it will automatically put us into a lousy state where we do not feel like doing anything.

Positive Words that Empower Us
I *can* do it
I *will do* my best to do it
I *love* maths (love is an empowering and powerful word)
I am *good* at languages

Negative Words to Avoid
I *cannot* do it
I *will try* my best (try is a word that lacks power)
I hate maths (the word 'hate' weakens us)
I am bad at languages

LESSONS FROM LIFE: YOUR WORDS CAN TURN ON OR TURN OFF YOUR BRAIN

In fact, the words that we say to ourselves are so powerful that they can literally turn on or turn off our brain! Have you experienced a time when your mother asked you to look for the ketchup in the kitchen and you replied, 'I do not know where it is!' After she urged you to go look for it, you walked into the kitchen repeating to yourself, 'I do not know where the ketchup is. I do not know where the ketchup is.' True enough, you looked around the kitchen and did not see the ketchup. Then you called back to mum saying, 'I cannot see the ketchup'. She then replied, 'Look properly, it's there!' You continued to repeat to yourself, 'I can't find the ketchup'. Then, your mother walked right into the kitchen and grabbed the ketchup from right under your nose and said, 'Here it is! Are you blind?'

Although the ketchup has always been there, your eyes missed it because you kept telling yourself that you could not find the ketchup! The same thing applies to your life! If you keep saying that you cannot pass maths, then you will never be able to pass it. You are giving your brain the command to shut down and stop learning maths. However, when you say to yourself that maths is easy to learn, your mind opens up the possibility of learning maths!

ASK YOURSELF THE RIGHT QUESTIONS

Very often we also talk to ourselves by asking ourselves questions. If you just thought, 'Do I do that?' then that is a question, isn't it?

The kind of questions you ask yourself is also very important to whether you feel motivated or discouraged. For example, when we fail a test after studying hard, we may ask, 'Why do I always fail?' or 'Why am I so careless?' or 'Why do I always screw up?' If we get dumped by our girlfriend or boyfriend, we may ask, 'Why do these things always happen to me?' By asking such questions, we will feel even worse and get stuck in a lousy state!

Instead, you should ask yourself questions that will motivate and empower you! If you fail a test or get a poor mark on a project, ask, 'What can I learn from this?' By asking this new positive question, you keep yourself in a powerful state to improve yourself. You also feel more motivated to study harder next time. Similarly, if something bad happens to you, respond by asking, 'What good can come out of this?' By changing the questions you ask in your mind, you will become a more positive and motivated person!

WHY DO I ALWAYS FAIL? ➡ **WHAT CAN I LEARN FROM THIS?**
WHAT IS WRONG WITH ME? **WHAT IS POSITIVE ABOUT THIS?**

IT IS NOT WHAT HAPPENS TO YOU, IT IS HOW YOU RESPOND

I mentioned earlier that no matter what happens to you, you can control how you feel and the state you are in. One way is to control the words you use to respond to what happens. For example, if someone comes up to you and says, 'You are a stupid good for nothing idiot who will never succeed in life!' How do you think you will feel? Most people will say that they will feel terrible, rejected or discouraged.

In actual fact, the way you feel will depend on how you choose to talk to yourself. If you respond by telling yourself, 'Maybe he is right. I am stupid and a good for nothing idiot.' Then you will be in a lousy state and will not be able to perform. However, you can choose to respond by telling yourself, 'That's ridiculous! I have what it takes to succeed and I will prove it!' In this way, you will feel empowered to perform at your best!

> **CHOOSE TO ALWAYS TALK TO YOURSELF IN A WAY THAT WILL EMPOWER YOU!**

CONTROL YOUR THOUGHTS THROUGH YOUR MENTAL IMAGES

You have learnt how the words you use affect your state of mind and how you feel. The second thing we need to learn to control that affects our state are the images we make in our mind!

We often feel lazy and unmotivated because we make images in our mind about how difficult, tedious and time consuming studying will be. As a result, we will not feel like studying. We always find ourselves depressed at times because we keep playing images inside our mind of how someone cheated us or reprimanded us, or how we failed at something.

You must understand that like a movie director, you can control what pictures and movies to play in your head. You can choose to stop playing pictures of boring, depressing stuff and only focus on seeing motivational, happy pictures in your mind!

Controlling the Intensity of your Feelings

Have you noticed that we feel different intensities of happiness, motivation, laziness or depression? Sometimes we may feel a little bit motivated, whereas at other times, we may feel very motivated and sometimes extremely motivated. We can also feel a little sad at times and extremely depressed at other times.

Wouldn't it be great if we could control how intense our feelings are? We can intensify and increase feelings of happiness and motivation. At the same time, we can reduce lousy feelings. Well you can! You do so by changing the way your mind makes images. What do I mean by this? Let's do an exercise to find out!

Exercise

I want you to close your eyes and think of a time in the past when you felt very good about yourself. It could be a time when you scored an 'A' for a test or you won a competition.

Now, as you think of that moment, do you get the feeling of confidence and happiness? Good. Now I want you to notice if the image in your mind is:

Black and white or in colour   _____

Near or far   _____

Bright or dim   _____

Large or small   _____

A still picture or a movie   _____

Associated or disassociated   _____

On the left, right, top or bottom   _____
of your mental screen

* *An associated image is one in which you are reliving an experience by looking through your own eyes. A disassociated image is one in which you are watching a movie of yourself, reliving an experience from a third person's perspective.*

Now I want you to play with that image in your mind. As you do so, notice if the feeling gets stronger or weaker. If your image is black and white, make it in full colour. If the image is far away, bring it close to your face. Similarly, if the image is dim and small, make it huge and bright! Change the location of the image on your mental screen until the feeling gets more intense. If it is a still picture, make it into a moving movie. Finally, if you are looking at yourself in the image, then step into your own body so that you become fully associated and are looking through your own eyes.

Welcome back. If you played with your image, you would have noticed that it changed the intensity of your feelings. Like most people, your feelings will get stronger and more intense when you:

- Change it from black and white to colour
- Bring it from far to very near
- Enlarge the size of the image
- Turn it from a still picture into a movie
- Make it brighter
- Make it sharper
- Change from a disassociated image into an associated image

Similarly, when you do the opposite, the feelings will get weaker and disintensify!

Know when to Intensify and Disintensify your Feelings

So, how can you use this to help you in your life? Whenever you are in a lousy state, you can reduce the lousy feelings by changing the image in your mind, i.e. making the image small, dim, disassociated and push it far away.

When you are feeling happy and confident, make that feeling stronger by making the image in your mind big and bright. Fully associate into the image, turn it into a movie and bring it close to you.

How to Totally Change a Lousy Feeling

Suppose someone or something depressed you. For example, let's say that a classmate insulted you this morning and you are still feeling depressed and maybe even angry. If you are like most people, you would keep thinking about it the whole day, playing those lousy pictures in your mind. Your whole day might be spoilt and you will not be in the mood to perform at your best.

Instead, you can choose to change the pictures in your mind to something that will immediately change your lousy feeling into one that is neutral or even happy.

Here is what you can do. First disassociate yourself from the picture if you are currently looking at the whole episode through your perspective. Step out of your body, taking ten steps and pushing the picture further away until it is one quarter of its size.

Now, take that image and make it dim and dark. You can also make the image black and white and blurry. Now, be a bit outrageous and imagine that little Mickey Mouse ears are growing from your friend's ears and his nose is swelling up to a big red tomato. Finally, put that image in your hand and toss it towards the sun and see it explode into a million pieces.

How to Get Instant Motivation

Have you ever been in a situation where you needed to start getting some work done but you just felt too lazy and tired? Remember that what you are feeling is simply a state of mind which you can change in an instant! Let's use what you have learnt so far and follow the following steps.

1. Create an Image

Think of a time in the past when you felt totally motivated and energised. It could be a time when you were really excited about something. Make a clear image of it in your mind.

2. Intensify the Feeling

Now, intensify the feeling by stepping into your body and fully associating with the image as if you were really there. Next, turn the image into a movie and make it large, close and in full colour. Increase the volume of the sounds and voices that you hear around you.

3. Change the Way You Use Your Body

At the same time, I want you to radically change your body to match exactly how you felt when you were totally energised and excited. Stand up tall and jump around if you want. Throw your shoulders back, breathe deeply and put the expression on your face as if you were really excited.

4. Change Your Words

Now, change the words you say to yourself. Say to yourself in the most exciting voice you can think of: 'Yes!' 'I'm taking action now!' 'I feel excited!'

 **I want you stop reading and try this now**

THE POWER OF ANCHORING

Another powerful way which I use to transform my state of mind into a powerful state is to use anchors. What are anchors? Anchors are things you see, hear or feel that can immediately put you into a certain state.

You already have many anchors around you that can transform your state of mind. Unfortunately, many of your anchors are negative ones that put you into a lousy state. Examples of anchors are your bed, the sound of your teacher's voice, your school textbooks or the examination hall.

For many students, a look at their bed triggers a state of laziness, their school textbooks trigger a state of laziness, the sound of their teacher's voice may trigger boredom and the examination hall may trigger the feeling of nervousness. All these are lousy anchors that we must get rid of.

At the same time, we need to create some positive anchors. This is so that when we see, hear or feel these anchors, they will trigger in us a super-motivated state.

How Do We Create New Anchors?

Whenever we are in a very intense emotional state and there is a stimulus (something we see, hear or feel) that is repeated over and over again, what happens is that the stimulus gets linked to the emotional state. So the next time we see, hear or feel the same stimulus, it will automatically trigger that same emotional state. The stimulus has now become an anchor!

For example, let's say that you are in a very happy and excited state. Now, while you are feeling this, you clap your hands in a certain way over and over again. After a while, the clapping (stimulus) gets linked to the happy feeling. Next time you feel lousy, simply clap your hands in the same exact way and it will trigger that state of happiness and excitement. This is a very powerful technique which I have used many times!

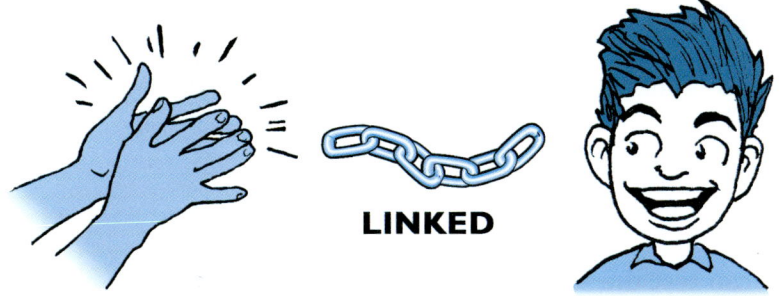

Create Your Own Powerful Anchors:

So what I want you to do now is to create your own powerful anchors! Here are the steps:

1. Put yourself in a powerful state

First, use what you have learnt about changing your mental images and your body posture to put yourself into an intense positive emotional state. You can put yourself into a state of motivation or excitement.

2. Apply the stimulus

Next, as you are in this intense emotional state, apply a unique stimulus that you want to use as your anchor. It could be an anchor you see, hear or feel. For example, the anchor could be clapping your hands or pumping your fists like Tiger Woods (an anchor you can feel). It could be saying something to yourself like, 'Yes!' (an anchor you can hear). Another powerful anchor is using motivational music from a movie for example (an anchor you can hear). I personally like to use the theme from the movie 'Rocky' or 'Star Wars'.

3. Repeat it a Few Times

Now, repeat this anchor at least five times as you remain in the positive state.

4. Test and Apply

Finally, you can test the anchor by getting into a neutral state and then firing off the anchor (i.e. pumping your fists or playing the music). This should trigger the positive state again!

LESSONS FROM LIFE: SUPER ATHLETES USE ANCHORS

The technique of anchoring is nothing new. In fact, it is often used by top athletes to get themselves into a positive state where they can perform their best. Next time you watch a basketball, football, baseball, tennis or golf game, observe how these superstars make certain unique gestures before they play. What they are doing is firing off their anchors. For example, Michael Jordan sticks out his tongue, other basketball players mumble to themselves before they shoot at the free throw line. Some baseball players spit before they pitch the ball.

Chapter 17

The Final Countdown

AS THE DAY OF THE EXAM DRAWS NEAR...

As examination day draws near, you will start to enter the final phase of your preparation. In this chapter, I will describe the entire process of how you can put yourself into an optimal state of preparedness for the examinations using the concepts covered earlier.

By this time, you should have prepared Mind Maps® of all your relevant study materials and compiled a list of the different types of application questions and steps to solve them (see Chapter 11). You should have also completed all assignments, projects and tests and analysed the mistakes made in them. The final preparation should comprise a revision of everything that you have covered, rather than a first time study of the material. It should not be your first effort at grappling with the material.

YOUR OBJECTIVE IS UNCONSCIOUS COMPETENCE

How is it that there are 'A' scorers, students who can complete their examination papers with time to spare and score 'A's while others simply run out of time? The answer lies in the difference in the level of competence that the two groups of students study to. Students who always run out of time merely study to a stage where they understand the subject, but are not adept or skilled at it. They still need time to think about and analyse a test question before answering it. This stage is known as the level of conscious competence.

Successful students, on the other hand, always study to a stage of unconscious competence. They revise their work to a stage where they can instinctively answer the questions without having to analyse the problem consciously. Their familiarity with the materials and methods helps them arrive at solutions quickly and competently.

CREATING AN OPTIMAL LEARNING ENVIRONMENT

To study effectively, it is important for you to first create an optimal learning environment. You should choose to study consistently at one place so your mind gets into the habit of working whenever you are there. The study area you choose should have the following characteristics:

Let There Be Light

The environment most conducive to learning is one that is brightly lit, preferably with yellow light. This is because fluorescent (white) light is glaring and may lead to headaches.

Check The Temperature

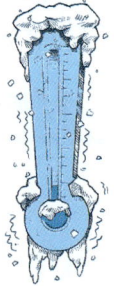

A temperature that is too high will tend to make you feel drowsy. Try, as far as possible, to study in a place that is a little colder than what you would normally like. The reason is that a lower temperature will keep you more alert. The optimal temperature for the brain is 19° Celsius.

Free Yourself Of Distractions

Unless you have great discipline or willpower, always ensure that your study area is free from distractions like TV, telephone, video games, comics or magazines or a bed.

Don't Pig Out!

Do not eat a big meal before a study session. It often makes you drowsy because a lot of energy and blood is directed to your digestive system. This makes it difficult to cope with the extra food. Try to avoid red meat (burgers), sugar or white flour (found in cakes and pastry) before studying, as these food types reduce your brain's ability to store information.

Bach For Background Music?

Play music in the background whenever you study. Music is rhythmic and listening to it has a synergistic effect which enhances brain power. The best kind of music to use in learning is Baroque music because it maintains a rhythm of sixty beats per minute which puts the mind in a relaxed state (alpha state) so that learning can take place.

Individual Or Group Study?

Is it better to study alone or in a group? It depends. Group study allows you to pool resources and knowledge. However, if you choose to work with students who are ill-disciplined, you will be distracted. So, always approach those who are more resourceful and more disciplined than you are. In this way, you can only be influenced for the better.

Individual study, on the other hand, guarantees minimal distraction, but it also means that you will not be able to share and compare notes with other students. The bottom line is that you should study individually, and at certain times, arrange group study sessions.

PLAN A STUDY SCHEDULE EARLY

About two months prior to the examinations, draw up a detailed study schedule of what you intend to study each day, right up to the day your first paper begins. This will ensure that you cover all the necessary subjects on time.

How Early Should We Start Preparation?

Work backwards from the date of your first paper. You must calculate how much time you will need to effectively cover all the subjects involved. Try to allocate five days for emergencies that may crop up. However, always imagine that the five extra days do not exist, or you may be tempted to procrastinate.

How Much Time Should Be Allocated To Each Subject?

Although the amount of time you should allocate to each subject is unique from person to person, you could follow these guidelines:

1. Spread out Study on a Particular Subject

Instead of cramming the study of a particular study, like geography, over a few days, it is better to study just one or two chapters each day over a longer period of time, say ten days. Spreading the study of a subject over a few days ensures that your mind has time to digest the information and organise it before moving on to another 'chunk' of information.

2. Plan for Daily Study Sessions

Remember that in order to achieve the greatest number of high points of recall, you should always plan a study session of up to a maximum of two hours.

After each study session, wait for at least half an hour before starting another session. Within each study session, always take a break between two and five minutes. Your study sessions should be divided into four separate periods of not more than twenty-five minutes each. During each study break, your mind should be as relaxed as possible.

3. Plan for Third and Fourth Revisions

You also need to schedule revision times for each subject. Remember that to keep your memory in an optimal condition, you have to revise whatever you have learnt in ten minutes, 24 hours, a week and a month. The first two revisions (i.e. with ten minutes and 24 hours), are normally done in the study sessions you have already planned for. You only need to make additional study slots for the third and fourth (if necessary) revisions for every subject. I suggest that the fourth revision of a particular subject (like physics) be planned on the day before that particular paper.

STUDYING DURING A STUDY SESSION

As mentioned earlier, a two-hour study session should be sufficient time to cover a subject chapter of average length. For slightly longer chapters, you may need to use two study sessions. For each study session, you should cover the following:

1. Revise the Previous Day's Work

Ideally, you should be able to re-create in your mind the entire Mind Map® based on the chapter you reviewed the day before, without referring to your notes. You must also review the application questions and homework assigned to that particular chapter.

2. Commit the Chapter to Memory

For the day's chapter of study, go through your Mind Maps® thoroughly and then use the memory systems like the Link System and the Number System to commit the key points to memory. You should do so until you are able to cover the Mind Map® and from memory, recite every last point.

3. Practise the Application Questions

Besides ensuring that you have committed all the facts to memory, you must practise doing all the different application questions related to that chapter. You should then check to ensure that you have used the correct steps to solve each type of question and have the correct answer. Even though you may already know the answer, you should still practise doing it. By re-doing the questions, you are installing the knowledge into your level of unconscious competence.

* Recall from Chapter 11 that for each chapter, you should compile in a notebook all the different types of application questions and the steps to solve them. You compile the application questions from various sources such as your homework, assignments, assessment books, textbooks, school tests, past-year examinations and other schools' test papers.

4. Do An Overall Revision Of Today's Material

This should take you no more than ten minutes. Remember that you should always revise when your memory peaks ten minutes after each study period.

A STUDY SCHEDULE

An illustration is given of how you can create a study schedule for yourself, using all the concepts we have discussed so far. In this illustration, I will assume that the following subjects will be included in your final examinations:

Subject	Abbreviation	Number of Chapters	Examination Date
Mathematics	Maths	10	18 November
Geography	Geog	12	28 November
History	History	10	22 November
Physics	Physics	12	24 November
Chemistry	Chem	10	25 November
Literature	Lit	12	27 November

The study schedule is presented on pages 254–255. In particular, note that in planning the schedule:

1. A five-day buffer (13–17 November) is given for emergencies, although revisions are planned within it.

2. We start by working backwards from the day labelled 'End Of Study'. This day is the first day of the buffer period.

3. A final review, normally the fourth revision, is done on the day before each paper. For example, the final history review takes place on 21 November, which is the day before the History exam.

4. As far as possible, a mix of different subjects is planned for each day's study.

5. Before starting each day's work, a revision (within 24 hours) is done on subjects studied the previous day. This is indicated with an asterisk.

6. If one week has passed since you last studied a particular subject, do an overall revision of the entire subject.

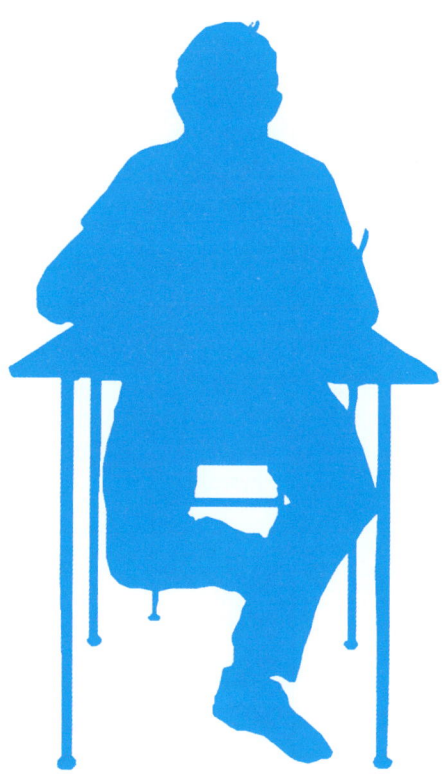

A STUDY SCHEDULE (I)

October 2014

Sunday	Monday	Tuesday	Wednesday	Thursday	Friday	Saturday
			1	2	3	4
5	6	7	8	9	10	11
12	13	14	15	16 Start of preparation	17 Physics 1, 2, 3	18 ✱ Physics 4, 5, 6
19 ✱ Physics 7, 8, 9	20 ✱ Maths 1 History 1 Physics 10	21 ✱ Maths 2 History 2 Physics 11	22 ✱ Maths 3 History 3 Physics 12	23 ✱ Maths 4 History 4	24 ✱ Maths 5 History 5	25 ✱ Maths 6 History 6
26 ✱ Maths 7 History 7	27 ✱ Maths 8 History 8	28 ✱ Overall Physics Revision (1 week)	29 ✱ Maths 9 History 9	30 ✱ Maths 10 History 10	31 ✱ Geog 1 Lit 1 Chem 1	

I Am Gifted, So Are You!

A STUDY SCHEDULE (II)

November 2014

Sunday	Monday	Tuesday	Wednesday	Thursday	Friday	Saturday
30						1 ✵ Geog 2 Lit 2 Chem 2
2 ✵ Geog 3 Lit 3 Chem 3	3 ✵ Geog 4 Lit 5 Chem 6	4 ✵ Geog 5 Lit 5 Chem 5	5 ✵ Geog 6 Lit 6 Chem 6	6 ✵ Geog 7 Lit 7 Chem 7	7 ✵ Overall Maths Revision Overall History Revision (1 week)	8 ✵ Geog 8 Lit 8 Chem 8
9 ✵ Geog 9 Lit 9 Chem 9	10 ✵ Geog 10 Lit 10 Chem 10	11 ✵ Geog 11 Lit 11	12 ✵ Geog 11 Lit 12 End of Study	13 ✵	14 Extra 5 days (for emergencies)	15
16 ✵ Overall Chem Revision (1 week)	17 ✵ Final Maths Review	18 Maths Exam	19 ✵ Overall Lit Revision (1 week)	20 ✵ Overall Geog Revision (1 week)	21 ✵ Final History Review	22 ✵ History Exam
23 ✵ Final Physics Review	24 ✵ Physics Exam Final Chem Review	25 ✵ Chem Exam	26 ✵ Final Lit Review	27 ✵ Lit Exam Final Geog Review	28 ✵ Geog Exam	29

Chapter 18

The Final Battle

Although it is almost guaranteed that a well-prepared student will pass well, it may take more than preparedness to score distinctions. This is because well-prepared students may not produce their best work under the stressful conditions of an examination. In this chapter, I will be pointing out some of the most common mistakes that students make under examination pressure. We will also look at precautions you can take to ensure that you give your best, on this all-important day.

PUT YOURSELF IN AN EMPOWERING STATE

If you have gone through all the steps of the study process and are well prepared, the only thing that could spoil your chances of getting your 'A' is being in the wrong state of mind. If you are in a lousy state such as anxiety, depression or nervousness, you could end up 'going blank' or making lots of careless mistakes.

So the first thing you need to do is to put yourself in the most empowering state like what I have taught you in Chapter 16: Getting Empowered…In An Instant. Remember that your state of mind will affect how you feel. How you feel will affect your actions and your results. When you are in a state feeling absolutely confident, excited and empowered, you are going to produce your very best. Here are a few things you can do!

1. Arrive Early to Get Relaxed

It is always good to arrive early for an examination. Firstly, it guarantees that you will not be late for the paper and secondly, being early allows your mind to relax before it is put to work. Remember that your mind performs at its best when you are in a relaxed state.

2. Get your Mind Off the Exam

It will definitely help if you could chat with your friends about anything that could take your mind off studying, but never talk about the examination or the study material. Most of all, never ever study on the day of the examination. This is the best way to sabotage your mind. Doing so will put you in a more tense state and the new material will only confuse you and interfere with any information that your mind has so well sorted out and integrated during your sleep.

3. Use the Power of Words

In Chapter 16, we discovered that the words you use on yourself can empower you or destroy you. Never allow that voice inside your head to say things like 'I'm nervous', 'I'm dead', 'I hope it is not too difficult', 'Oh no!' Instead, do what world champion boxers do. Keep telling yourself, 'I'm getting my A', 'This is easy', 'I can do it', 'No problem'.

Even when you find yourself stumped by many difficult questions, never allow yourself to talk negatively. Once you get into a lousy state, it will be all over. So, keep talking positive.

4. Put Yourself in an Empowering State

Before the exam, get yourself into an empowering state by thinking about a time in the past when you felt totally confident, unstoppable and powerful. See that picture clearly in your mind and make that image big and bright. Make sure you are fully associated with that picture and that it is in colour.

Next, make sure you are in an empowering physiology. Breathe the way you would be breathing if you were totally confident. Put that determined look on your face. Throw your shoulders back and walk as if you were unstoppable.

You can use the power of anchoring you learnt to trigger an empowered state. Listen to 'Rocky' or Olympic theme songs from your CD player just before the exam. Put the power moves that you have developed (like pumping your fists in the air or snapping your fingers and shouting 'Yes!') into action.

Once you are at the peak of your empowered state, you can begin to tackle the paper.

SCAN THE TEXT

The first thing you should do when you start the paper is to read through all the instructions and scan the entire paper from beginning to end before starting to attempt any questions. Scanning helps you to plan the order in which to answer the questions as well as how much time to spend on each section.

A WORD ON TIME

A lack of time is the undoing of many students, whether they are prepared or not. So, it is important that you keep track of the time by glancing at your watch every time you feel the need to. In order to avoid running out of time, you should:

Allocate Your Time Wisely

Always plan in advance the amount of time you will spend on each section and, subsequently, on each question. This should mostly be done during the dry runs.

Plan For Extra Time

You should also plan for an extra 'check-back time' of at least 15 minutes. This time can also be used as an emergency measure, if you happen to exceed the time you have allocated for your questions.

APPROACHING THE QUESTIONS

Easy First, Difficult Last

It is not always a good idea to answer the questions in the sequence in which they are found. This is because, at times, very difficult questions may be put at the beginning while easier ones are at the end. When we encounter such a situation, we may continue working on a difficult question till we find that we have spent too much time on it. Consequently, we rush through the rest of the paper only to find that we have no more time left for even the easy questions. The consequence is failure. To avoid this, you should do either one of the following:

1. Whenever you find that you are stuck with a difficult question, immediately circle the difficult question and go on to the next one. You can return to it after you have finished answering all the easy ones.

2. Answer all the easy questions first before proceeding with the difficult ones. Always leave the ones that require a lot of thinking, analysis and writing to the end, when you have finished most of the paper. This is because these are often best done when your mind is in a more relaxed state.

Don't Get Carried Away

Very often, students get so excited about answering a familiar question that they write on and on until they find that they have wasted too much time on it. Avoid giving too much information.

Never Give Up

Difficult questions, especially if they are put at the beginning of a paper, often have the effect of demoralising you. When this happens, you will probably not even be able to answer the easy questions that come later on

because you would have formed the belief that it was a difficult paper that you could not handle.

If this happens to you, take a deep breath, relax and do not give up. Skip the problematic questions and tackle the easy ones that boost your confidence. When you go back to the difficult questions finally and find that you still cannot figure out the answers, never leave the answer space blank because that will guarantee you a zero for that question. Instead, write down whatever you do know as long as it contains a germ of logic. Not only have you nothing to lose but you may still be awarded some marks and that could make the difference between a pass or a fail mark.

ANSWERING THE QUESTIONS

There are two rules you should follow in answering any kind of question. They are:

1. Always Read Critically

Always read each question slowly and carefully before attempting to answer it. Students often read the first few words and assume that the question is the same as one that they have done before in earlier tests and homework. You may end up giving an answer that is totally out of point.

Remember that it takes only one word to change the meaning of an entire question. If we do not read carefully, we may miss that crucial word and misunderstand the whole question. So, always be alert to critical keywords that appear in the question.

For example, do not read 'and' where the questions say 'or'. Also, do not confuse 'which of the following statements are true' with 'which of the following statements are <u>not true</u>'.

2. Give The Right Amount Of Information

Never dive into a question without knowing what is actually required. If you do so, you may give too little information, too much information or information that is totally irrelevant.

The first step is to know how much information to give. The marks allotted to each question is often a very good gauge. If a question is awarded five marks then you would normally be required to produce five points, and so on.

Now let's take a look at how you should answer specific categories of questions like multiple choice and essays.

MULTIPLE CHOICE – THE TRICKIEST OF ALL

Many students assume that multiple-choice questions (MCQs) are the simplest of all the question structures. This is because the answer is already given to you, and you only need to select.

My advice is to never underestimate MCQs. In actual fact, they are the most tricky of all. Very often, examination setters will make the choices so close that it takes not only just knowledge, but careful skill to select the right choice. If you are not extremely clear about the concept, you will probably get the question wrong. MCQs are also where most of the careless mistakes are made. So here are a few strategies to excel in this area.

1. Read Critically

As always, read the question very carefully. Do not assume that it looks familiar to one you have done before. The change in one word can change the entire meaning of the question. For example 'all of the above' and 'none of the above' are extremely similar, but drastically different. (I have made numerous mistakes in this area myself.)

2. Give Your Answer First

Before you look at the four or six choices given, always write down your answer first on the side of the page. Then, compare your own answer to each of the choices.

3. Read All the Choices

Many students make the terrible mistake of ticking what they think is the correct answer without reading through all the other choices. 'The other answers must be wrong', is what they tell themselves. Always ensure you read through each of the choices before you give the answer. The reason is that there may be a more correct answer.

4. The Strategy of Elimination

If you are not sure which answer to select, you can use the process of elimination. Here are a few techniques you can use to eliminate the wrong choices.

a. Eliminate the obviously wrong choice.

b. Eliminate the partly wrong choice. These are the choices that seem correct but there are one or two words that make it wrong.

c. Eliminate answers that are inherently correct, but unrelated to the question.

d. Eliminate the choice that is very different from all the other choices. It is normally wrong.

e. If there are two choices that are very similar, one of them is usually the correct choice.

f. If there are two choices that are exact opposites, one of them is usually the correct choice.

ESSAY QUESTIONS

In order to excel in essay questions, you must prove that you are able to recall the appropriate facts, demonstrate that you understand how to apply them to the question and be able to organise the facts in the best possible way.

Mind Map® for Planning Essays

A very useful tool to help you to recall and organise your facts is the Mind Map®. Before you jump in and write your essay, always spend ten minutes to develop a plan for the essay. Use the Mind Map® technique to sketch the plan out in pencil. The Mind Map® will help you trigger key points as well as allow you to see the best way to group and arrange your points.

An important reason to come up with a plan is so that you can see your overall essay structure before you even start writing. At this stage, you can decide what facts to put in and the best order to put them in and which points to be placed in the first paragraph, second paragraph and so on. In general, your essay can be divided into an introduction, the main body and the close. It is important that in the close, the main ideas/arguments are summarised and a stand is taken. The most common mistake students make in essay questions is to write out of point. Planning your essay first ensures that this does not happen.

Only when you are totally satisfied with your Mind Map® plan (spend no more than 10 minutes) should you start to write your essay.

YOUR FINAL MOMENTS

After answering all the questions, you should ideally have fifteen minutes left to spare, as you had initially planned. It is vital that this time be used to double-check your answers. You will definitely begin to see some errors you have made in understanding the questions, or giving the answers. It is also now that you will begin to see facts which you may have forgotten to put down.

So, how do we double-check answers? Double-checking in the last fifteen minutes should include these points:

1. Re-read the questions to make sure that you have understood them correctly.

2. Re-read your essay and short-question type answers and make sure these answers are to the point and free from grammatical and spelling errors. Also ensure that no important points have been left out.

3. If time permits, recalculate (preferably using an alternative method) all mathematical questions to see if you get the same answer. If you are short of time, simply read through your workings.

4. As for multiple-choice questions, check that you have not missed any of them out. More importantly, when the answers are given in a separate answer booklet, check that the answers you have given correspond to the correct questions. Lastly, never leave any question unanswered.

YOUR DESTINY IS YOURS TO CREATE

Well, you have certainly come down a long road, haven't you, whoever you are and wherever in the world you are. In the moments you have spent reading the book, you have learnt many simple, yet powerful concepts that can change the way you study, forever. You have realised that the beliefs you have about who you are and what you can do will ultimately determine the results you produce. You know that if other students can achieve good results, then so can you. It is only a matter of acquiring the skills and strategies. You also now know about the infinite capacity of your brain. You realise that given the right keys, you can access the genius within you. You have learnt these keys, haven't you? You are cognisant of how to use both sides of your brain using techniques like Mind Mapping® and the Memory Systems which you can put into effect to create the compelling future that you have planned for yourself and which you read about in the chapter on goal setting. You are capable of self-motivation and have turned into a competent time manager. Procrastination is not for you!

I urge you to take action now, as you turn the final page of this book. Take out your school textbooks, create a few Mind Maps® and use the memory techniques to see how fun and easy learning can be. Use your diary to plan your time for the coming week. You may even want to write in your journal more empowering goals for the future.

Remember, just because you have not done well in school in the past does not mean that you will not do well in the future. The success of your future depends on what you do today. So, go out there and start to plant the seeds for an abundant harvest.

Finally, I wish you all the best in your journey to success. I hope that you will write to me or that if we meet one day at a seminar you will tell me your success story.

Until then, be sure to live your dreams!

BIBLIOGRAPHY

Bandler, R. and Grinder, J., The Structure Of Magic II (California: Meta Publications, 1975).
Bandler, R., Time For A Change (California: Meta Publications, 1993).
Bandler, R., Using Your Brain For A Change (Utah: Real People Press, 1985).
Buzan, T., How To Make The Most Of Your Mind (Cambridge: Colt Books, 1989).
Buzan, T., The Mind Map Book (London: BBC, 1993).
Buzan, T., Use Your Memory (London: BBC, 1989).
Covey, S. R., The 7 Habits Of Highly Effective People (New York: Fireside, 1989).
Dilts, R., Applications Of Neuro-Linguistic Programming (California: Meta Publications, 1983).
Dilts, R., Changing Beliefs Systems With NLP (California: Meta Publications, 1990).
Dilts, R., Grindler, J., Bandler, R. and Delozier, J., Neuro-Linguistic Programming: Volume 1 (California: Meta Publications, 1980).
Jensen, E., Brain Based Learning and Teaching (san Diego: Turning Point Publishing, 1995).
Jensen, E., Super Learning (San Diego: Turning Point Publishing, 1995).
Mukerjea, D., Superbrain (Singapore: Oxford University Press, 1997).
O'Conner, J. and Seymour, J., Training with NLP: Skills For Managers, Trainers and Communicators (California: Harper Collins Publishers, 1994).
Ostrander, S. and Schroeder, L., Super-Learning 2000 (New York: Dell Publishing, 1984).
Ostrander, S. and Schroeder, L., Super-Memory, The Revolution (New York: Carrol Graff, 1991).
Ostrander, S. and Schroeder, L., Cosmic Memory (New York: Carrol & Graff, 1991).
Robbins, A., Unlimited Power, (Great Britain: Simon and Schuster, 1988).
Robbins, A., Awaken The Giant Within (New York: Summit Books, 1991).
Rose, C., Accelerated Learning, (New York: Dell, 1987).
Rose, C. and Nicoll, M. J., Accelerated Learning For The 21st Century (New York: Dell Publishing, 1984).
Shone, S., Creative Visualisation (London: The Aquarian Press, 1984).

AKLTG's Life Transformational Programs

Personal development

- Patterns of Excellence™
    - Module 1: Breakthrough to Success
    - Module 2: Leadership & Charisma
    - Module 3: NLP™ practitioner certification
- Wealth Academy™
- Pattern Trader Tutorial
- Wealth Academy Forex

Professional development

A wholly-owned subsidiary of AKLTG, Growth Catalyst is our one-stop training solution for professional development, with core expertise in customised corporate training, consultancy and professional conferences.

- Strategic Business Planning
- Sales excellence
- Presentation & public-speaking
- Interpersonal relations
- Leadership
- Team-building

Youth development

- I Am Gifted!™ Holiday Camps for students aged 6 to 19 years
- 21st Century Skills Training & Life Skills Workshops
- Outdoor Education (Adventure & Leadership) Camps
- School-based motivational talks
- Transformational Teaching Series for educators

Pre-school development

Designed to cultivate balanced left-right brain development, our childhood education program unlocks your child's creativity in problem-solving and fosters innovative thinking. Your child will also develop:

- Divergent thinking
- 3D-spatial reasoning
- Motor skills
- Language & listening skills
- Moral values

For general enquiries, call (65) 6881 8881 or send email to info@akltg.com

Adam Khoo Learning Technologies Group
www.akltg.com

SINGAPORE
Adam Khoo Learning Technologies Group Pte Ltd
Management office
107 Eunos Avenue 3 #03-02 Singapore 409837

Centre for Personal & Professional Excellence
991 Alexandra Road, #01-05 Garden Office, Singapore 119964
Tel: (65) 6881 8881 Email: info@akltg.com

Adam Khoo Learning Centre Pte Ltd
Square 2
10 Sinaran Drive #04-27 Singapore 307506
Tel: (65) 6765 5516 Email: novena@aklc.com

Century Square
2 Tampines Central 5 #04-09 Singapore 529509
Tel: (65) 6783 2093 Email: tampines@aklc.com

West Coast Plaza
154 West Coast Road #01-75 Singapore 127371
Tel: (65) 6777 2128 Email: westcoastplaza@aklc.com

Sembawang Shopping Centre
604 Sembawang Road #03-08 Singapore 758459
Tel: (65) 6556 1826 Email: sembawang@aklc.com

MALAYSIA
Adam Khoo Learning Technologies Group Sdn Bhd
B-2-12 TTDI Plaza, Jalan Wan Kadir 3, Taman Tun Dr. Ismail, 60000 Kuala Lumpur, Malaysia
Tel: (603) 7725 0212 Email: infomy@akltg.com

INDONESIA
PT Adam Khoo Learning Technologies Group
Jakarta office
Wisma 46 Kota BNI, 2nd Floor, Suite 2.05
Jl. Jendral Sudirman Kav., 1 Jakarta 10220
Tel: (62) 21 574 7511 Email: Indonesia@akltg.com

Surabaya office
Adam Khoo Centre
Ruko Surya Inti Permata B 52-53
Jl. Jemur Andayani 50
Surabaya, Indonesia

CHINA
优拓咨询(大连)有限公司
大连市中山区五五路32-2号
安达商务大厦409室
邮编: 1166000
电话: 0411—82703262 电邮: china@akltg.com
网站: www.iamgifted.com.cn

VIETNAM
Adam Khoo Education
22 Nguyen Binh Khiem
Da Kao Ward, District 1
Ho Chi Minh City, Vietnam
Tel: (84) 8 3911 9050
Fax: (84) 8 3911 9055
Website: www.adamkhooeducation.com.vn

LICENSEES

SINGAPORE
Adam Khoo Learning Centre
Telok Kurau branch
190 Changi Road #01-01A Singapore 419974
Tel: (65) 6447 0900
Email: telokkurau@aklc.com

INDONESIA
PT Adam Khoo Learning Centre
Pondok Indah branch
No. 9 F, Jl. Sultan Iskandar Muda, Arteri Pondok Indah, Jakarta 12240
Tel: (021) 729 1029 Email: pondokindah@aklc.com

BSD City branch
No. A/21, Jl Pahlawan Seribu, BSD City Serpong Jakarta 15321
Tel: (021) 5316 4349 Email: bsd@aklc.com

Pantai Indah Kapuk branch
Rukan Manyar Blok D No 1, Jl Pantai Indah Selatan
Jakarta Utara 14470
Tel: (021) 5694 7725 Email: pantaiindahkapuk@aklc.com

Kelapa Gading branch
The Club Gading Mas 2nd Floor, Jl Boulevard Raya No. 1
Belakang Balai Samudra, Jakarta Utara 14240
Tel: (021) 4585 938 Email: kelapagading@aklc.com

Graha Famili branch
Jl Mayjend Yono Soewoyo
Komplexs Graha Festival Kav.3
Surabaya, Indonesia 60228
Tel: (62) 31 900 1277 Email: grahafamili@aklc.com

CHINA
广州宝捷利教育(咨询)有限公司 (Partner Office)
广州市白云大道南金钟大厦410，411室
邮编: 510405
电话: 020—26097765 / 020—86183711

VIETNAM
TGM Training (Youth Program Licensee)
Ho Chi Minh City office
47, Street No. 9, Him Lam Town,
District 7, Ho Chi Minh City
Tel: (08) 6264 7902 Email: lienhe-hcm@tgm.vn
Website: www.tgm.vn

Ha Noi office
Level 6, Ha Noi Ngoi Sao School
Trung Hoa - Nhan Chinh, Ha Noi, Vietnam
Tel: (04) 66 755 998 Email: lienhe-hn@tgm.vn
Website: www.tgm.vn

Growth Catalyst Viet Capacity Training (Growth Catalyst Licensee)
Block TT2, row A, No.10, Bac Linh Dam
Dai Kim Ward, Hoang Mai District
Ha Noi, Vietnam
Tel: (84) 91 303 70 66
Email: tam.dt@gcv/edu/vn
Website: www.gcv.edu.vn

Adam Khoo Learning Centre
22 Nguyen Binh Khiem
Da Kao Ward, District 1
Ho Chi Minh City, Vietnam
Tel: (84) 8 3911 0066
Fax: (84) 8 3911 9055
Email: hcmc@aklc.com
Website: www.aklc.com.vn

INDIA
Sixth Sense Learning Strategies Pvt. Ltd. (Youth Program Licensee)
Plot no 10, Road no 12
Anand Banjara Colony, Banjara Hills
Hyderabad – 500 034
Andhra Pradesh, India
Tel: (91) 40 2339 9566 / (91) 40 2339 8566 / (91) 939 0303 666
Email: info@sixthsenscindia.com
Website: www.sixthsenseindia.com

Eureka Learning Technologies Private Limited (Youth Program Licensee)
3-C Behere Arcade, Prabhat Road
Pune 411 004, India
Tel: (91) 20 2543 5391 / (91) 20 2543 5392 / (91) 20 2543 5393
Email: info@eurekaeureka.net
Website: www.eurekaeureka.net/transformational-learning/

UNITED ARAB EMIRATES
Eureka Learning Technologies Private Limited (Youth Program Licensee)
Website: www.eurekaeureka.net